THE LEGAL THEORY OF ETHICAL POSITIVISM

To Beth,
who won't read it,
and Emily,
who just might,
with love

THE LEGAL THEORY OF ETHICAL POSITIVISM

TOM D. CAMPBELL
Dean of Law, The Australian National University

Dartmouth
Aldershot • Brookfield USA • Singapore • Sydney

Published by
Dartmouth Publishing Company Limited
Gower House
Croft Road
Aldershot
Hants GU11 3HR
England

Dartmouth Publishing Company
Old Post Road
Brookfield
Vermont 05036
USA

British Library Cataloguing in Publication Data
Campbell, Tom
Legal Theory of Ethical Positivism. –
(Applied Legal Philosophy Series)
I. Title II. Series
340.112

Library of Congress Cataloging-in-Publication Data
Campbell, Tom, 1938–
The legal theory of ethical positivism / Tom D. Campbell.
p. cm. — (Applied legal philosophy)
Includes bibliographical references.
ISBN 1-85521-171-8 (hb)
1. Legal positivism. I. Title. II. Series.
K331.C36 1996
340'.112—dc20 95-34908
CIP

ISBN 1 85521 171 8

Printed and bound in Great Britain by
Hartnolls Limited, Bodmin, Cornwall

Contents

Series Preface

The objective of the Dartmouth Series in Applied Legal Philosophy is to publish work which adopts a theoretical approach to the study of particular areas or aspects of law or deals with general theories of law in a way which focuses on issues of practical moral and political concern in specific legal contexts.

In recent years there has been an encouraging tendency for legal philosophers to utilise detailed knowledge of the substance and practicalities of law and a noteworthy development in the theoretical sophistication of much legal research. The series seeks to encourage these trends and to make available studies in law which are both genuinely philosophical in approach and at the same time based on appropriate legal knowledge and directed towards issues in the criticism and reform of actual laws and legal systems.

The series includes studies of all the main areas of law, presented in a manner which relates to the concerns of specialist legal academics and practitioners. Each book makes an original contribution to an area of legal study while being comprehensible to those engaged in a wide variety of disciplines. Their legal content is principally Anglo-American, but a wide-ranging comparative approach is encouraged and authors are drawn from a variety of jurisdictions.

TOM D. CAMPBELL
Series Editor
The Faculty of Law
The Australian National University

Preface and Acknowledgements

This book started out as a project designed to provide a brief exposition of Legal Positivism as a normative political philosophy which was to be followed by a series of applications within different areas of law exploring the advantages and disadvantages of channelling governmental power through the formulation and administration of specific rules. Owing to the breadth of the task it has turned out to be more substantially a book concerned with the general theory of 'Ethical Positivism', as I have named that aspect of the positivist tradition which presents moral justifications for a system of government through positive rules and requires adherence to an ethics of positivism on the part of legislators, administrators, judges and citizens.

The illustrative applications which remain concentrate on various topics concerning freedom of expression so that a significant portion of the book focusses on free speech as a particularly challenging area for a political philosophy which opposes the imposition of abstract rights through judicial power and favours the articulation of concrete rights through democratic debate and the enactments of accountable legislatures. Since it is part of the argument of the book that the formulation of acceptably specific rules requires clarity and decisiveness in the selection of priority purposes, the chapters on free speech involve discussion of substantial issues which go beyond illustrating the implications of Ethical Positivism and are of independent interest in terms of the analysis and justification of law with respect to freedom of expression.

Even so, the discussion of Ethical Positivism remains rather sketchy, at least with respect to the justifying arguments which would be required to render the theory thoroughly convincing. The reader is advised to expect the contextual staking out of a position rather than its comprehensive vindication. I believe that this largely expository project has considerable significance as a way of reconciling the most persuasive ideological critiques of legalism with a constructive approach to law reform in a postmodern environment. At any rate, it has proved a formidable enough task to outline an approach which deconstructs the standard caricatures of Legal Positivism as inherently insensitive, inegalitarian and impractical and identifies an ideal of a fallible but legitimate legal process as a necessary ingredient of progressive political endeavour.

My debts in this enterprise arise principally from the constant stimulation of colleagues and students at Glasgow University and the Australian National University and generous leave granted by both institutions. I also acknowledge the substantial assistance provided by the Australian Research Council. In personal and intellectual terms I owe much to the writings, conversations and enthusiasms of Neil MacCormick and Frederick Schauer. They are not, however, to be implicated in the outcome.

This preface also gives me the opportunity to mention the cheerful and trusting involvement of John Irwin who, as the managing director of Dartmouth Publishing Company, adventurously took on the Applied Legal Philosophy series and has continued to provide unobtrusive support and encouragement. The community of legal philosophers owes him a great deal.

It is, however, my wife, Beth Campbell, who has, more than anyone else, made it all seem worthwhile.

Tom D. Campbell
Canberra

1 Introducing Ethical Positivism

Introduction

In legal theory, Legal Positivism is generally taken to be the view that the concept of law can be elucidated without reference to morality, and that it is the duty of judges to determine the content of and apply the law without recourse to moral judgments. To many people, lawyers and laypersons alike, this seems outrageous. If the law is not deeply imbued with our moral convictions, how can it command our respect? If law can be law without being moral then our legal obligations can be no more than coercion. Nor does it seem that the actual operations of law are intelligible unless they are brought into some sort of supportive relationship to at least part of the morality of the community in question.[1] Legal Positivism must, therefore, be mistaken in theory and perhaps immoral in practice.[2]

It is the thesis of this book that the belief in the amoralism (and certainly the immoralism) of Legal Positivism is profoundly mistaken. For while it is correct to say that Positivism insists on the practical importance of the distinction between morality and law and equally correct to say that Positivism holds that judges should not themselves normally make moral judgments in the course of their judicial activities, these positions are commended on the basis of foundational moral views about what law and politics should be all about. My purpose is to bring to the fore these ethical aspects of Legal Positivism, to defend them against philosophical and political objections and to illustrate some of their implications in relation to human rights and, more particularly, freedom of expression.[3]

'Ethical Positivism' is the label chosen to identify the sort of theory that centres on the ethical functions and prerequisities of positivist models of law. The legal theory of Ethical Positivism (hereafter LEP) is not an analytical view about the semantics of 'law' or the deep meaning of legal discourse, nor is it a descriptive/explanatory theory about the best way to understand law and its social functions. Rather,

LEP is a moral theory about the exercise of political power which it views as the activity of seeking to control and coordinate in a morally defensible manner the conduct of large numbers of people. The particular focus of LEP within political philosophy is the proper modus operandi of the state as the main institution through which political power is exercised in the modern world. The framework for its analysis is a discussion of the acceptable form of the organised use of collective power over a whole society. LEP is thus essentially a critical (justificatory/condemnatory) theory of the state and contemporary political process.

In brief and highly simplified summary, LEP presents an aspirational model of law according to which it is a presumptive condition of the legitimacy of governments that they function through the medium of specific rules capable of being identified and applied by citizens and officials without recourse to contentious personal or group political presuppositions, beliefs and commitments. LEP depends both on the analytical thesis that law can be conceptually, argumentatively and operationally separated from morality and on the sociological thesis that actual legal systems can approximate to a situation where their laws are administered in a rule-deferential manner. However, the organising and motivating force of LEP is a substantive political view about the moral significance of the positivist vision of what a good legal system looks like and how it contributes to a just, effective and democratic polity.

LEP is a broad approach within legal theory. It covers a variety of ways of unpacking the political ideal that government should be conducted through the creation and (separate) application of specific and objectively operable local rules. LEP emphasises that it should be the task of courts both to express and to limit the legitimated political will of a community via the impartial implementation of its rule-formulated decisions. Courts ought to assist in maximising the effectiveness of constitutionally legitimate government activity but must do so in a way which facilitates control of those failures and abuses which it is part of the function of the positivist model to identify and check. LEP is, therefore, a highly political theory of law, albeit one which concentrates on the legal contribution to political objectives which flow from the form and process of law, rather than its specific contents.

The Ethics of Positivism

The label 'Ethical Positivism' signals that LEP goes beyond what is sometimes called Institutional or Normative Positivism, the view that law consists of a system of rules, where rules are understood in cognitive and institutional terms rather than as reducible to near brute facts, such as sanctions and commands.[4] The Ethical Positivist endorses the basic ontology of rules which characterises Normative Positivism but argues for this view of law on prescriptive rather than philosophical grounds.

In the terminology of contemporary theory, LEP subscribes to the 'separability thesis', namely the view that law and morality *can* be separated (in that, for instance, legal decisions need not draw on moral premisses) but rejects the 'separation thesis', if this is construed as the claim that law and morals actually are separate, for LEP acknowledges that this is not generally the case.[5] Rather, LEP represents what might be called the 'prescriptive separation thesis' according to which the identification and application of law ought to be kept as separate as possible from the moral judgments which go into the making of law. This is to adopt as a prescription, rather than an analysis, the contention of Joseph Raz that the tests for determining the existence and content of a law should be value-free.[6] It goes further than H.L.A. Hart, whose rule of recognition, which sets out the criteria for identifying first order legal rules, can include moral criteria, a position which has been described by W.J.Waluchow as 'inclusive legal positivism'[7] and by Hart himself as 'soft positivism'.[8] However, there is no actual disagreement here as Hart's position is a descriptive one whereas LEP is a prescriptive theory which does not deny that actual legal systems routinely permit the moral judgments of judges a major role in legal process.

The term 'ethical' is preferred to 'moral' because it better connotes a system of second order moral reasons which have bearing on the design of institutionalised practices and the ways in which those entrusted with institutional roles conduct themselves. Somewhat arbitrarily, I take the term 'ethical' to point us towards the appraisal of complex institutional patterns and roles, which have to be seen largely in terms of their instrumentality for a range of morally significant human objectives, in contrast to the 'morality' of more direct one to one social interactions. The label 'Ethical Positivism' indicates that law is to be valued as an institutionalised way of doing things which serves important societal purposes.

Further, it is part of the theory that the effective accomplishment of these purposes calls for ethical conduct on the part of participants in their various roles, as judge, as lawyer, as policeman and as citizen, a matter of role morality as distinct from personal morality.[9] This ethical conduct will standardly involve role occupants presumptively subjugating their own moral beliefs about what would be substantively good law in favour of their moral commitment to obeying formally 'good' law. This requires participating in and fostering a community of understanding, in the legal profession and beyond, which embodies certain types of relatively 'objective' standard as to how legal disputes are to be settled and what counts as a sound legal argument. The main thrust of this ethic is a subordination of personal views to the morality of the role which recognises the moral priority of the overall objectives of the system and the duties of the individual as performing a part within that system.[10]

A sub-theme is that, when the pure positivist model is inapplicable or impracticable, or where the legal system in question falls short of the positivist ideal, courts can properly be viewed as having a certain moral authority which derives from their institutionalised impartiality with respect to the parties in dispute and, to a lesser extent, the interest groups whose political differences are manifest in litigation. The impartiality of courts is very limited in relation to value disputes, but to the extent that they are not parties to the conflicts that they are required to resolve courts have a degree of moral legitimacy which can make them appropriate sources of minor changes in the substance of law, provided that these law-making activities are subject to legislative review with respect to their precedential force.[11]

That the conjunction of 'ethical' with 'positivism' is a somewhat jarring combination is a tribute to the extent to which Natural Law theory has come to be identified with the moral approach to law.[12] Indeed, it is a considerable propaganda blessing for Natural Law theory that it is easy to pillory Legal Positivism as unfeeling and insensitive on account of its efforts to distance law from morality. Assumptions of the amoralism, even the immorality, of Legal Positivism persist despite the evident value commitments of Legal Positivists from Thomas Hobbes to Jeremy Bentham and John Austin to H.L.A. Hart, Neil MacCormick and Joseph Raz.[13] In this context, the apparent oxymoron, 'Ethical Positivism', has the heuristic merit of expressing in an arresting manner the insight that the justifying grounds of Legal Positivism can be viewed as primarily ethical, rather than analytical, descriptive or explanatory.

In so far as classic Legal Positivism has moral associations these are, of course, generally of a utilitarian variety. Legal Positivists of the English-speaking world trace their ancestry to Thomas Hobbes, who embraced the absolutist state as a way to maximise the fulfilment of desire, particularly pleasure, and minimise that to which people are averse, particularly death.[14] The greatest Legal Positivist of them all, Jeremy Bentham, and his follower John Austin, were part of the reformist movement, Philosophical Radicalism, which taught that law and its sanctions have a particularly important role in directing the selfish actions of individuals towards outcomes which serve the greatest happiness of the greatest number.[15]

While such utilitarian explications of the term 'ethical' in 'Ethical Positivism' draw attention to the hoped for beneficial consequences of positive law in the sort of institutional terms that characterise LEP, it is as well at the outset to emphasise that the theory is not tightly bound to such a limited theory as Benthamite utilitarianism. As we will see, the purposes which law may serve are by no means confined to the minimisation of pain (harm) and are rarely extended as far as the maximisation of human happiness (benefit). Other, non-hedonistic, objectives may be involved, such as distributive justice and individual autonomy (whether or not these bring happiness or freedom from harm). Legal process may also be valued simply as fair process, independent of its outcomes. LEP is morally eclectic and politically tolerant. One attraction of LEP as an aspirational model of law is that it can be taken to serve the values of a wide range of particular philosophies, individualistic, communitarian, hedonistic or pluralist.

Certainly, there is an historical association between Ethical Positivism and individualistic or libertarian ideologies in which the self-sufficient individual is all-important and the activities of states are to be kept to the law-and-order minimum. However, Legal Positivism is not tied to the ideology of its origins. Law as a system of rules can serve collective as well as individual ends, and the individuals involved may be constituted in large measure by their social roles, group affiliations and societal environment without undermining the assumptions of LEP. Indeed, respecting the purposes of sovereigns as the source of legal authority can have a distinctly holistic ring, particularly where the sovereign is conceived in democratic terms.[16]

In general, the sovereign power aspect of Legal Positivism carries few of the connotations of those liberal forms of the 'rule of law' which present law as a morally neutral framework within which autonomously constituted individuals are free to pursue their private objectives under the umbrella of a non-partisan state. An element of this model will exist and may be welcome to the extent that law embodies rules of mutual convenience which aid social cooperation, but, in most areas of morally justified legal restraint and permissibility, law takes some sort of stand on the allowable range of individual and group activities. What sort of stand should be taken is, for LEP, an open question which is normally best left for independent political determination outside the legal system.

A Positivism of Rules

It is central to LEP that a system of law ought to be a system of rules.[17] Further, the rules in question must be 'real' rules, that is rules which have, in Raz's term, 'exclusionary force' in that they function in decision making partly by excluding considerations which are not indicated by the rule in question, even if such considerations would otherwise have been relevant.[18] To adopt the metaphor popularised by Dworkin in relation to rights, for LEP, rules are trumps. No mere 'rules-of-thumb' or general guidelines to aid decision makers will suffice for the decisive role of rules within the state.[19] In addition, if they are to fulfil this role, rules must have considerable specificity, clarity and mutual consistency.[20] While rules in a positivist system must be 'general' in the sense of universal as opposed to particular (referring to classes of person and events rather than individual persons and instances), they need not be general in the sense of applying to all persons and must not be general in the sense of being vague or unspecific. Positivistic rules, as we shall see, are as specific as is necessary to capture the perhaps controversial political choices relevant to the conduct in question and must be at a level of abstraction which makes them effective instruments for their social purposes and, at the same time, enables citizens to assess the fairness of the distinctions drawn between types of person and conduct in question. The prime purpose or function of law is to facilitate political choice. The core limitation on legal subservience to political decision making is that political authority must be mediated by such rules and not simply a matter of ad hoc particularistic decrees or discretions.

We will see that there are a number of powerful normative arguments which support LEP's commitment to rules. Many of these are based on the utility of rules in relation to the control and coordination of conduct. Less frequently noted is that rule format is also appropriate for expressing and hence for assessing proposals for morally justified limitations on human freedom in the promotion of welfare and justice. Rules are often opposed to principles, but in fact rules are the best expression of principled decision making. By expressing the maxim of the action that is required, prohibited or empowered, rules encourage rational, in the sense of reasoned, decision making in a form which exhibits the moral issues at stake, namely the desirability of the *type* of conduct in question.[21]

Rules also have a role to play in facilitating meaningful democratic choice by presenting precise choices in an intelligible form. They are also a significant ingredient in any system which seeks to combat the majoritarian difficulties which concern such classic democratic theorists as Rousseau and John Stuart Mill.[22] Finally, rules serve to provide a structure for such community life as is possible in large and complex societies.[23]

For these reasons LEP affirms the centrality of rules in relation to the legitimacy of claims to impose mandatory requirements on the members of a society. This entails that courts should ideally be limited to the application of rules politically arrived at in other fora.

However, LEP is not a pure Formalism which reads laws without regard to their purposes, although it is a foundational tenet of the theory that rule application can and ought to be relatively detached from the ulterior purposes of such rules, particularly if this takes the adjudicator beyond what is apparent from a contextual understanding of the rules themselves. In particular, LEP is opposed to the Formalist pretence of deducing legal decisions from broad abstract concepts, such as 'coercion', 'contract' or 'title'. The move from broad to specific requirements involves a series of moral and political choices, not a mechanical extrapolation from key concepts. Moreover, a rule cannot be interpreted without an understanding of the situations to which the rule is intended to apply and the general nature of the political choice that was involved in its formulation or retention.

LEP is, of course, in substantial conflict with the sort of prescriptive Legal Realism that seeks to encourage acceptable outcomes from legal process by a pragmatic judicial assessment of their consequences without deferring to the well-formulated prior decisions of rule-creating authorities. LEP requires citizens and adjudicators to interpret and respect laws as carefully worded formulations of specific political choices, representing one among the many political determinations that could be made on the issues in question within that community. Law courts should not be simply arenas for the determination of an outcome that the participants deem socially or economically desirable. LEP does not deny the reality that specific rules are often absent or ignored, or that there are systems in which judges are encouraged to take rules as no more than tentative guidelines, but such matters are to be portrayed as unwarranted departures from the positivist model and deplored as unethical dereliction of legislative and judicial duty.

The desirability of the basic positivist model is enhanced by conjunction with democratic institutions, such as elected legislatures and freedom of the media. Institutionalised democracy is crucially dependent on the ideal of government through rules, for rules provide an effective focus for making ethical choices about legitimate coercion and make it feasible to exercise some control over the power of officials within democratically approved boundaries. However, the merits of the model are not entirely extinguished in non-democratic systems. It is accepted that the cumulative advantages of government through rules are morally defeasible, particularly where the substance of legislation is so evil as to outweigh the benefits of the legalism of the system in question. LEP generates strong but overrideable moral presumptions in favour of the legitimacy of governments which operate through specific rules impartially administered. Moreover, LEP, being concerned primarily with the form rather than the content of ruling, is compatible with a wide range of substantive political philosophies, although, as we shall see, the values which underlie its appeal do have direct relevance to material as well as formal matters. LEP has, therefore, considerable potential as a consensual framework for law makers as well as law applicators. In particular, forms of both Rights Theory and Economic Analysis of Law can be tied into the positivistic model without serious modification, provided that the rights or the economic assessments are determined by legislators and not by courts.

In other ways also, LEP is not a complete political philosophy, for it allows that there are more basic sources of legitimacy, such as the consent of the governed and the pursuit of the general good (incorporating public and individual goods) which may legitimate at least some governments' actions which do not conform to the positivist model. However, many elements of the justification of government through rules themselves draw on notions of consent and the common good, so that there is no simple opposition between rule through positive law and these, more fundamental, ideals.

The values on which LEP draws include those traditionally associated with the idea of rule of law:[24] liberty, effectiveness, systematic allocation of power and at least the potential for fairness in the distribution of benefits and burdens. However, the positivist version of 'the rule of law' in terms of visibly enacted empirically applicable and suitably specific rules relates to other values with a more evident social dimension, such as cooperation, community, non-discrimination and equality of welfare.

The rationales for government through specific rules are, in combination, sufficiently powerful to make approximation to the positivist model a condition of government legitimacy, such that serious and consistent departures from the model may serve to delegitimate governments, so depriving them of any justified authority they might otherwise possess. In this way LEP can be as radically destabilising as any anarchist critique. Ultimately, such moral judgments involve a balancing of factors which cannot be reduced to a rigid formula. Nevertheless, we may reasonably contend that LEP sets out a model which is a necessary ingredient of an acceptably democratic system and a mitigating aspect of non-democratic regimes.

Some Implications of Ethical Positivism

The practical import of LEP is explored as the analysis of the book unfolds, but it may be helpful at this stage to mention just some of the political implications of the approach.

First, LEP, especially in its democratic mode, has a preference for statute law over common law as better adapted to expressing current political choices in a positivist manner, while accepting the need for clarification of statutory enactments and sometimes delegated legislative authority by precedent-creating judicial decision. Established common law systems can develop acceptable positivist rules, in their (often covert) creative law-making mode, but as vehicles of legal development they are broadly undemocratic and tend to breed confusion through the indeterminacy which derives from loose analogical reasoning under whose guise judicial legislation normally takes place.[25]

Second, LEP is opposed to the extensive use of judicial or administrative discretion directed only by general standards. For instance, it argues that the alleged benefits of inserting 'moral' escape clauses relating to such matters as 'unconscionability' can never be more than peripheral in an acceptable system of commercial law.[26] On the other hand, we will see that LEP favours that positive law should be couched at a level of generality which matches the justified purposes of government, so that judicial reasoning must involve the interpretation of rules in the light of their overt and publicly stated purposes.

Third, LEP is hostile to Alternative Dispute Resolution where this involves imposing decisions outside a framework of specific rules and is thought to dispense with the need for law as a social regulator. This does not imply that the methods of law are always to be preferred in settling conflicts. Indeed, law is often a second-best strategy to be applied where agreements cannot be achieved by other means. It is where coercively imposed mandatory decisions are involved that Alternative Dispute Resolution is suspect as potentially oppressive and unprincipled.[27]

Fourth, LEP rejects constitutional arrangements whereby court-administered human or fundamental rights are used as a higher locus of power than the electoral and representative institutions within modern democratic politics. This is not because LEP is hostile to the idea of basic human values which ought to be respected in all systems, but because it declines to give the power to define the content of fundamental rights to persons who are not accountable for what are in effect major legislative decisions.[28]

These apparently conservative points do not depend on any light dismissal of evidence of the limited success of government through law in combating the dominant prejudices, biases and oppressions at work in all societies. Indeed, LEP can be seen as a framework for the powerful critiques of false claims to political and legal objectivity. However, its modest but important claim is that, given the appropriate political and legal culture, specific rule governance can have an important role to play in moving societies towards the attainment of general prosperity, effective humanity and social justice. It follows that, while Legal Positivism in general has been the whipping-boy of many communitarian, socialist and feminist theorists, it can be argued that LEP is better adapted to serving important aspects of collectivist, egalitarian and humanitarian ends than available alternatives. There may be Socialist Positivists and Feminist Positivists as well as Libertarian ones.[29]

The Scheme of the Book

The legal theory of Ethical Positivism is expounded and defended in the first six chapters. Following the general overview presented here, Chapter 2 sets out the context of the theory through an analysis of the intractable problem of dealing with inherent danger of establishing governments that are strong enough to deliver effectively the benefits which legitimate the existence of states, a problem which is described as 'the tragic paradox of politics'. Chapter 3 carries this through into a consideration of the nature and functions of rules and their role in ameliorating the practical detriments arising from the paradox of politics. Chapter 4 uses the preceding analysis to develop and defend LEP in the context of current legal theory, preparing the way for Chapter 5, which concerns the ethics of lawyering, and Chapter 6, which deals with the proper limits of interpretation in judging, a topic which is central for establishing the plausibility and practicalities of LEP in the processes of rule identification, rule following and rule application, including the vexed matter of how LEP can respond to second-best situations in which there are insufficient or inadequately specific authoritative rules.

Chapters 7 to 9 are more applied. They illustrate and commend LEP through an examination of various approaches to the legal regulation of communication, with particular reference to defamation. These chapters on freedom of expression have their own intrinsic interest and objectives, but they also serve to indicate the practical significance and feasibility of LEP.

Overall, no more is claimed for the book than that it makes explicit and plausible an approach in legal theory which may give a sense of direction to those who are persuaded by the prevalent criticisms of conventional Legal Positivism, which point to its unwarranted pretensions and traditional ideological biases, but remain convinced that rule-centred law reform is still a worthwhile and important goal in any democratic polity that is serious about countering injustice and inefficiency.

Notes

1 With variations in emphasis, these arguments may be found in Finnis (1980), Detmold (1984) and Beyleveld and Brownsword (1986).

2 The immorality argument relates to the alleged affinity of Positivism with unconditional obedience to evil regimes. The classic dispute in Fuller (1958) and Hart (1957–58) has been revived in Dyzenhaus (1991).

3 See Campbell (1988a). In writing of 'Ethical Positivism' I do not imply that there is a readily identifiable and cohesive school of such theorists. Rather, the position is constructed from themes and aspects within both historical and contemporary authors. The nearest approximations to the position I adopt are some recent essays by Neil MacCormick, particularly MacCormick (1989) and elements of Frederick Schauer's 'presumptive positivism', in Schauer (1991). Schauer notes that normative issues have always been one aspect of Legal Positivism: 'For generations, legal theorists have been debating the conceptual validity, descriptive accuracy, and normative desirability of a perspective on law known as *positivism*, which under one view, is the systematic embodiment of a rule-based perspective on normative systems' (p.197). In commending his account of the role of rules in legal decision making, Schauer notes that 'If this normatively appealing picture of the role of rules is also descriptively accurate for many legal systems, it provides for us a new way of looking at an old issue' (p.197). Conversely, Alexy (1989b, p.169) notes that the necessary connection of law and morals can be interpreted as a normative argument.

4 Thus MacCormick and Weinberger (1984).

5 For this terminology, see Coleman (1982a) and (1989).

6 Raz (1985, pp.39–40).

7 Waluchow (1994, p.4). Waluchow uses 'exclusive legal positivism' for the view that 'excludes morality from the logically or conceptually possible grounds for determining the existence or content of valid law'.

8 Hart (1961, 2nd edn, 1994 p.250).

9 On role morality, see Emmett (1966) and Downie (1971).

10 See Chapter 5.

11 Adam Smith erects an entire moral and legal theory on the limited idea of impartiality as non-involvement in the dispute under consideration. See Smith (1976).

12 Similar paradoxical terminology is to be found in MacCormick (1985), the general drift of which I applaud. However, his thesis differs from mine to the extent that he is centrally concerned with giving moral reasons for substantive law not embodying too much of the dominant social morality, a position he calls 'moral disestablishmentarianism'.

13 This may arise from the confusion of Legal Positivism with Philosophical Positivism, the view that all knowledge is empirical in its basis and that moral evaluations, being non-empirical, do not give rise to knowledge. An extreme version of Philosophical Positivism is Logical Positivism (see Ayer, 1936). Most Legal Positivists have not been Philosophical Positivists, but see Lee (1989). In terms of the classical Positivists, Hobbes is most evidently embedded in political philosophy: see Boyle (1987). A similar interpretation of Hart is given in Simmonds (1993, p.154) with respect to the idea that Hart identifies as the most 'important' features of law those relating to security.

14 Hobbes (1990, Part I, Chapter 6).

15 The resultant artificial harmony of interests is a basic theme of the Philosophical Radicals, including James Mill's theory of democracy. See Mill (1821).

16 On this theme, see Campbell (1983), especially Chapter 6.

17 In what follows I adapt Hart's analysis of a legal system and distinguish primary rules of conduct and secondary rules relating to the recognition, alteration and interpretation of first order rules (Hart, 1961).

18 Raz (1975, pp.35–45, 73–6).

19 For 'rules-of-thumb', see Schauer (1991) and Alexander and Sherwin (1994).

20 In this, as in some other respects, LEP echoes Fuller (1969) but does not take up Fuller's famous thesis that formal legality is necessarily productive of substantive justice.

21 For this essentially Kantian approach in relation to law, see Lamont (1981).

22 Rousseau (1963) and Mill (1910).

23 Here I adopt the analysis of Durkheim (1933) in relation to complex societies.

24 An example is the 'thin' model of the rule of law put forward by Summers (1992, p.213):

> Citizens ought to be governed, but only by persons duly authorized by law to govern, *and* citizens ought to be governed only in accordance with precedents, statutes and other forms of law all of which ought to be reduced to rules that are:
> (1) general
> (2) determinate and clear
> (3) applicable to official and subject alike (as appropriate)
> (4) public
> (5) constant through time
> (6) uniform within the jurisdiction
> (7) free of conflict with other rules
> (8) susceptible of compliance.

However, Summers takes all these standards to be subject to the discretionary duty of the judge to have regard to equity at the point of application. Unfortunately, this qualification undermines the normal rationale of the cluster of requirements, namely to promote the predictability of official coercion. See Waldron (1989).

25 For a radically opposed view, see Allan (1993).

26 Kronman (1980) rightly points out that such concepts invite decisions based on background values such as distributive justice.

27 See Fiss (1984) and Brunet (1987).

28 See Chapter 7.

29 See Chapter 10.

2 The Tragic Paradox of Politics

Introduction

Every legal theory requires a political setting and no political philosophy should lack a theory of law. These truisms are routinely ignored, even by those who hold that politics concerns the state and acknowledge that the state is primarily a legal institution. The de facto division of labour between legal and political theorists – deriving, in part, from their institutionalised separation within academia – fragments what should be an integrated enterprise: the elucidation and defence of a principled and comprehensive justification and critique of the roles and procedures of law and state.

In neither sphere does the distancing of legal from political analysis routinely take the form of denying the significance of the other. However, many political theorists simply take the institutions of law as given and unproblematic, assuming the end product of the political process to be law making, in practice ignoring law application, compliance and policy implementation. Legal philosophers are often equally at fault in omitting genuine consideration of the political process from which law emanates and to which it is ultimately accountable.[1]

Amongst those theorists who do attend to the legal–political nexus are to be found, at one extreme, those who believe that it is possible to conceive of the legal and political functions as theoretically distinct and separable, however much they may often be mingled in actuality. At the other extreme are those who take the view that there is no way, either in theory or practice, that politics and law are separable. The former approach, following the tradition of Hans Kelsen, generates legal theories which exclude the political considerations from legal theory as a matter of theoretical principle.[2] The latter approach, characteristic of the Critical Legal Studies movement, generates work which concentrates on exposing the political nature of processes which are claimed to be purely legal.[3] Somewhere in between lies Dworkin's *via media*, a theory which is to be commended for its explicit attention to the political theory of jurisprudence, although ultimately the basis for the distinction between the two spheres is inadequate.[4]

The argument of this book is that there are both moral and political reasons for seeking to distinguish in analysis, and separate in practice, the legal and political functions, at least in certain respects and to a significant extent, but that there are equally strong moral and political reasons for acknowledging openly both the political nature of the acceptable rationales for distinguishing law and politics, and the inevitable and sometimes desirable residual politicality of some important legal operations.

Political Philosophy

There are no tenets in political philosophy that command general assent. This applies to conceptual matters relating to the analysis of the 'political' itself as much as to issues concerning the proper content of specific political decisions. For some theorists, politics is quintessentially about power, that is the capacity of some people and groups to get others to do what they wish, whether or not they would independently have so acted.[5] For other theorists, politics is about the pursuit of a society so organised that there is no room for unwilling or manipulated acquiescence in such common decision making as is required for the general good. Thus conflict and consensus models of social and political processes diverge on what politics is about and not just on what particular political systems and decisions are correct.[6]

It may be assumed that a degree of irreconcilable conflict is inevitable in any actual polity, in that choices will always have to be made between incompatible but equally defensible courses of action, but that the pursuit of consensus, especially in relation to such conflicts, is at least part of what politics is about and something to which law can contribute. In crude terms, conflict theory is descriptively more correct, while consensus theory has the edge as a morally superior (and at least partly realisable) model of politics. Without making any strong assumptions as to the actual balance of conflict and consensus elements within polities, it will be assumed that this balance is a variable of immense moral significance. Thus, even if we define the state in terms of the distinguishing characteristic that it, with some success, claims the possession of a monopoly of coercive power, we need not draw the conclusion that coercion is the inevitable essence of the state's activities in the sense that it must always be the dominant characteristic of all political relationships.[7]

For contemporary polities at least, there is a requirement for a more or less centralised decision-making process to determine national and external community objectives and how these are to be pursued. In the modern – and even in the postmodern – world there must be some decisions made relating to the society as a whole which are binding on its constituent parts. However broad or narrow its actual or proper scope, however decisions are made and applied within its bounds, contemporary societies cannot survive without a state.[8]

The necessity of statehood is derived in part from the fact that, without a state, any society lacks the preconditions for preventing itself being split into parts or gathered up into one or other actual state. Boundaries and organised defence are de facto requirements of an independent and continuing society. The necessity of statehood is multiplied by the identification of the least controversial prerequisites of tolerable existence: internal order in relation to material possessions, reproductive relationships and economic activity.[9] While such ordering functions can be performed by relatively unchanging traditional or customary norms, albeit with some sort of enforcement mechanisms, it is almost uncontroversial to point out that modern economies require a measure of centralised decision making, certainly in relation to the basic structure within which individual and group economic conduct takes place, and also as a way of entering into agreements with other independent societies, or states, and other similarly essential public goods. Such centralised decision making cannot be conceived of except in a social context, that is within a relatively stable customary pattern of social relationships, but this context does not render states redundant. However much a society may rely on custom and tradition, its adaptability to modern conditions requires that there is some means for introducing changes into this inherited structure and dealing with challenges to its authority within its territorial boundaries.[10]

To these banalities may be added others concerning the pervasive disagreement between members and groups within a polity regarding both the proper ways of making and enforcing decisions which are binding in that society, and the principles and goals which ought to determine the content of these decisions. These disagreements stem from conflicts of values, conflicts of interest and differences in knowledge, all of which have individual and group bases.[11] Underlying such basic disagreement about the role and substance of state activity there are more immediate practical conflicts over who it is that should do and get what in the social and economic interactions of any social group, the very conflicts which give rise to some of the necessities for states. Further, these disagreements and conflicts do not arise between social and economic equals. Independent of state activity, some persons and groups have more capacity to achieve what they want and value than do others with whom they are in dispute or competition. Thus inequalities of capacity lead to inequality of holdings.[12] The inequalities may be in physical strength, intellectual capacity and personal persuasiveness, and the resulting inequalities may be in charisma, wealth and hence in power. The inequality of outcomes arises from the operation of these different capacities in particular economic and social environments and the scarcity of what is valued by those in competition for whatever it is they desire.

This developing thumbnail sketch of the political dimension of human life concentrates on basic societal necessities rather than desirable possibilities. However, states may also be more positively beneficial in relation to the communal objectives that they, perhaps alone, can generate or enable in complex societies: the cultural achievements made feasible by the pooling of resources, the sustenance of interdependent ways of life which are deemed to be intrinsically desirable, the focus for a sense of communal identification as an ingredient of individual wellbeing, the provision of an infrastructure for creation and distribution of substantial quantities of material goods and multiple other objectives made possible by the cooperative opportunities of a central decision-making process which helps to sustain and adapt organised conformity within a given territory.[13]

The most evident forms which the benefits of a political structure take are the reduction of harm and the production of benefit through the prohibition of harmful, and the prescription of beneficial, conduct. This is primarily the role of criminal law.[14] If this has an unduly utilitarian ring to it, much the same point can be put in terms of the prohibition of wrong and the prescription of right conduct, with no implication that wrongness and rightness is always to be given substance in terms of human harms and benefits.[15] This conduct control function of the state is also a feature of those perhaps less coercive and less centralised constraints exercised through the medium of societal rules and social pressures. States both extend this community-based function to cover all those within large territorial boundaries and develop it through the introduction of mechanisms to enforce and adapt conventional behavioural rules. Given that the control of conduct in these regards is never going to be completely successful, states are expected to exercise the capacity to rectify harms done and make up for potential benefits lost, either by way of compensation or through punishments and rewards. Such rectification is both a precondition of ensuring tolerable adherence to conduct and a requirement of fairness. This is primarily the role of corrective justice.[16]

The remedy of those other unacceptable inequalities which arise without evident human wrongdoing but are nevertheless susceptible of amelioration, illustrates more positive functions of states.[17] There are many ways in which states can have a role in furthering the objectives of social justice on the basis of such criteria as relative merit, need or contribution, all of which presuppose some commitment to the idea that individuals are of equal worth, despite their unequal conditions and the unequal worthiness on which corrective justice concentrates.[18]

These rationales for state activity relate principally to what may be called the incidence and distribution of naturally harmful/beneficial (and hence wrong/right) actions. However, many harms and benefits derive, intentionally and unintentionally, from the deployment of the organised activities of a number of persons directed towards good or bad objectives. Such systemic or organisationally produced goods require that obligations be placed on various individuals or categories of person regarding actions which are not in themselves harmful or beneficial, or right or wrong. This makes sense within an organisational system being created or activated for these purposes. Economic systems with extensive division of labour are one obvious example. These organisational goods will include the maximisation of individual utilities within the relevant group, some of which can be regarded as simply the sum of individual benefits and others of which may be seen as public goods, in that they relate to benefits which either cannot be attributed to particular persons or cannot be limited to particular persons or groups within a society. Such public goods may be thought of as the distinctive provenance of the state, as no individual or group of individuals has an interest in creating goods over which they can have no private benefit or distributive control.[19]

Organisational goods (that is benefits which can only be derived from complex and interrelated activities of a number of persons) are characteristically associated with utilitarian values. However, they can also take in other moral goals, such as the attainment of justice in society where this involves the organised pursuit of such ideals as the equal or just distribution of benefits and burdens within groups or society as a whole. Systematic as distinct from ad hoc social justice is one such organisational good.

Underlying such manifestly political functions states also have a role in the sustenance of reliable mutual expectations which make it possible for members of such a large society to act in the light of knowledge of how others will conduct themselves and to follow conventions which facilitate individually beneficial social arrangements without the constant requirement for ad hoc interpersonal negotiations.[20] The benefits which derive from these conventional arrangements may be called 'conventional goods'. They include the convention-based mutually beneficial interactions of groups as well those which ease the path for individuals to attain their personal objectives.[21] This type of social benefit may be derived from the existence of any complex social structure (such as a system of property rights and obligations) as well as from particular institutionalised conventions (such as promise keeping, or the etiquette of avoiding physical contact in public places), but there are important differences between orderings of social interactions which function within a group so as to produce what may be regarded as a group objective, such as the output of a manufacturing process, and social conventions which enable individuals and groups to follow their personal objectives or enjoy some private benefit. The latter are conventional as distinct from organisational goods. Conventional goods are more prepolitical than organisational goods and less amenable to deliberate change and manipulation. The substance of the distinction is that organisational goods involve the coordinated mutually supportive activity of a group directed to a shared output, while conventional goods relate purely to facilitating the self-directed actions of individuals and groups.

Nearly all the advantages of conventional goods can be derived from societal systems without states, and indeed without politics as a distinct arena of social life, simply by the emergence of societal codes of conduct and customary complex economic and sexual arrangements. Indeed, overt organisational creations can be highly destructive of useful social conventions.[22] The argument for a centrally located and enforceable decision-making function, or state, depends a great deal on the assumption that such societal arrangements are unsustainable in large-scale societies without an overt political underpinning. Some sort of centralised political structure is necessary to modify customary systems in intended directions and within limited periods of time and to harmonise these with more explicit organisational aims.

We may schematise the *justificatory benefits* of states as:

1 the maintenance of the mainly physical necessities for the *survival* and flourishing of large groups with territorial boundaries under contemporary conditions;
2 *control of naturally harmful* (either directly or indirectly) or intrinsically wrong conduct;
3 *encouragement of naturally beneficial* (either directly or indirectly) or intrinsically right conduct;
4 rectification of wrongs or the correction of fault-related harms (*corrective justice*);
5 creation of morally acceptable distributions of good and harms (*social justice*);
6 facilitation of ordered mutually supporting conduct with desirable outcomes: *organisational (mainly public) goods*;

7 support for uncontroversial coordinated conduct for the mutual benefit of individuals and groups through the sustenance of standard social practices: *conventional goods.*

This incomplete and oversimplified but nevertheless formidable list of possible benefits of political society could be supplemented by considering what social life would be without states, even though some of them are catered for outside the confines of states.[23] They are itemised here partly to underline the initial prima facie case in favour of states and partly because they are important for the analysis of the next chapter, which concerns the various societal functions of rules and laws.

Given these potential benefits of state activity, the moral case for statehood would appear overwhelming and the sceptical reader may well come to the view that we are simply setting the scene for a classic liberal legitimation of contemporary statehood. Certainly, to this point, this account ignores the 'downside' of all such state activities, particularly in situations of unequal power and conflicting values, interests and knowledge. Thus any system for arriving at collectively mandatory decisions in conditions of disagreement and differences of interest will involve some element of coercion, either by way of direct use or threat of force, or by manipulation through the control of scarce resources. Furthermore, states present the constant danger that this coercion will be exercised in the interests of powerful groups and individuals, whose pre-existing social and economic power may be not only defended, but greatly extended via control of the machinery of state.[24]

Moreover, the benefits which can be obtained from states may only be enjoyed at potential high cost even in terms of the survival values which underpin the most basic rationales for having states. Thus it is clear that states and modern warfare are inextricably linked. More generally, because states are primarily means for the efficient pursuit of collective ends, their very efficiency makes them extremely dangerous. A thoroughly bad state may result in a worse societal situation than anarchy with only voluntary cooperation.[25] The central problem of political philosophy is how to maximise the benefits of states while minimising their costs. This problem is a grave one because the sometimes tenuous prospect of benefit is almost analytically tied to the risk of serious harm. This ambivalence of state power is the central paradox addressed by political philosophy.[26]

The analysis so far does no more than reaffirm the hopes and dilemmas presented classically by the Enlightenment theorists from Hobbes through Locke, Hume, Smith and Rousseau to Kant and John Stuart Mill. All these philosophers sought a scheme of values and socially viable institutions to justify and yet limit state power.

We still grapple with these issues through their articulations of the nature of authority, liberty, utility, justice and rights. No longer, however, do we live in an Enlightenment world. Our confidence in the capacity of reason or custom to provide workable solutions to the paradox of politics has all but gone. We recognise that current pluralisms of race, class, gender and culture cannot readily be transcended by universal values or engineered into authentic consensual politics.[27] On the other hand, excluding the extremes of postmodernism, we cannot easily accept that conduct is justified merely because it conforms to existing cultural patterns, however horrendous these might be in terms of our own cultural values, or that cultural loyalty legitimates anything.[28]

Something of the Enlightenment critiques continue in the constant exposure of 'injustice', 'oppression', 'hierarchy' and 'inefficiency', but the intellectual and moral bases for these critiques (all of which presuppose that there is a better way of doing things) are cruelly vitiated by the lack of a common epistemology of values or an agreed methodology of social science. Such fundamental problems will not of course be adequately pursued, let alone resolved, here. They must simply be noted and taken account of in the argument which follows. However, the sceptical analyses of postmodern value uncertainty have direct bearing on the 'downside' of the moral balance sheet of states. Many of the justificatory benefits of states depend on some agreement as to what goods are worth pursuing and at what price, and how such goods and prices are to be ranked. But how, on contemporary epistemological assumptions, are such agreements feasible?

Rampant value pluralism and non-cognitivist meta-morals leave us with little to utilise but individual self-interest, and even the philosophical underpinnings of such residual Hobbesian rationality is destabilised by postmodern accounts of the self which, in casting doubt on the persistence of individual identity, undercut the basis for the appeal to long-term self-interest.[29] Moreover, such consensus as remains does not exclude, and indeed may centre on, community values of sharing, humanity and collective fulfilment which are far removed from the sceptical individualism fostered by epistemological subjectivism.

What I have called the paradox of politics is the tension between the societal need for centralised coercive authority and the dangers involved in any human beings having such power over others. The paradox is tragic in so far as both the need for and the dangers of government stem from the same features of the human condition: the vulnerability of individuals and small groups in situations where scarcity, or perhaps human nature itself, generates the drive to dominate and control others. Contemporary uncertainties over the objectivity of values in general and the perhaps related incapacity to agree as to the basic terms of social existence in pluralistic societies exacerbate the paradox of politics. De facto relativities and moral uncertainty seem to call for a definitive role for government in determining standards which cannot be socially agreed, hence pushing us towards a Hobbesian view of the state as the arbitrary fount of our knowledge of right and wrong.[30] On the other hand, value scepticism renders strong government suspect, and the ethos of such societies gives us no basis for confidence in the capacity of politicians, officials and judges not to abuse the extensive powers of the modern state. We thus both need and fear decisive political authority.

Some such scenario underlies the perennial theme of the nature and justification of political obligation, the requirement that individuals must obey the rules or orders of designated persons, whether or not they wish to do so or agree that they are morally defensible. How can such obligations be justified and the limits of its justification established? This classic conundrum of political obligation requires further analysis in relation to the major justificatory concepts of political philosophy.

Freedom and Autonomy

The need to justify any claim to political authority may arise purely from the presupposition that human freedom or autonomy is an undeniable good, a good which is compromised by coercive power. It is not, however, clear that freedom is in itself of significant value. We must, therefore, seek to identify the nature and extent of the necessary as well as the avoidable costs of political obligation for the sort of human freedom that counts, which, in its fullest sense, we may call 'autonomy'.[31] Deploying, for the moment, the traditional concept of negative liberty or negative freedom as the absence of external restraint, it may seem that states destroy freedom because they always use or threaten to use literal force against their subjects as a means of external restraint. In this case freedom is certainly to be valued in the light of the negative connotations of its absence. Given that physical coercion is evidently undesirable, certainly in so far as it is assumed to involve pain and fear of pain, freedom, as the absence of such coercion, is clearly to be valued as the better option.

However, if we bracket off the brute unpleasantness of physical coercion, it is not so clear that freedom in the negative sense of the absence of constraint is an intrinsic good. Indeed, it seems clear that freedom is often valued only instrumentally as a precondition of actions and decisions that people wish to take and is therefore axiologically dependent on the worth of those objectives. At the very least, some freedoms, that is the absence of constraint in relation to specified sorts of conduct, are more important than others. This in itself indicates that undefined negative 'freedom' may be of no significance whatsoever to those who are 'constrained' from doing only that which they have no wish to do.[32] It can certainly be argued that there is moral significance in people getting what they want, both because this tends to be pleasing to those individuals, and on the grounds that it is a manifestation of autonomy. 'Autonomy' may be defined as the effective exercise of choice in terms of whatever the individual values (goal autonomy) and effective exercise of choice in relation to the means for the pursuit of valued goals (instrumental autonomy). Again, both aspects of autonomy may have (empirically defeasible) utilitarian worth. They may also be ascribed intrinsic value as relating to the essence, or perhaps simply the most important aspect, of what it is to be human, the making of choices and the pursuit of goals.[33]

Even assuming that the freedom we are discussing takes in this more positive idea of autonomy as acting in accordance with one's wishes, the value of such freedom depends a great deal on whether it is analysed as a normative or a factual condition, that is, whether freedom is the *right* to do as one pleases or whether it has to do with the existence of the *actual or 'material' opportunity* to act in accordance with such desires.[34] As a normative concept, freedom may involve no more than Hohfeldian 'privileges' or liberty rights, that is the absence of any obligation not to do the desired action.[35] Alternatively, freedom may be interpreted as a claim right, with correlative obligations, either of a negative sort (not to interfere with the specified conduct) or of a positive kind (to give some degree of assistance to the person with the right so as to enable her to perform the action in question).

As a factual condition, freedom as material opportunity can be interpreted to mean the existence of all the physical and psychological preconditions of action in relation to the specified activity. These preconditions can usefully be divided into (a) the absence of external obstacles to doing that which the person is physically and psychologically capable of doing (Hobbesian freedom) or (b) the presence of such capacities, necessary for the performance of the action, as are internal to the person concerned (sometimes called 'positive' freedom).[36] As a normative condition, my freedom, of whatever sort, may be of no real significance if either (a) I do not wish to do what I am under an obligation not to do, or (b) I do not have the material opportunity to do what I am not normatively free to do (that is, which I have an obligation not to do) even if I do wish to do it. Factual freedom also may have no real significance (a) if I do not wish to do that which I have the material opportunity to do, or (b) I am precluded, by acceptance of normative restrictions, from doing that which I otherwise want to do. However, in this second case, we may, of course, value the material opportunity to act contrary to normative restrictions which we do not accept. Indeed, it might be argued that normative freedom is significant only if it does curtail our factual freedom. This certainly follows if we interpret such obligations purely in terms of sanctions, for in this case normative obligations are de facto material restrictions on opportunity (assuming that sanctions are effective or are thought to be effective by the relevant group). This is, however, insufficient to cover those cases where individuals act from an acceptance of the obligation as a justified requirement, in which case, from the internal point of view of the agent, there is a clear distinction between material and normative freedom. I may be able to do that which I may not do.

This analysis suggests ways in which political authority, that is the right to place obligations on others (in the case of the state, *all* others in a given territory) and utilise coercion in case of non-conformity to those obligations, may be rendered less problematic. First, the obligations in question may not bear on what those affected wish to do or not to do. Thus I may have a political obligation not to kill but have no wish either to kill or to have the choice whether or not to kill. We may call the absence of such obligations '*natural non-significant freedoms*' – 'natural' because they relate to non-moral desires, and 'non-significant' because they involve no conflict with the natural desires we happen to have. Could such obligations have any function since, by definition, the persons concerned are required not to do only that which they do not wish to do? And is a state which creates only this sort of obligation going to be able to fulfil the requirements which justify its existence, such as the prohibition of commonly perpetrated harmful acts? The most that can be claimed here is that some of the rationales which justify states arise from the harmfulness of the conduct that *some* individuals, but not others, wish to perform, so that obligations to refrain from such harmful conduct restrict (if effectively enforced) the factual freedoms only of those who desire to act in ways that are considered by others to be harmful. The smaller the membership of this class of persons, the less there is a problem with the obligations in question.

It may also be noted that most of the coordinating functions of states render obligatory things which have in themselves no great significance for subjects in that they are indifferent to them, so that there is no loss of significant freedom in accepting such requirements except to the extent that opportunity costs are involved. This is in practice a highly important and pervasive type of law and it is noteworthy that it imposes little real threat to significant freedom.

A second way in which political authority can be rendered less problematic is where the affected individuals voluntarily accept the obligations which arise from its exercise. If this acceptance is based on the fact that they do not in any case wish to do that which they are now required not to do, then the second case collapses into the first. What other interpretation of their willing acceptance of obligations can be offered? One such is that the creation of an effective obligation on all members of a society may change the situation from one in which the individual wishes to do something to a situation where he or she no longer wishes to do it. Thus I may wish to kill anyone who kills my friends and may object to the obligation to refrain from so doing. But in a society where an effective obligation against homicide is created I may no longer have cause to regret that I am not permitted to indulge in revenge homicide because the situations giving rise to this desire no longer occur. Thus the consequences of regulation may alter the desires which would otherwise oppose that regulation. In this case we are dealing with what may be called *organisational non-significant freedoms*. Limiting such freedoms has no actual impact on those affected although, if circumstances change, they may do so.

A third class of non-significant freedoms derives from the operation of moral convictions. The analysis presented so far is compatible with an amoral model of human nature whereby individuals are characterised only by Hobbesian or natural desires and instrumental rationality. If we add to this picture a moral dimension such that we accept that individuals and groups have beliefs about what they ought to do irrespective of political authority, then a more complex picture emerges. Thus a moral individual (that is an individual with a morality) may wish to act in a certain way but believe that she morally ought not to do it. In this case, where a political authority requires that she not do that which she believes she ought not to do (although – contra her moral beliefs – she desires to do it) then we might be inclined to say that this is not a serious infringement of her freedom, in that her moral self does not wish to do the act in question. Indeed she may be grateful that she is required to do that which she believes she ought to do but might not otherwise do because of her morally uncorrected desires. We may call these *moral non-significant freedoms*. However, it is in the nature of morality that individuals should make their own choices about the performance of morally questionable conduct. Removing this freedom may undermine their status as moral agents and thereby infringe their dignity. Indeed, maximising such 'moral' freedom is often presented as the prime justification for promoting autonomy and consequently features as a leading argument for anarchy. It is arguably better that people make bad moral choices for themselves than that they are required to act in accordance with correct moral standards. Yet enforcing a morality that is approved by the subject does not seem so serious an infringement, and the harm involved may be readily overridden if benefits can be shown to flow from the restriction. Political obligation is at least less problematic where it coincides with moral obligation, as perceived by the subject.

Moral non-significant freedoms arise in relation to organisational obligations, where the benefit which grounds the obligation is achieved through cooperative activities, as well as obligations to refrain from naturally harmful conduct or to engage in naturally beneficial activities. Indeed, it is under the former guise that many of the prima facie benefits of states may be found. Thus, if the individual subject morally approves of the state's pursuit of social justice even when it disadvantages that individual, the loss of freedom involved may be regarded as morally non-significant.

Moralising our picture of human nature is, however, a two-edged sword. State prohibitions may be unwelcome because they prevent individuals doing what they believe they ought to do even if they do not, morality excluded, wish to do it. Indeed, this may be thought an even less acceptable limitation of normative freedom than simply interfering with amorally desired conduct. Thus the state may prevent individuals entering into agreements for the common good which give effect to their moral desire to promote the welfare of the group in order to appropriate their resources for the general good as conceived and pursued by the state. Nevertheless, the existence of the three types of non-significant freedom outlined above demonstrates that there is not always an irreconcilable clash between political obligation and significant freedom. So much may be taken from at least some readings of consent theory, without drawing on the absurdities of primordial contracts or the speculations of hypothetical consent models.[37] The problems of political obligation are certainly reduced in so far as indifference or consent, moral or amoral, characterise the attitudes of subjects to the specific requirements of their state.

Two major areas for grave concern remain. One is the spectre of natural and moral pluralisms, the existence of different desires and different moralities, particularly when these erode the bases of community by undermining mutual social expectations. The other is the problem of keeping political authority within the sphere of non-significant freedoms. Pluralism of desire is a matter of sociological and psychological fact, even if we allow that there are some basic universal wants shared by all humankind. We may all desire happiness but our conceptions of happiness vary enormously. The political problems which arise from the pluralism of desire derive from the fact that proscriptions which do not affect the material opportunities of persons who desire, say, security do affect the material opportunities of those who desire, say, a life of excitement. Factual irreconcilables arise from such causes and render impracticable the objective of freedom-neutral obligations for all subjects. Of course, similar desires lead to conflict in situations of scarcity, but their resolution is morally less problematic since the same proscriptions may be applied equally to all those involved.

Solutions to the problem of plural desires may be sought in the sphere of second order desires. Thus the most obvious tactic when faced with a pluralism of desire is to favour those types of desire which are statistically most frequent, thus minimising the incidence of significant unfreedoms. This may be endorsed wholeheartedly by a utilitarian morality but only with reservations by which one incorporates an element of distributive justice according to which membership of a majority is not always in itself a morally relevant ground for priority allocation. A policy of equal desire satisfaction, if practicable, serves to obviate the distributive justice difficulty but it cannot eliminate the need to pick and choose between preferences in the determination of which significant unfreedoms to override.

Other solutions to this problem may be sought in moral judgments to the effect that some desires and their associated styles of life are more acceptable than others. Again, these value judgments may take a majoritarian form, in which case we respect the values of the majority as a way of preserving a maximum of factual freedom. Or we may take a participant moral view and judge according to the subject's assessment of right and wrong desires. While the latter may appear more relativistic than the former, both rest on an individual moral judgment, albeit a second order one as to the proper way of determining political obligation. The decisive advantage of the majoritarian approach, both to choosing preferred desires and in selecting the way of selecting such a decision procudure, is that it is more capable of providing a definitive result even in a pluralisitic society.

If it turns out that, in one way or another, some desires are less worthy of respect, then this certainly reduces the clashes of obligation and significant freedom, for we can be unconcerned about those restrictions which are significant only for those with immoral, or proportionately less moral, desires. But how are we as individuals or as members of a potential majority to make such moral evaluations and have sufficient confidence in them to use them to discount what others regard as a diminution of their significant freedom? Whatever the epistemological problems of establishing an objective morality, they are as nothing compared with institutionalising such an epistemology so that it can be harnessed or institutionalised to overrule only objectionable majority moral opinion.

While the intervention of moral judgment may help us to mitigate some of the problems of natural or desire pluralism this merely takes us on to the difficulties of moral pluralism, which is even more problematic than desire pluralism to the extent that it seems less acceptable to require someone to act against their morality than it does to require them to act against their amoral desires. This would seem to generate a strong argument for non-interventionist states in situations of pluralism generally. But this is not generally so. Non-intervention often results in greater loss of significant freedom than does intervention aimed at increasing significant freedom. Whichever morality we adopt, if we prohibit those acts which are harmful in that they reduce the significant freedoms of others (as defined by that morality), significant freedom is enhanced.

Moreover, it is only by cooperative endeavours – which are bound to affect what some moral minorities regard as significant freedoms – that a vast range of material opportunities, and therefore the goal of individual autonomy, can be realised. Widespread valuable freedom is likely to involve possession of material opportunities which may be possible only through a highly active state. We are therefore in the position of requiring a trade-off between freedoms, some of which have more significance than others. At this point the idea of freedom, particularly in its fuller version as autonomy, begins to look highly ambivalent as between the acceptance or rejection of political obligation and the extent of the proper functions of the state. Everything would appear to depend on the particular nature of the state's activities, although, as we shall see, much also depends on the manner in which the state adopts and carries out its particular selection of policies which bear upon significant freedoms.

Utility and Rights

The contention that political obligation is not necessarily antithetical to significant human freedoms cannot be taken to imply that such obligations, and only such obligations as do not conflict with significant freedoms, are justified. We cannot assume that freedom, significant or otherwise, is the sole or overriding political value. All that can be argued at this stage is that justified state activity should seek to minimise interference with significant freedoms.

Despite its economic and hedonistic connotations, 'utility' is, perhaps, still the best label for those goals which serve as grounds for the restriction of significant freedoms by citing the overall advantageous consequences of so doing. Indeed, if we incorporate freedom as one of those goals which human beings desire and equate utility with the sum of their desire satisfaction, freedom may be subsumed within the rubric of utility, which is, indeed, what utilitarians seek to do.[38] Certainly, the bulk of the justifying benefits we attributed to states are capable of narrowly utilitarian formulations. Thus the necessity for survival is a prerequisite of all utilitarian goals. Behavioural control may be conceptualised purely in terms of prohibiting acts which cause negative utility and permitting or requiring acts which have positive utility. Notoriously, the corrective and distributive goals of state action are less amenable to utilitarian analysis, but it is usually at least arguable that the preferred corrections and distributions are those which increase the sum of human happiness or desire fulfilment.

If we go so far as to adopt the principle of utility, whereby all choices, including choices about the proper role of government, are morally subject to the test that every action must maximise the total happiness or desire satisfaction within the relevant group, the extent of government action may seem alarmingly massive and open-ended. To counter this prospect, it is sometimes suggested that that utility is relevant to government only with respect to its negative formation, the minimisation of pain, suffering or desire frustration.[39] Even this 'negative utilitarianism' seems to threaten very extensive state involvement in the details of everyone's life. And, in any case, given that any individual is likely to accept minor suffering in order to obtain great pleasure, negative utilitarianism seems morally arbitrary by excluding this tactic in the mass.

Famously, the traditional liberal principle which is used to circumscribe the scope of undiluted utilitarianism is that, apart from limiting the freedom of individuals to preserve the freedom of others, intervention in the conduct of anyone is validated only by the grounds that this intervention serves to reduce the occurrence of significant harms to others.[40] This 'harm principle' rules out state action on paternalistic grounds, that is intervention which purports to be justified on the basis that it is of benefit to the individuals whose freedom is curtailed by the intervention. Exceptions are allowed in this regard only in connection with those who are not capable of rational conduct, the assumption being that such persons are members of readily identifiable groups, such as children, or the mentally handicapped, who can thus readily be treated differently.

The libertarian position is that state control should be further limited by a number of 'rights' in addition to the right to negative freedom. Such rights would standardly include the right to life, to liberty and to acquire and transfer property.[41] The list of such rights may be extended to cover at least all the traditional civil and political rights from the right to a fair trial to the right to vote (and even the right to bear arms). This line of thought, which I will call the 'rights approach', seems to offer real guidance as to the proper scope of government activity, at least in the negative sense, in that it makes clear what states may not do, even if utility requires it. It is an important approach, in that it provides the principal justification for political systems which contain Bills of Rights which are interpreted and applied by courts to check the power of elected legislatures in their assumed pursuit of general utility.[42]

Given that Bills of Rights are clearly attempts to deal with the paradox of politics by placing effective checks within states on the abuse of governmental power, it may seem obtuse to reject the institutionalisation of human rights as a contribution to the philosophy of political obligation. If we follow in the tradition of John Locke and identify the natural rights which both define and constrain the activities of the state then it may seem an excellent idea to have a judicial body to determine whether the conduct of government is such as to justify our continuing trust. Unfortunately, however, the content of such rights either must be stated very simply, in which case it is unclear what they precisely involve, or else spelt out with some degree of specificity, in which case they are highly controversial. If they are stated very simply, as is normally the case, the determination of their detailed application in cases of controversy is effectively a matter of judicial legislation. In this case the paradox of politics is not evaded since the court can use its constitutional power to impose its view of the proper content of the rights in question. It may be argued that constitutional courts have less power for evil than government since they do not have the same material resources at their disposal, and can only strike down legislation or illegitimate government activity rather than perpetrate any positive harm. However, there is a sense in which constitutional courts with the authority to administer Bills of Rights have more power than government since government cannot, if the Bill of Rights is entrenched (and perhaps it must be to curb governmental abuse), overrule the court, while the court can overrule the government. Moreover, the idea that a power to nullify can do less harm than a power to carry out a policy is simply wrong as it cannot be assumed that government inactivity is less threatening to human interests than government activity. In the terminology of the approach, this point can be made by saying that governments are able to prevent violations of human rights between citizens and groups in a way which is severely threatened by the powers of a constitutional court in charge of a Bill of Rights whose decisions served to protect vested sectional interests.

This situation would pertain even if there were a defensible moral epistemology which produced a reliable consensus as to the specific content of human rights. But there is no such epistemology and no such consensus. At the most it can be said that most people in many cultures agree on certain general values and on some fundamental interests that are common to all humankind. For these reasons, which are elaborated in Chapter 7, the rights approach does not solve the tragic paradox of politics, but simply transfers it to another branch of government. The upshot of this discussion is that we cannot utilise the idea of rights, or acquire any morally definite list of fundamental rights, to settle the vexed question of the proper scope of state activity. Even if we could, it is not clear that this would enable us to trust any unelected and irremovable body of persons to interpret and apply these rights without bias. As it is, all that we can hope to identify is a range of significant human values, including the relief of suffering and the maximisation of desire satisfaction. Although we may wish to pursue these values by enacting rights to protect the relevant interests, this mechanism gives us no guidance as to what the content of these rights should be. This is a matter which, in the nature of moral epistemology, must be settled by political debate and political choice.

Justice

One important political value which is often related to rights, and equally often opposed to utility, is justice. We have already considered corrective justice (the putting right of intentional or negligent wrongs) and social justice (morally acceptable distributions of benefits and burdens), to which we may add formal justice (treatment in accordance with the relevant rules or institutionalised rights). If we take justice to be a particular political value rather than simply a catch-all for all major political ideals then it clearly has to do with distribution of benefits and burdens between individuals or in society as a whole, perhaps particularly those that are the outcome of societal existence.[43] Competing conceptions of justice can readily be formulated in terms of the criteria for determining which distributions are just, the standard ones being desert, need and entitlement (as determined by existing rules, rights or expectations). Where justice comes in to counter or modify the dictates of utility, it is usually to suggest that the way in which utility is created and the way in which it is distributed should take cognisance of the deserts, needs and entitlements of those involved.[44]

Each of these terms and their interconnections requires careful analysis, and their more specific designations and priorities involve us in moral as well as conceptual choices. My own preference is for a scheme which gives a central organising role to the idea of moral desert as the basis for justice in all its manifestations, but does not endorse the normal contention that justice is always the overriding political value.[45] It is just that people get what they deserve but there may often be other more important objectives, such as the humanitarian imperative to combat suffering or the economic need to increase the productivity of impoverished societies.

Alternative criteria of substantive justice include distribution in accordance with contribution (which may be seen as a version of the desert approach which measures merit by contribution) or distribution in accordance with need (which would seem to be a principle of humanity rather than justice, but none the less important for that).[46] These different values in distribution are difficult to prioritise and order, which means that it is not feasible to look to the idea of justice as the measure of the propriety of governmental functions. While we may seek to resolve these matters by the adoption of sophisticated decision procedures, such as those of Rawls, Ackerman or Habermas,[47] or by the deployment of some highly unspecific principles such as 'equal concern or respect' or 'equal human worth', such methods do not produce a level of interpersonal agreement sufficient to provide an authoritative view of the nature and limits of justifiable governmental activity.

The difficulties involved in arriving at a defensible moral consensus on matters of justice are increased if we extend justice, as is commonly done, to cover all priority values, for these are disparate and, in some cases such as the trade-off between desert and utility, largely incommensurable. Moreover, it is particularly in matters of justice that the significance of treating like cases alike comes to the fore. The idea (normally called 'formal justice') that benefits and burdens should not be distributed randomly but in accordance with set criteria is independent of the idea (normally called 'material justice') that these criteria reflect certain acceptable principles or standards. Exactly what moral status we should give to pure formal justice is far from clear, but there is certainly a rooted conviction in western societies from the time of Aristotle that if person A is to suffer or benefit as a result of governmental processes (judicial or otherwise) then all persons who are relevantly similar to A ('all As') should suffer or benefit to the same extent.

That said, it must be noted that formal justice is a matter which concerns us whether or not we are dealing with matters of substantive justice. Thus if, on utilitarian grounds, burdensome tasks are allocated on the basis of ability to perform them well, it will be regarded as unfair (formally unjust) if only some persons with the appropriate capacities are called upon to perform the task in question. Further, the significance of formal justice may be related to conventional and organisational goods, for whose attainment it is necessary to have largely unquestioning conformity to the patterns of conduct which facilitate individual conduct or connect together to produce the public good in question. Formal justice may therefore be viewed largely as a manifestation of the role of organisational goods, with the independent importance of justice for the limitation of both significant freedom and the claims of general utility being primarily a matter of the importance of presumed equality, modified by desert, for the acceptable ordering of a society that involves the entitlement to use force for its implementation.

Given our assumption of moral pluralism, the contention that political authority can be justified only by reaching an approximately correct balance of freedom, utility and justice takes us to an epistemological form of the paradox of politics. The existence of moral pluralism is one of the chief grounds for the need for states, namely to settle the difference of opinion as to how members of a single society should live together, yet the operation of states requires us to make complex moral choices that are amongst the most controversial and divisive possible. It looks as if only an objective epistemology can provide us with the legitimation of the methods which are necessary to deal with the problems of pluralism. There seems to be no possibility of governmment by means of value-neutral rules.[48]

Democracy

We now have to ask whether the state functions which may be used to justify political obligations have any particular connection with types of government, defined in terms of the locus of power: democratic, oligarchic or monarchical. So far, the analysis has been to do largely with the substance of goals that justify states. However, the discussion of freedom led us into the contention that the arguments against government are reduced if the content of the obligations does not conflict with significant freedoms. Building on this, it was argued that subjects' freedom is also not significantly restricted if they believe the restrictions on what they wish to do are justified in terms of their own values, even if they conflict with their own desires.

Similar considerations reduce the problem of political obligation where the other rationales for government, such as the utilities we considered or the goals of justice, which are candidates for overriding restrictions on significant freedoms, are such as to command the assent of the subject. This reduction is greatest where the number of subjects who concur with the principles which justify the activities of the state in question is maximised. The maximisation of assent does not by itself require democratic institutions in the sense of direct participation in government or in the election of representatives to govern on behalf of citizens. In theory the activities of any state could, by luck or design, meet with the approval of its subjects, whether or not they have in any sense explicitly consented to the arrangements in question.

One argument for democracy is that such approval is more likely to exist where there has been a chance to elect a government and exercise some control over its activities. The link between approval and democratic procedures is strong in the case of direct participation in decision making, provided that those involved have some understanding of what it is they are choosing. In the case of standard representative government based on voters' choices between competing political party candidates, the assumption that voting produces congruity of values between government and voters depends on highly contingent assumptions about the extent of the knowledge of candidates, parties, their policies and the machinery of government. Only where adequate information on these matters is available does the argument from maximising approval have any real purchase.

A further assumption in this central argument for democracy is that voters have some sort of continuing control over those elected to govern on their behalf. Essentially such control rests on the sanction of not re-electing an incumbent government. This crucially depends on governments meeting with continuing approval and not just on getting elected in the first place, but, again, this approval does not work for the purposes of the argument unless it is based on genuine knowledge of what it is that the government is doing.

To make the argument for representative democracy work, there has to be some approximation to direct democracy in which citizens have an equal share in actual decision-making power. This suggests that all major decisions should be formulated and presented for discussion in a way which approximates to what is involved in direct participation, not simply in legislation (because we cannot assume as yet that this is the dominant governmental mode) but in whatever particular decisions call to be made in the exercise of the functions of government. Given such preconditions, there are grounds for commending representative democracy on the basis that it is the best institutional mechanism for maximising the extent of subjects' approval for the conduct of government and thus helping to maximise significant freedoms.[49]

The model of democracy as outlined so far is essentially the classical utilitarian argument for representative democracy developed by James Mill and later utilitarians. Representative democracy is an institutional device for achieving an artificial identity of interests between governments and governed. We may call it the *self-protection justification* of democracy.[50] Complementary to this model is the argument that democracy is a desirable expression of individual and group autonomy simply because it is an exercise in self-government, whether or not this works to the benefit of those whose autonomy is being expressed. This *autonomy justification* of democracy feeds neatly into our earlier discussion of significant freedom, particularly if we conjoin it with the self-protection model as a way of emphasising the significance of the freedom in question. It is a justification which is, however, vulnerable to the objection that the very objectives which justify the existence of states may be undermined by the incompetence of electorates. This is another manifestation of what I have called the tragic paradox of politics, in that there is no evident way of institutionalising an effective means of making an impartial assessment of an electorate's relative competence.

There are, of course, equally many arguments against democracy, at least as it has been defined to this point. Of major importance are arguments relating to the position of minorities, which are discussed shortly. Prior to the problem of minorities is the view that there are stronger arguments in favour of government by an elite of informed and able persons. The rationale for government by an able minority is powerful in relation to government as a utilitarian device for attaining maximal satisfactions, since there is little evidence that majorities are particularly capable of knowing what will best contribute to their collective self-interest. The contrary considerations have to do with the difficulty in placing government in the hands of able persons (indeed, representative as distinct from direct democracy may be seen as the best way to go about trying to do this) and the impossibility of controlling those who are appointed. The strongest argument for democracy as against able oligarchy is that no group is to be trusted not to abuse the power which government gives them or to take the trouble to find out what it is that their subjects actually want.

All these considerations follow from a conception of democracy which is limited to majority control over elected representatives. We have yet to deal with the problem of minority interests within democratic systems. The argument from maximising approval is clearly a second-best type of argument in that it logically entails that the greater the approval the more justified is the government, with unanimous approval being the aspirational ideal. Further, unless we have the unlikely scenario that everyone has an equal share of the experience of being in a minority on matters of equal significance to them, we have to accept that democracy has particular problems over the fact that the some people disproportionately benefit from a majoritarian system. There are two standard ways of dealing with this problem. The first is to place restraints on the way in which majority decisions are reached. The second is to place limitations on the content of the decisions which majorities have the authority to make.

Restraints on the way in which majority decisions are reached involve attempts to moralise the decisions. These attempts rest on the view that a majority decision based on pure self-interest has less political legitimacy than one which manifests a majority opinion as to what is useful, right or just for the whole society. Rousseau presents a strong form of this analysis in *The Social Contract* when, in arguing that government should express the 'general will' rather than the 'will of all', he contends not only that all citizens should be in roughly the same social and economic circumstances (in which 'each has enough and none too much') but that in making their legislative decisions in a system of direct democracy they should be able to debate and vote only on general rules which affect everyone equally rather than on particular matters which would favour some more than others. Since all citizens are in roughly the same situation and they are limited to matters which affect them all equally, there is no taint of partiality or selfishness in the outcome.[51]

This utopia is clearly unrealisable in complex societies but the same rationale holds and can be applied to some extent. Few rules are so general that they apply to all citizens equally. An approximating example would be a per capita tax on every voter, but then not all subjects are entitled to vote. However, since we cannot assume that voters are in a situation of rough economic equality, even such a rule would not meet Rousseau's expectations since some will be disadvantaged much more than others. The nearest approximation that is likely to exist is a rule which affects everyone in a situation in which all are equally likely to be and which affects everyone to the same extent. The right/duty to vote might be one example.

Nevertheless, at the other extreme, Rousseau's ideal excludes decisions which benefit named individuals and groups at the expense of others. And, in the area of criminal law in particular, it argues forcefully against criminal sanctions which do not apply to all persons in that society, save where they are shown not to be responsible for their conduct. Of particular significance in representative government is that no exclusions should be made in favour of those elected to governmental positions. However, in reality nearly every law must apply to a certain category of citizens (those who have incomes of a certain amount, those who steal, those who are farmers, and so on). While these classifications may not represent necessarily fixed caste or status groups, inevitably individuals in some groups are more likely than those in other groups to fall within them. Usually the most that can be required, therefore, is that benefits and burdens be applied on the basis of *relevant* criteria, the assumption being that being in a majority is not, at this stage in the process, a relevant criterion.

It is a contention of this book that it is a necessary condition of attaining this objective that democratic legislatures adopt rules which embody criteria that are candidates for being assessed as relevant or irrelevant, appropriate or inappropriate. Little can institutionally be done to ensure that defensible choices are actually made by such legislatures, but at least they can be given the opportunity to make decisions on the basis of their honest assessment of relevant criteria for differential treatment, and this means deciding what rules to adopt. Democratic theorists are, however, increasingly unwilling to leave the matter there, and seek to introduce some substantive limitations to what it is that majorities may decide. Thus it is argued that we must rule out majorities making decisions which are racially or gender biassed, or interfere with certain basic rights of citizens, such as to a fair trial or to freedom of movement in and out of their country.

Only some of these substantive limitations on the legislative rights of majorities can be viewed as implicit in the democratic process. No rationale for democracy is compatible with giving majorities the right to deny the vote to any adult group resident within its territory. Most democratic rationales are incompatible with denying to any group the right to obtain and communicate information relevant to the making of political choices. It is, however, difficult to fit all minority protection rights into the presuppositions-of-democracy basket, particularly those rights which set limits to the extent to which governments can intervene in the 'private' lives of citizens with respect to such matters as sexual conduct, religious practice and freedom of association for non-political purposes.

Such specially protected rights designed to safeguard the interests of those threatened by unjustifiable government action can be viewed as ways to cope with the paradox of politics, the tragic incompatibiity of the need for government and the need for protection against government. If the paradox is genuinely insoluble, and it may well be just that, then the idea of such rights, whether or not they are constitutionally entrenched, is at least a way of reminding citizens and politicians of the problem. It is the contention of LEP that this will only be the case when highly generalised rights are given relatively precise rule formulations and that this is not a suitable task for courts. However, the fact that there are strong arguments both for giving the power to make such precise formulations to courts which are above the normal political process and for giving that power of articulation to democratically controlled representatives is yet another manifestation of the paradox of politics.

Summary and Critique

This somewhat breathless survey of the political context of legal theory attempts to explain the Positivist's ambivalent approach to the state, aiming to render it efficient in relation to its justifying goals and at the same time seeking mechanisms to control its illegitimate and destructive tendencies. Our analysis has raised some grounds for hope in that we have seen that not all the liberties lost through state authority are necessarily significant liberties and that there are good reasons for holding that both utility and justice provide bases for restricting some significant freedoms to some extent.

We have begun to explore the difficulties that such an enlightenment scheme generates in a postmodern world by considering the role of democratic institutions in attaining justified agreement in areas of deep moral diversity and practical controversy. When this comes to the question of protecting minorities, the discussion begins to home in on the possible centrality of rules as the format for the content of what justifiable political decision making ought be about. In the next chapter, analysis of the general social functions of rules clarifies further the ways in which rules can play a central part not only in the limitation but also in furthering the acceptable activities of government.

Looking to the function of rules to provide a medium for both the greater efficiency of government and for lessening its abuses runs up against that large and persuasive body of legal philosophy which sees rules as but weak tools for any purpose apart from that of giving a false appearance of legitimacy to systems which are basically oppressive and indefensible. In the view of these critics, the legalistic cure compounds the disease, for it legitimates inequality through the appearance of political neutrality.[52] A riposte to this potentially devastating critique follows later, but it is helpful at this stage to indicate that the LEP accepts the critique if it is aimed at the contention that even positivistically well formulated rules are always sufficient to guide and control government. Not only is LEP only a partial political philosophy which has relatively little to say about the proper content of many political goals, it is also an approach which emphasises that the ethics of the way rules are handled is as important as either the morality of their form or the value of their content.

What LEP offers is a conceptual framework for an institutional arrangement whereby effective and defensible political decisions can be made, enforced, supplemented and revised. The contention is that, in seeking a just and effective form of social organisation, there is far more to be gained by improving the quality of legislation and adjudication along positivist lines in the light of critical appraisal of actual performance than there is in jettisoning the ideals of rule-based rights and duties together with the processes and ethos of impartial adjudication. Government through rules may be more than an impractical and counter-productive strategy which diverts attention from the political nature of legal adjudication.

Notes

1 In the United States these distinctions are greatly blurred by the overt political role of the Supreme Court, which gives rise to an enormous literature that is directed towards the articulation of a form of moral/political reasoning appropriate to its deliberations.

2 See Kelsen (1967).

3 See Boyle (1992).

4 Thus Dworkin (1986) and, by way of criticism, Alexander (1987).

5 For instance, Dahl (1957, p.203) and Weber (1968, vol.1, p.53), which defines power as 'the probability that an actor in a social relationship will be in a position to carry out his will, regardless of the basis on which this probability rests'; more specifically, power determines who prevails in situations of conflict.

6 For the role of consensus in social life, see Parsons (1937), Habermas (1987) and some feminist theories, as in Young (1990).

7 See Giddens (1984, p.257).

8 But not necessarily a 'sovereign state' in the sense of an organisation possessing unlimited de jure coercive power.

9 Anarchist theories dispute not so much the necessity for such regulatory functions as the inevitability of their coercive forms. See Miller (1984) and Burnheim (1985).

10 Thus Hart (1961) takes it as axiomatic that there must be 'rules of change'; see also Parsons (1951) on adaptation as a functional prerequisite of society.

11 Interpretations of these disagreements range from deterministic analyses in terms of economic self-interest to sincere and reasoned moral and empirical disagreements about values and the means for their realisation.

12 This is a fact that is generally neglected by libertarian theorists who regard such resultant inequalities as essentially just. See Nozick (1974).

13 Arguments for the promotion of otherwise unobtainable goods are not logically distinct from those which see the state as necessary for the prevention of otherwise unpreventable evils, since the distinction between promoting goods and preventing evils is relative to the starting point from which the positive and negative terms derive their meaning.

14 However, some civil law, such as torts, can also be justified by its role in altering conduct in a socially desired direction.

15 On a pure retributivist view, the infliction of pain on morally guilty persons is an end in itself.

16 On some meritorian theories, all aspects of justice can be viewed as corrective: Sadurski (1985, p.101).

17 Hayek's influential argument against the 'redistribution' of what has not been distributed in the first place is little more than a verbal quibble: Hayek (1976, pp.62–100).

18 On equal worth and unequal worthiness, see Campbell (1988b, pp.31–5).

19 See Smith (1976), Olson (1965) and Hardin (1982).

20 See Hobbes (1990, Chapters 14 and 15), Hume (1978, p.548) and Axelrod (1984).

21 See Lewis (1969).

22 Hence Burke's general critique of revolutionary change: Burke (1990).

23 This accounts for the heuristic benefits of historical accounts of fictional social contracts as originating social and political institutions and the appeal of Rawls's ahistorical construct of an 'original position': Rawls (1972).

24 Hobbes is prepared to accept this consequence but those who are more doubtful about the comparable evils of anarchy are less sure that the price is worth paying.

25 Burnheim (1985, p.221).

26 This may sound a rather dated way of stating a problem which is central to the postmodernist critiques of the Enlightenment tradition, critiques which take the failures of liberal democracy to mark an end to the prospect of legitimating states. However, the nihilistic demythologising of classical political philosophy can be seen as an assertion of an extreme form of the paradox of politics. See Lyotard (1984).

27 Rawls (1993) has given up on anything but local consensus and the boldest remaining attempt to transcend localism, Habermas (1989), remains merely programmatic. See Rorty (1989).

28 The complexities of cultural pluralisms are worked out more clearly in classic debates about moral relativism than in contemporary discussions within postmodernism. See Bernstein (1983) and Hollis and Lukes (1982).

29 See Parfit (1984).

30 Hobbes (1990, Chapters 17 and 18).

31 See Lindley (1987).

32 This point is well made in Dworkin (1981).

33 For a fuller exposition of these distinctions, see Campbell and Hegginbotham (1991, Chapter 2).

34 See Campbell (1974b).

35 Hohfeld (1919, p.143).

36 Berlin (1969).

37 The most appealing form of the theory is where the granting of authority to government is a trust and may be revoked: Locke (1960).

38 In the 'ideal' utilitarianism of Moore (1903), freedom is one of the multiple desirable ends which right acts maximise. Hedonistic utilitarians relate the value of freedom to its instrumental role in promoting happiness.

39 Acton (1969).

40 Mill (1910) and Feinberg (1985).

41 Nozick (1974) has a limited list of such rights; Raz (1986, Chapter 10) has a more extensive and open-ended range.

42 Thus Dworkin (1977).

43 This is the somewhat arbitrary assumption in Rawls (1972).

44 This is the essence of Dworkin's distinction between the function of legislatures and the function of courts: Dworkin (1977, Chapter 7).

45 See Campbell (1988b, pp.6–8).

46 See Campbell (1974a).

47 Rawls (1972), Ackerman (1977) and Habermas (1987).

48 See Raz (1986, Chapter 5).

49 Schumpeter (1950) and Downs (1957).

50 The classic statement of this theory is to be found in Mill (1821).

51 Rousseau (1963) and Pateman (1970).

52 See Hutchinson (1986).

3 The Roles of Rules

Introduction

The overview of the political context in which legal philosophy must be viewed which is sketched in the previous chapter may appear something of a digression from the task of explicating Ethical Positivism. This is not so. In the case of a prescriptive theory of law, the nature of law is a matter of its function within a preferred political system. What we take law to be, and how we relate it to other aspects of society, is largely determined by a wider political philosophy.

Nevertheless, the organising theme of the previous chapter is designed to lead into the more specific question of the particular contribution of law within preferred polities. The tragic paradox of politics, according to which states are both highly necessary and extremely dangerous, leads on to the hope of a partial resolution emerging from the dual role of rules as both the facilitators and the circumscriptors of state power. Rules are an essential part of morally defensible government.

Further, the multiple value bases of political justifications in a pluralist society, together with the epistemological barrenness of the notion of moral rights as a method of arbitrating between them, brings to the fore the necessity for democratically oriented political discussion and decision over the whole spectrum of government activity. Our analysis of the concept of liberty has indicated that nothing can be shown, a priori, to be off-limits for states, and no simple determinations of social and political issues can be demonstrated to be so evidently correct as to avoid the need for debate and compromise. Utility in its various contents, freedom and autonomy in both their valuational and instrumental guises, formal and material justice in different varieties, all give rise to complex forms of individual and public goods, both conventional and organisational. There is no easy way through this morass of trade-offs between significant freedoms, priority social goals, prime individual interests and basic fairnesses. Each society has to work painfully towards generally acceptable values as expressed in principles and more specific standards on which to base its communal and cooperative existence. In this chapter it is argued that such a process must involve a deal of rule creation, testing and reinvention.

Beyond debate about the substance of the precise norms that are to govern social interactions there must also be a choice of the rules that are to govern the making of rules, the second order rules that constitute the political framework of a society. Unless we despair of finding defensible working agreements within a tolerable form of social organisation, we have to conceptualise and institutionalise how communal decisions are to be made and applied despite the complexities of our social problems and the divergencies of our values and their prioritisation. In this context, also, it is arguable that it is more advantageous to make the mode of selecting binding rules central than it is to rest our hopes on the choice of the best leaders or affirmations of the most appealing social goals.

This chapter provides reasons for these contentions, first, through an analysis of rules which brings out the sort of institutional forms to bear in mind when commending the political roles of rules; second, by outlining general non-statist advantages of societal rules; and third, by suggesting the political advantages of rules through drawing on the justificatory state values analysed in the last chapter and the processes for resolution which are associated with democratic ideals.

Rules: The Preliminary Analysis

At the extremes, actual systems of law may be defined either in terms of rules or in terms of courts. Since courts are hard to identify without recourse to their constitutive rules, and are routinely thought of as applying pre-existing rules, at least to a degree, rules or rule-type norms are essential to all theories of law. Positivism is distinguished from other legal theories mainly by its emphasis on the centrality of rules or rule-like norms and their analysis as defeasible human creations which communicate power and affect conduct.[1] Those theorists who do not concentrate on rules tend to give them a focal part at least in the presentation of what counts as a legal system, even if they go on to emphasise how much more there is to law than a system of rules. If not exclusively so, law is about the rules, the sort of rules that lay down what we may, must or must not do or omit to do.[2] This remains so to a surprising extent, even for those theories that emphasise the plasticity of rules and the yawning gap between paper rules, actual judicial determinations and the effects of both on human conduct.

For Hart, the principal theoretical challenge is to determine when a rule may be said to be a rule (social or legal) within a particular society; that is, he is concerned with what may be called 'societal rules' and how they relate to the idea of obligation.[3] The difficulty of this enterprise is that regularity in observable conduct is not conclusive as regards the social existence of a rule, for members of a society may, for one reason or another, fail to conform to the rules of their community and behave in a regular manner for reasons unconnected with the existence of rules. Hart's famous answer to this problem is to combine the requirement of general conformity with the likelihood of adverse reaction towards such limited non-conformity as there may be, adverse reaction which takes the form of criticism of the rule violation which effectively endorses the rule as the justificatory basis for the censure. In the case of obligations, justification here is given substance in terms of a belief in the social importance of the rule in question.[4] Yet such an analysis clearly presupposes the meaningfulness of rules independently of their acceptance within a particular, or indeed any, community. The 'rule' which is used to criticise non-conformity to a practice which is believed to be useful must be identifiable without reference to empirical regularities or particular acts of criticism, otherwise we could not make sense of using a rule to justify criticism of conduct.

Taking our cue from another pivotal Positivist, John Austin, we might identify this prior sense of 'rule' with the idea of a general command.[5] Since, however, it seems possible to conceive of a rule without a commander of that rule and it is undesirable at this stage to presuppose an account of rules which seems biassed at the outset towards the overtly political aspect of Positivism, it is better to start with the explication of the operators 'must' and 'may' as the irreducible modalities which, when combined with the use of universals (or general terms), constitute rules. However, linguistic usage suggests that rules do not all have this prescriptive or permissive character.[6] Thus, if we say that 'violence in response to violence is the rule', we mean simply that violence is a common or normal response to violence. Similarly, we may say that, 'as a rule, Australians are lucky' or 'Queensland is hot'. It is possible to dismiss such descriptive uses of the language of rules as representing nothing more than an ambiguity in our terminology which is of no particular significance. Certainly, descriptive generalisations have their own distinctive features. Thus the idea of an empirical rule is often restricted to those generalisations which fit the formula 'as a rule', meaning 'normally', whereas the generalisations in prescriptive rules are rarely confined to those which require certain conduct only normally. To say 'Australians must pay their taxes' is not readily construed as 'Most Australians should pay their taxes' or 'Australians should normally pay their taxes'. However, we will see that prescriptive rules usually presuppose descriptive generalisation, in that they make social sense only on the assumption of certain descriptive regularities. Thus 'Queenslanders should stay inside in the middle of the day' makes sense if we know that the average day in Queensland is hot. And so, while we may restrict our attention to what may be called 'normative' or 'regulative' rules, we will first explore the nature of their generality that they share with descriptive rules and then analyse the deontic operators 'may' and 'must'.

Rules are essentially general (in the sense of 'universal') in that they relate to types of conduct and and usually to types of people rather than individual actions and particular persons. This generality has two aspects. First, it involves or presupposes classifying particulars as having certain characteristics in virtue of which they are assigned to one type rather than another. However, such universal terms may be used in particular instructions as well as in rules. 'Do not sit down in that puddle' (in which the particulars or tokens are identified by the use of the universal terms 'sit' and 'puddle') is not a rule, while 'Do not sit down in puddles' is a rule.[7] In practice, societal rules are not simply general, in that they employ universal terms rather than particular names or identifiers. They are also general in that they require or permit a degree of repetition or non-repetition of the type of conduct in question by certain types of all persons.

The scope of a rule follows from the description of the conduct, and often the circumstances in which it occurs, as connoted by the universals involved.[8] Similarly, a rule may indicate the type or range of persons to whom a rule applies: the persons whose conduct is in question. While it could be argued that 'You, person P, are not to sit in puddles' is not a rule because it is addressed to one specific individual, whereas 'No-one is to sit in puddles' is a rule, there seems little awkwardness in the idea of rules which apply to only one person (such as the person who formulated the rule) although such rules may have limited use. We may take it, therefore, that the degree of generality in the addressee(s) of the rule is a variable which may be eliminated altogether without the rule ceasing to be a rule (although arguments for having rules on account of their generality can apply equally to the range of persons to whom it is addressed as to the scope of the rule). Interestingly, and this is a point to which we shall return, the possibility of this particularity of range does not hold for moral rules because of the requirement that moral rules be universalisable; that is, the requirement that they hold of all similar persons in similar situations.[9] Together the statement of the scope of a rule and the range of those to whom it applies or is addressed may be called the 'descriptive element' of the rule.[10]

These somewhat arbitrary fixed points, which serve to get the analysis of rules under way, gain significance when attention is switched to the purposes or functions of rules. Rules have universal terms to delineate their scope because this is necessary if they are to fulfil a type of role or associated collection of roles within social life. It is difficult to specify this role at the appropriate level of generality. 'Guidance', 'direction', 'regulation', 'governance' all pick out different emphases for what may be generically labelled 'prescriptivity'. What they have in common is the idea that conduct conforms to certain patterns through those involved being aware that they are required or permitted either to behave or not to behave in specified ways. Prescriptivity is such a basic concept in human experience that it is illuminating to point out that the intelligibility of prescriptive language depends on pre-existing assumptions about the freedom of individuals to make such choices as relate to the prescription, and the awareness of individuals that they have options or alternative possibilities for action or inaction between which they have the capacity to choose. The language of 'must' and 'must not' does no more than indicate that this choice is purportedly removed from them with respect to the specified conduct, while the operator 'may' serves to indicate that an existing prohibition (a 'must not') does not apply. What is removed is not the material capacity to act in one way or another but the belief that it is for them to decide whether or not to act in such ways. All that is required here for the language to be meaningful is a very bare conception of mandatoriness or non-optionality. What this mandatoriness amounts to is a fundamental question in all normative theory.

Contrary to much standard analysis, such prescriptive meaning does not in itself provide a reason for action. It states that something must or must not be done, not why it must or must not be done. If the prescriptive language is used by a person in authority or a person with power then it will generate reasons for action, but these derive from the authority or the power and not from the prescription itself. If there is a reason for having the rule then this reason may endow the rule with a normative force related to that reason, but the meaning of the rule, including its prescriptivity, does not depend on either the existence or the justification of that reason. A purposeless, arbitrary or baseless prescription is still a prescription.

This is a fundamental point, for it frees prescriptivity from reductionist analyses either in terms of 'good reasons' or in terms of sanctions. The bare meaning of prescriptive language is independent of whether or not there is a good reason for that prescription or whether there is a sanction for non-compliance. 'You must do this' is meaningful without any hidden implications that there are good reasons for doing it or that you will be made to suffer if you do not. Prescriptions do not require analysis in terms of providing reasons for action. Indeed, it is precisely because they do not carry reasons with them that they require justification, particularly as, by definition, they have the effect of restricting choice (or, in the case of permission, presuppose such an existing restriction) and thus potentially interfere with significant freedoms.

The rationality-neutral status of prescriptive language is not altered by its incorporation in the general descriptive element of rules. General prescriptions are equally meaningful without accompanying reasons for action and are equally in need of external justification. This may be lost sight of because the language of obligation is (helpfully) analysed via the notion of societal rules, in that our obligations are what is required of us as members of a society, a polity or a jurisdiction by the authoritative rules which are accepted as legitimate in these spheres. However, rules without justified authority carry no sense of obligation or, if they do, it is a very meagre sense of 'obligation' which does not capture anything beyond the concept of non-optionality.[11] What has to be allowed is that there is a bare notion of a mandatory rule that expresses only the ready intelligible, if philosophically elusive, idea of a prescriptive requirement: non-optionality or mandatoriness. This need be no more substantial than what is involved in understanding what it is that makes any rule a rule, whether it be a rule of a game, a language or a simple social practice. All that is involved here is the notion that, within a certain sphere, certain matters are, or are not, to be done and are therefore not a matter of individual choice. This minimal prescriptive effect of all rules is a meagre sense of obligation, which captures the simple idea that a rule, in its own terms, removes certain options from those to whom it applies.

Thus Warnock, in considering the role of rules within morality, writes that a rule 'exclude[s] from practical consideration the particular merits of particular cases by specifying in advance what is to be done whatever the circumstances of particular cases may be'.[12] This notion is sometimes explained in terms of the idea of 'exclusionary reasons', that is as a type of second order reasons which require us to pay no heed to the sort of first order reasons that normally govern our conduct in the absence of rules. Thus Raz analyses rules in terms of a combination of a first order reason for action, as stated in the rule, together with a second order reason directing us to refrain from acting on other first order reasons.[13]

This is a fruitful analysis, but we do not need to take up the idea that exclusionary reasons are actually reasons of a motivational or justificatory sort rather than bare instructions not to take such reasons into account. Exclusionary reasons do not motivate or justify, rather they serve to indicate that we are to exclude reasoning and simply apply the rule itself. They are thus anti-reason, not a type of reason, either first or second order. We are then led on to consider what reasons we could have for obeying such instructions, but this takes us beyond the analysis of the prescriptive rules to a consideration of their purposes and so to the justification and ethics of rule following.

Something of this notion of exclusionariness is echoed in Schauer's conceptions of the 'entrenchment' and 'stickiness' of rules, qualities which he identifies with the way in which rules resist modification in the light of their uses in particular circumstances. Entrenchment has to do with the way in which, although all generalisations may be oversimplifications with respect to complex reality, they have to be retained nonetheless for the purposes of ordinary discourse. While in conversation we may modify our terms to suit these changing circumstances, there are limits to this malleability of language, and in the case of regulative rules this applies even more to prevent us changing the content of the rule to adapt it to the general purpose it serves in the specific circumstance with which we are confronted. 'Under this decision mode, the decision maker treats the generalisations as more than mere indicators, but as supplying reason for decisions independent of those supplied by the generalisations underlying justification.'[14] Thus, according to Schauer, 'rules are necessarily sticky, resisting current efforts to mould them to the need of the instant'.[15] This, perhaps, is the explanation why prescriptions are not generally of the form 'as a rule' even if the descriptive generalisations which they presuppose are probabilistic.

These ideas of entrenchment and stickiness relate to Schauer's contention that rules have to be seen in purposive terms, in that they are adopted to solve specific types of problem. His favoured example is the phenomenon of the unruly dog in a restaurant giving rise to the rule 'No dogs in the restaurant', which then resists modification even when the restaurateur is confronted by a guide dog or the Queen's corgies. Despite the fact that rules have purposes, it seems an aspect of rule direction, Schauer notes, that we resist looking behind the rules to their purpose in order to vary the descriptive element of the prescription. This point may be made more strongly by resisting Schauer's too easy assumption as to the purpose-related nature of rules, at least in terms of the analysis of the meaning of rules. For, while rules are adopted for purposes and these purposes may well serve as the justification for creating the rule, having such purposes is not written into the idea of what rules are. Indeed, the same rule may serve many or no purposes. What should be accepted is that rules have the function of removing choices and hence of removing consideration of the reasons for such choices. The fact that we may have reasons for removing such choices does not make the meaning of the rule itself purposeful, although it does begin to provide some explanation as to why rules are peremptory in force and sticky in meaning.

Quite apart from implicit sotto voce reservations and qualifications which may be assumed to attach to particular utterances, the exclusionary force of rules is not an all-or-nothing business, and may be quite limited, depending on the conventions and assumptions governing rules of that type in certain contexts. Even within its allotted scope, a rule has greater or less valiance in relation to competing rules or reasons for action. The idea of 'force' here is potentially more specific than weight, a variable which relates to the significance of the substance of the rule, but has the same function in relation to decision making in cases of conflict.[16] The force of a rule is a function of its prescriptivity, not its content, and may vary from overwhelming to nothing more than applying other-things-being-equal, that is, when there is no countervailing reason or rule which applies. However, if there is no force behind the exclusion then it cannot be said to be an exclusion at all and, on the analysis, there is then no rule.

Entrenchment and stickiness may be less applicable to some rules, namely rules which are simply practical guides to uncontroversial ends based on empirical experience. In the case of such 'rules of thumb', where the purpose of the rule is an implicit part of its meaning and the nature of its instrumentality is clear, they are more readily subject to modification in the light of experience and in the light of particular circumstances which make it clear that following the rule will not be effective for the purpose in question. As Schauer notes, however, rules of thumb do not have the categorical prescriptive force of regulative rules in normal circumstances.[17]

We have seen that it is a common mistake to think that the meagre sense of obligation, the meanings of the operators 'may', 'must' and 'must not', are intelligible only if they are filled out in some way, for instance by relating them to the threat of force or the social pressure that may be used to back them up, or by giving them a moral or prudential content or background. It is similarly a mistake to reduce the force of a rule to an assessment of the significance or weight of its content. These mistakes may arise from the assumption that the making of a rule in itself provides those to whom the rule applies with reason for conforming to it. However, the bare idea that certain actions must be done or must not be done leaves it an entirely open question whether or not there are societal or other pressures for conformity to it, or whether there are good or indeed any reasons for compliance. From the point of view of those to whom the rules apply, the existence and intelligibility of the prescription is one thing, the identification of the reason – if any – for obeying it is another. This is so, even though it is clear that societal rules usually call for obedience. Normally, the context of the articulation of obligation-creating rules carries with it the assumption of certain reasons for conformity, such as the desire to play a game or, in the case of language, the need to communicate and, more generally, the desire to please those who subscribe to the rules in question, but the bare sense of a normative requirement is separable from all these reasons and from the specific contexts of its deployment – hence the 'meagreness' of the simple sense of obligation that is expressed in the use of all socially prescriptive rules. Rules are prescriptive but involve no inherent reason why the individuals to whom they are addressed should conform to them; that is, they do not in themselves establish what may be called 'material obligation'.[18]

This takes us again to the reasons for having rules, which is a wider question than asking about the purpose of each particular rule. The justifiability in question must be something more than the legitimacy, validity or authority of the rule in question within its normative system, since none of these in itself provides us with reasons for action.[19] In addition, the justifiability of obligation-imposing rules does not need to be absolute in the sense that it cannot be overridden by other considerations. Furthermore, because we are dealing with a system of obligation discourse, the justificatory reasons in question relate not to the content of the obligations but to the acceptance of meagre obligation qua obligation; that is, the justification for following the requirements addressed to us irrespective of our opinions as to their content, at least to some extent. In other words, material obligation is established by the existence of justificatory reasons for following rules rather than being guided by our own moral judgment or other preferences about the rightness or wrongness of the actions required by the rules.

Having distinguished meagre from material obligation, and related it to the notions of exclusionariness and stickiness, we can move on to identify the types of reason that are standardly given for complying with different types of meagre obligation and thus identify material types of obligation that do analytically incorporate reasons for action. This will enable us to arrive at a clearer understanding of the roles which rules play in the different aspects of social life.

Rule Rationales

Taking up the analysis of justificatory bases for material obligations, we must remind ourselves that such bases should not be directly dependent on the specific content of the obligations in question, although we will see that complete content independence is unattainable. We are not here dealing with justifications of rules that depend directly upon their particular content, for example the prohibition of specific types of naturally harmful conduct and the prescription of specific types of naturally beneficial actions. However, we are making assumptions to the effect that some forms of conduct are harmful to a degree that justifies some sort of restricting societal response. Nor are we concerned with purely prudential reasons for action which are central to the justification of rules of thumb, that is rules directed towards guiding us as to how to achieve our desired objectives. It will be assumed at this stage that such rationales do not serve to justify 'real' or exclusionary rules since their force is overridden by the individual's belief that they do not serve his purposes in particular circumstances. While it is clearly possible to mount arguments to the effect that all obligations are reducible to long-term self-interest, it will be assumed that the sort of rules in which we are interested require more than prudential justifications.

Before going into these matters in more detail, it is appropriate to foreshadow that rule rationales involve the evocation of values to which appeal has been made in Chapter 2, both in the justification and the circumscription of political obligation. We will see, however, that these rule rationales are not confined to the benefits of laws. Indeed, it will become apparent that much justified political authority involves the endorsement, reinforcement and application of prepolitical societal rules.

The Diversity of Rationales

The myriad of rule rationales may be roughly characterised into those relating to coordination and those relating to control. The former have to do with the facilitation of orderliness, cooperation and distributive patterns. The latter are about the encouragement of intrinsically or instrumentally beneficial or welcome conduct and the discouragement of intrinsically or instrumentally harmful or unwelcome activities. While many rules have both coordination and control aspects (indeed, an element of control is involved in all large-scale coordination) the distinction can be analytically useful in helping us to appreciate the complexity and variety of rule functions.

Under the heading of 'coordination rules' come all those rules which relate to the social utility of having practices which enable people to anticipate the conduct of others and thus more successfully achieve their objectives either personally or in cooperation with others, one of the societal functions which is fine-tuned rather than initiated by law making. Coordination rules may be subdivided into types or aspects of rules: (a) *facilitative rules*, which enable agreements to be made and enforced (such as the rules of contract); (b) *convenience rules*, which provide for otherwise morally arbitrary individual choices to be made in according with publicly known and accepted criteria so as to avoid unnecessary conflict and costly negotiations (such as rules of the road); (c) *distributive rules*, which are designed to bring about desired patterns of contested benefits and burdens (such as property rules and much taxation law); and (d) *output rules*, which are designed to organise the production of desired goods (such as rules of the workplace or bureaucratic rules) for public benefits as well as for those directly involved.

In most cases of coordination rules a wide measure of rule conformity is usually a prerequisite of functional effectiveness, and it is clear that such conformity requires that the rules in question be treated, in their context, as conclusive reasons for action and that the interpretation of their content be sticky in that it cannot be varied unilaterally to suit the particular participant. However, the exclusionary force and stickiness of the rules will vary with the category of rules in question. Thus, while disregard for facilitative rules such as contract rules can have deleterious consequences for the facilitation of particular arrangements, its effects tend to be more localised than, for instance, disregard for convenience rules, such as regulatory traffic laws. Neglect of distributive rules has a more incremental effect on the attainment of distributive patterns and its precise impact will depend on the conformity of others. The significance of each act of conformity/non-conformity will depend on the overall workings of the system and the extent to which justice and not simply effectiveness is at stake.

Output rules gain their significance from their role in promoting the specific objectives and here the importance of conformity will depend not only on the rule-governed participation of others but also on its effects on the outcome goals in question. Clearly, output rules depend for their utility on their part in promoting the social objectives which are desired by their creators, as when distant policy goals are achieved through complex taxation and commercial regulations which have a purely instrumental role whose significance is barely if at all understood by those to whom they apply. The value of such rules is that they further the organisation of large numbers of individuals and groups in ways which make the pursuit of complex social objectives feasible. This bureaucratic function is normally best served by unthinking conformity to and application of these rules, but where individuals or officials are in a position to appreciate failure in their intended instrumentality, extensive discretionary powers to modify or abandon the rules in particular cases may be appropriate unless there is scope for abuse through the discretion being exercised for the private benefit of the official. Common to all these categories is the factor that, to some degree, the significance of individual conduct in relation to the rules depends on its impact on the organisational system. Non-conformity matters not so much for its immediate consequences as from its subsequent and cumulative effects.

Control rationales for rules depend more on the general need to prevent directly harmful and encourage directly beneficial behaviour. This may be done by educational efforts to internalise habitual obedience or an awareness of the social benefits of having such rules, or by attaching sanctions that deter and perhaps reward the relevant conduct. Such rule justification is not, of course, entirely independent of the content of the rules in question but, granted that there are harmful and beneficial actions, rules, particularly sanctioned ones, have an important role in reducing the former and increasing the latter, so they are a desirable social mechanism in this regard. In contrast to coordination rules, conformity to harm/benefit-controlling rules is worthwhile in each and every case, irrespective of what other people may do. There is also strong reason for high levels of both exclusionary force and stickiness owing to the fact that there are so many social forces at work which are directed towards ignoring or reinterpreting the rules so as to avoid their evident behavioural implications. Thus individuals and groups will tend to play down the force or vary the meanings of rules to suit their own interests, particularly when they are in the heat of activity rather than reviewing their own past or future conduct.

Societal rules are so varied and so often indeterminate in their function that it is impossible to give a comprehensive and readily agreed classification of rule types. Thus rules which fulfil the social function of forestalling social conflict by providing bases for resolving disputes may be regarded as coordination rules since, by having known dispute resolution rules, conflict avoidance is encouraged and convenience is increased. However, such rules may also serve to penalise certain types of harmful conduct, thus falling under both the umbrella of control and that of coordination. To a greater extent than standard control rules, dispute prevention/resolution rules serve their function independently of their content, for in considerable measure, in this sphere, any rule is better than no rule. On the other hand, where such rules are inefficacious in that they do not command agreement, they may provoke rather than reduce social conflict, and dispute resolution may often be better furthered by displacing the conflict-resolving rules in particular circumstances.

To this incomplete exploration of the types and functions of rules may be added other rule rationales which suggest functions that cut across our categorical schema, such as the psychological comfort and security of regularity and predictableness, and the symbolic function of rules as a focus for community identification and value commitment.[20] Further exploration of the significant properties of such societal norms in order to explicate in more detail the justification of the role of rules may be done under the rubric of several overlapping categories which apply to some extent to both control and organisational functions of rules: orderliness, fairness, socialisation and efficiency. In this analysis it becomes clear that the roles of rules overlap significantly with the justificatory bases of states explored in Chapter 2. This close and interesting relationship is taken up in what follows.

Orderliness

While adherence to a rule by even one individual in the circumstances to which it applies provides order in the sense of a recurrent pattern of conduct in identifiably similar circumstances, a number of individuals following different rules does not produce social as distinct from individual order. The orderliness arising from social norms is dependent on all individuals, or all individuals of an identifiable type, following the same rule in the same type of circumstance. Recurrent patterns need not be orderly, however, in the sense of excluding argument, conflict and fighting. To achieve order in the sense of harmony or smooth interaction, the rules must be such as to require conduct which has this particular result. This is most evident in rules for the ordering of situations of spatial proximity which produce physically incompatible modes of conduct on the part of those involved.

Since there are many different patterns of interaction which are compatible with smooth uncontroverted societal relationships, orderliness in this strong sense is relatively independent of particular rule content, but not entirely so. Societal rules are necessary for social order, but not just any rules will do. Where the content of rules is not such as actually to generate conflict and is capable of soliciting general conformity then we have the orderliness that generates the predictability and certainty which are preconditions of a harmonious and effective social order. The advantages of orderliness include the avoidance of conflict (which is unpleasant in itself and an unproductive use of time and energy), the reliance which can be placed on the conduct of others, which makes it clear what options are open to the individuals involved, and the psychological security which derives from a stable social environment.

Whether state-administered or not, the orderliness advantage of rules is a feature of all societal rules, but may form part of the justification for state involvement in the creation, sustenance and application of these rules when other social mechanisms are not producing the levels of conformity and clarity to sustain the necessary functionality of the rules. Large-scale societies with complex interactions and changing circumstances are likely to require extensive central authorisation and implementation of rules to maintain a level of order suited to their main types of interaction.

All these advantages are lost when the individuals concerned substitute their own judgment of what is appropriate for the directive of the rule, except in specific and specified circumstances. Foremost amongst these is where it happens that no-one else is involved, so that there is no potential conflict, reliance or uncertainty. Another special circumstance is where all those involved are able and willing to negotiate an alternative pattern compatible with orderliness in this specific circumstance. Both types of exception are subject to major reservations which may be maintained against all escape routes from rule conformity. The first reservation concerns the danger of partiality. Where such deviation is a perceived advantage to the deviators, they may be inclined to distort their perception of the situation so as to blind them to the fact that there are, for instance, others involved whose interests may be affected by the deviation. Quite apart from the unfairness that may be involved, this limits the extent to which the expected conduct of others can be relied upon, thus undermining the organisational benefits of the rules. The second reservation relates to the weakening of habit. Even if deviations in special circumstances are justified, such deviations can become habitual, thus reducing the likelihood of conformity in situations where the special circumstances do not apply. A third reservation relates to unfairness, in that allowing individual exceptions or mutual negotiations between those involved may lead to situations which are unfair to some of those involved. A fourth reservation concerns the inefficiency involved in individuals making costly appraisals of each situation with a view to possible deviation or negotiation. The first and second points may be viewed as part and parcel of the worth of organisation itself. The third and fourth points require further elucidation.

Fairness

We have already considered the issue of fairness in the context of the idea of formal justice: the principle of treating like cases alike, something which can happen only miraculously without the existence and application of rules which identify what situations and what treatments are alike.[21] It is easy to dismiss this formal sense of fairness as of little importance because so much more seems to depend on the substantive justice of the rules than their accurate and universal application. No doubt formal fairness is a powerful psychological factor and this provides important utilitarian grounds for taking some account of it, and in Chapter 2 we noted its general instrumental value in relation to organisational goods, but as an independent basis for respecting rules it does not always carry conviction.

A more telling version of formal fairness is the argument that if a certain outcome is right for one person then it must be right for all those in similar situations. So much follows from the belief that moral judgments are necessarily universalisable.[22] If an act is right in a certain context then it must be right in all identical contexts and indeed all contexts in which there is not a morally relevant difference. In this case a person who fares less well at the hands of a moral agent than another similarly placed person may properly argue that either she or the other person were not treated correctly. If the moral agent is not able to identify a relevant difference between the two situations then she must allow that one or the other has been dealt with wrongly.

It follows that, in all social circumstances where a person has a duty to treat others in accordance with moral standards, and this may be thought to apply a fortiori to anyone in authority over others, that person ought to make her treatment decision in accordance with a rule which captures the morally relevant criteria. On this assumption a person who is treated less well than another in a morally identical situation can use the fact of the difference in treatment to base a defeasible claim to have been wrongly treated. The claim may be defeated by evidence that it is the other person who was treated more generously than she ought to have been, but if this admission is not made, and no relevant difference is established, the claim stands. It may be argued that this shows that the 'wronged' person has been treated badly, but that this is a distinct moral assessment from any matter relating to the comparative treatment of the two persons. The legitimate complaint is that she was not treated as she ought to have been, not that she was treated worse than another similarly situated person. However, the language of fairness may still be appropriate in some such circumstances where the moral issue is one of distribution of a benefit or burden which is not in itself merited by any of the parties but calls to be allocated for reasons of utility. In these circumstances any relatively weak assumption of equal moral worth suggests that distribution should be made in equal portions. If this is not done then the wronged person may claim unfairness in the sense of an arbitrary departure from the appropriate distributive rule.

In most other cases justice enters the picture by way of the application of the appropriate substantive criteria of merit, need and so on. The injustice then arises because the correct rule has not been applied rather than because a different rule has been applied. It follows that substantive justice requires that persons be treated in accordance with rules which embody just criteria of distribution. Consistent rule application is therefore a necessary, not a sufficient, criterion of justice, for it may turn out that the rules are unjust, in which case consistent application multiplies injustice. However, unless it is demonstrated that treating persons according to their merits or some other relevant criterion can be achieved by means other than the application of rules, this is sufficient to establish that accurate implementation of rules is a prerequisite of a materially just society. Further, the rules in question must be genuine, sticky rules. Anything more fluid could not serve as a basis for the sort of interpersonal comparisons on which judgments of unfairness are based.[23]

The activities of states in relation to fairness are controversial to the extent that there is dispute over the proper content of rules and difficulty in attaining anything like proper administration of such rules as are generally acceptable, but, where fairness is taken as being a matter of great importance, then in situations of any scale and social complexity it is difficult to conceive of any sustained attempt to achieve fairness in society that did not involve a centralised effort to provide offical endorsement and administration of politically authoritative rules binding on all those involved. Even ad hoc readjustments of patterns of benefits and burdens require to be rule-governed, although the rules may relate to the achievement of an outcome rather than any specific way of achieving it. It should be noted that where the pattern is intended to instantiate material justice then this will involve rules which relate the outcomes to the conduct and character of those involved.

Socialisation

The role of rules within education in its widest sense is evident when we consider that the inculcation of any values depends on repeatedly giving instantiations as to what conduct is acceptable and unacceptable. An issue is, however, whether such 'rules' are mere rules of thumb, pointing unsocialised children and adults to the sort of thing that is usually acceptable and unacceptable, or whether they have the rigidity of rules with an exclusionary bite. This is clearly something which varies from society to society and is more or less appropriate according to the maturity of the individuals involved and the importance of the conduct in question. Small children with little understanding of the harm their behaviour can cause must be governed by strongly exclusionary rules, whereas mature adults who can appreciate the complex causality of the results of their conduct may have more latitude in their adherence. The details of such discussion depend in fact on the considerations of justice and utility which we consider elsewhere, for nearly everything depends on the rationale for the type of rule in question.

There is, however, a distinct rationale for having exclusionary rules which has direct bearing on the role of socialisation in building and maintaining community life. Quite apart from the organisational and other instrumental benefits of rules, adherence to the same set of rules is an important bonding mechanism which constitutes membership of a group and gives communal identity to the individuals concerned. Acceptance of the customs of a community is not just a way of being accepted into that community, it is part of what it is to be a member and part of what it is for that collection of individuals to constitute a community.[24] Contrary to the orthodox belief that rigid rules are required for impersonal associations or aggregates of individuals and not for closely knit communities which have multiple and continuing interactions, communities more than associations depend on a mass of complex rules. The contrast between the two types of social relationship is that associations must consciously create rules, whereas communities simply have them.

Efficiency

Rules, by their exclusionary force, simplify decisions. Rules limit the factors which need to be taken into account by the individual. They limit the matters which have to be discussed and decided by parties to an interactive enterprise; they limit the extent of the variety of human conduct that has to be anticipated in the formulation of a plan. Rules enable habitual, unthinking conduct in situations where time and effort spent on making choices have high opportunity costs. Of course, there are quicker ways of making decisions than using rules. Arbitrariness and chance are efficient in transaction costs but they are not so efficient in terms of achieved outcomes. Rules not only simplify decisions, they predict consequences, hence the choice of rule can be tailored to the outcomes desired from habitual conduct, and then revised if they do not work out as intended.

Societal rules are, however, usually rough and ready. They are not tailored to every circumstance, and can rarely be complex enough to take in all relevant variables.[25] There is therefore always a trade-off between maximal outcome and minimal decision costs. This is not a trade-off, however, that can be calculated on each and every occasion, otherwise the cost benefits of using rules would be lost, since it would be necessary to calculate on each occasion whether or not it is efficient to follow the rule or to start from scratch. Moreover, many rules are to be seen as the basis for continuing cooperation in situations where standard practices are of mutual benefit. Orderliness which embodies conventions of conduct in situations of some ambiguity, where all stand to gain from knowing how others will behave, generates a very important outcome in terms of efficiency, defined as the maximising of individual preference attainment. These benefits are simply not to be had unless shared rules are standardly followed. It is a commonplace that, however 'unregulated' markets may be, even the most competitive commercial situations cannot be efficient in relation to wealth production in the absence of a bedrock of control and coordination rules.

The characteristics and benefits of orderliness, justice, socialisation and efficiency which we have attributed to societal rules are supplemented and enhanced when we move on to the political dimension of obligations in which the centralised and purposive origins of the rules are more distinctive factors.

The Politics of Rules

We have seen that the LEP is a moral theory about the exercise of political power. We now have to relate this to our preliminary discussion of the societal roles of rules. In brief, the relationship is that some sort of centralised and effective authority is necessary in any large-scale society to ensure the necessary conformity to societal rules and organise, in particular, coordination rules, to effect certain societal outputs, such as defence, economic prosperity or survival, and a measure of social welfare, in an efficient and just manner.

We have seen that the advantages of states are various but centre on their potential for the avoidance of conflict, the facilitation of cooperation, the maximisation of individual welfare and the attainment of justice, both corrective and distributive. Clearly these objectives overlap substantially with the standard rationales for rules. Indeed, it is evident that most of the justificatory purposes for states relate to maintaining and enhancing the operation of societal rules. Such jurisdiction-wide effectiveness can in theory, and in reality to a degree, be attained by consensual means. But, while it is evidently desirable that non-coercive motivations be relied upon, they are not always sufficient to obtain the degree of conformity required for societal rules to fulfil their functions, and hence an organised system of sanctions may also be needed to encourage conformity. If opting out is not acceptable –on either efficiency or fairness grounds – mandatory and organised sanctions to support rule comformity may become necessary.

Quite apart from the issue of compliance, complex societies generate disagreements about the acceptable content of their rules. These divergences are sufficiently resistant to consensual reconciliation for there to be reason to avoid enforcing conformity. However, it is accepted that many choices have to be made between competing lifestyles and community objectives that require a measure of uniformity. Hence the argument for a state, as the monopoly power in a given territory, to give authoritative decisions as to disputed rule content.

Of course, it cannot be assumed that all state justifications emanate from the societal value of having rules. Indeed, there are strong arguments for saying that some acceptable state objectives are, in certain situations, better pursued by means of individual directives and the discretionary authority of mandated officials. However, rules are commonly necessary as means for the effective exercise of power. As instruments, rules enable power holders to establish approved patterns of conduct without the use of ad hoc individual commands. These patterns may be viewed either as desirable in themselves or as useful to further goals. Where these patterns or goals exemplify the objectives which justify states then the adoption of these rules as laws is indicated.

The effectiveness of rules as instruments of state action enhances the paradox that the capacities of states which make them valuable social institutions also render them peculiarly dangerous ones, in that they have the capacity, and their individual holders of power have the motivation, to misuse the powers given to them for personal gain or individual value gratification. This is the context in which we should view the normal defining feature of Legal Positivism: law as a system of posited and operational rules. The justification of states comes only in part from the instrumental function of the exercise of power through rules, that is from the approved objectives of states. That justification also derives from the fact that the exercise of power through rules, whatever its objectives, has advantages over the exercise of power without rules.

These rule advantages are additional to those applying to rationales for ordinary societal rules. Traditionally, the most important rule advantage for liberalism has been the opportunity government through rules affords to individuals and groups of avoiding sanctions through evasive action in the light of sanction-imposing rules, an opportunity which is not available if power is exercised in a non-predictable manner: we may call this the *liberty advantage*.[26] This liberty advantage has instrumental value for those affected by government in relation to their aims, but it also enables moral justification for holding individuals responsible for rule violations. At its humblest, the opportunity to choose makes it reasonable to hold the individuals responsible for their conduct and to blame and punish in line with any chosen violations. At its grandest this manifests respect for the individual; at least it removes the possibility of easy excuses for non-conformity. This advantage applies for all societal rules to which any form of sanction or criticism is attached, but has particular application in the case of mandatory rules conjoined with punitive consequences.

Rules also have a role in helping to channel power to its morally acceptable objectives, a phenomenon which we may call the *moral-form advantage*. The moral-form advantage derives from the fact that all conduct, including the justifiable exercise of power, must be principled, not arbitrary; that is, it must embody some principle or maxim, otherwise it cannot be moral because it cannot be evaluated from the moral point of view, such evaluation involving a decision about whether or not the maxim of the act is universalisable. As a matter of morality, acts are right and wrong only in so far as they exemplify acceptable or unacceptable types of conduct, where the type is identified through the description of the morally relevant features of the act. It follows not only that all acceptable rationales for government action must be universalisable, but also that governments morally cannot require citizens to behave in ways which are not candidates for moral legitimacy. General rules, in so far as they specifically required and permitted conduct in terms of classes of persons and types of conduct, can readily exemplify or be related to a maxim which is at least a candidate for universalisability. This means that the universalisability aspect of rule form is a necessary (but not of course sufficient) requirement for the morally justified exercise of political power.

Furthermore, where government is conducted through the choice of rules this facilitates rational decision making in government, partly by reducing the number of political decisions that have to be made, partly because they provide a manageable focus for working out how to achieve social maintenance or change. We may call this the *efficacious-choice advantage*. This advantage includes procedural rules for decision making which is a particular application of the coordinating function of societal rules applied to political organisations.

In this list of the political rationales of rules must be included their role in setting out the powers or rights of command of state officials: the *limited-capacity advantage*.[27] There is an efficiency rationale here in relation to the purposes of government through giving the power to officials which they need to carry out such tasks. Here too rules have an efficiency role, in giving officials the capacity to carry out specified objectives. Just as important, however, is the limitation of these powers within specified scopes and means: empowerment rules are limiting in that they do not grant all power and to them may be added further restrictions on the scope and method of the officials powers. On this edifice is founded modern administrative law.

So much applies to any form of government, democratic or not, but further advantages accrue to rule government in the case of democratic polities. In Chapter 2, democracy is analysed as a system designed to ensure (1) that political power is divided on equal terms between those affected by it so as (a) to maximise the autonomy of each individual and group, and (b) to achieve the benefits generally desired in a community; and (2) that certain fundamental interests of individuals and groups are inviolate or specially protected.[28] Within this democratic context, rules play further important roles:

1 Majorities can exercise more power through the choice of rules than they can through the choice of representatives alone. Control over representatives is enhanced by requiring them to act in accordance with rules and to govern via legislation, proposals for which feature in electoral manifestos and by reference to which performance can be assessed: this manifestation of the efficacious-choice advantage may be called the *democratic-control advantage*.[29]

2 Discussion and decision in legislative assemblies, direct or indirect, is moralised through the requirement that decisions are about rules not about particulars, particularly where the generalities are such that legislators and citizens are equally covered by the rules in question. This democratic application of the moral-form advantage of rules may be dubbed the *Rousseau advantage*, on account of its role in protecting minorities.[30]

3 As in all constitutional polities, rules are required to state with some precision the prerequisites of that process. In the case of democracy this involves giving specific substance to such ideals as freedom of speech, responsible government and equal electoral capacity. This *constitutional requirement* is an indispensable prerequisite for democracy, both with respect to its mechanisms and with respect to the rights of participation which must be firmly guaranteed for equal participation to be more than a formal possibility.[31]

Despite the impressive range of rationales for the operation of government through rules, they cannot and do not establish that all state power must be exercised in this way. Patently, some political decisions, such as in the conduct of war, the adoption of treaties and the location of capital cities, require decisions which are highly particularistic, although they can all be taken in accordance with rule-based authority assignation. Nor does the accumulation of positive arguments in favour of rule-governed states imply that any rule-governed state is morally legitimate. Clearly, the contents of the rules in question have to be put in the balance with the various advantages of rule format, and the balance may come out against any particular regime.

Nevertheless, the fact that so many of the affirmative rationales for states are generated by the value of rule conformity and so many of the defensive moves in the justification of state power against its opponents rely on the concession that such power may be tamed not only by democratic decision making but also by making the operation of the state a matter of choice and application of rules, rather than an agglomeration of individual commands, does tend to establish the central significance of government through rules as a necessary precondition of political legitimacy.

Critiques of Rules

The justificatory arguments for the centrality of rules in acceptable polities are not conclusive unless we also consider the condemnatory arguments against rules, arguments which emphasise the destructiveness of rules in relation to individual autonomy and community relationships, their encouragement of conformity, their inflexibility in the face of novelty and the coerciveness which is frequently involved in even the mildest forms of social pressure. The question of whether the benefits of rules outweigh their harmfulness depends on context and purpose and cannot in general be prejudged. It remains, therefore, an open question whether Ethical Positivism is a desirable ideal in any particular instance. However, the analysis of the political dimension or rules and rule enforcement does, as we have seen, engender important reasons why rule governance and rule abidingness are more readily justifiable than alternative political methods once it is accepted that significant liberties should be curtailed.

Many critical analyses of rules seek to undermine the claim that rules can limit the options of decision makers in any significant way, but other criticisms go along with positivist assumption about the relative determinacy of sense and concentrate instead on the undesirability of rule governance.[32] Some of these critiques deal with the inevitable lack of fit between rules and their objectives: the perpetual under- and over-inclusiveness which results from pursuing an objective with a blunt instrument that is not always going to give the result that is desired.[33] These points can be strong in relation to non-coordination rules where there is reason for those involved to look for interpretations of the rules which excuse them from doing what they do not wish to do. In the case of facilitative conventions it is easier to argue that rules would not be retained if they had insufficient specificity of meaning to serve as the basis for cooperative conduct.

More radical criticism is directed at the whole idea of solving problems through the application of rules. This critique is not directed at all the functions of rules, such as their coordinating role, but focusses on the need to find a better way of resolving disputes than in terms of rule-bound rights and duties, which imply that one party is in the right and the other in the wrong. Such an approach is said to generate rather than diminish conflict.[34] Thus communitarians see the concentration on law as putting all aspects of society under the dominance of legalistic rather than problem-solving thinking. Actual social relations, it is pointed out, are less formal and more open than the model of rules suggests. Indeed, those aspects of social relations that produce community are at variance with a rules and rights approach which encourages people to concentrate on their own interests in contradistinction to the wellbeing of others.[35]

In its feminist form, this argument is extended by the contention that seeing society in terms of rules and social problems as legalistic ones is part of gender-based domination. In its most recent phase, feminist jurisprudence offers powerful arguments to the effect that law and rules in general are a masculine enterprise and, more particularly, that the study of male domination through law reveals the sexual core of male violence and gender hierarchy. However, feminist thinking shares the general ambivalence of all communitarian theory towards the societal functions of rules, particularly coercive rules. Without wishing to repudiate the advances that can be made by the enactment of rules which are either gender-neutral or gender-empowering, I suspect that rule solutions are no solutions to underlying problems. Continuing gender inequality in employment, income and power, and the marginal effectiveness of legal solutions to domestic violence, rape and discrimination, prompt women to look elsewhere for real progress towards equality.[36] But not all feminists take such a negative view of the law's potential and continue to seek radical reform by redrawing the boundaries between 'public' and 'private' and thus between law and non-law, so that women can be protected more effectively in their sexual and economic relationships; or by proposing various devices for replacing a male with a female or gender-neutral perspective on legally relevant categories, such as what counts as 'work' in the context of accident compensation.[37]

The masculinity of rules is said, by some feminists, to lie in their combative nature: a perspective of contentious individualism rather than cooperation and caring. Thus Carol Gilligan holds that the tendency to see disputes in terms of rights and rules is essentially a masculine phenomenon.[38] Adopting something close to the traditional ideals of women as loving and men as competitive, Gilligan argues that a more caring approach to the failings of human relationships does not involve subjecting the participants to rules, but the conciliatory compromises of mutual give and take in the interests of all those involved. Dividing lines, simplistic dichotomies, closures of argument, all these simply manifest the imposition of male will over female conciliation. Thus, for Janet Rifkin, 'law is a paradigm for maleness' for 'the historical image of maleness – objective, rational and public – is the dominant image of law'.[39] Rifkin's argument is that the way in which rules abstract from reality, particularly gender reality, means that they are powerless to address discrimination which permeates human relationships. Thus gender-neutral rules solve nothing if the de facto situation is that women's position is such that they are adversely affected by such rules. Thus equal rule-formulated employment opportunity is of no value if women are not able to take up these formal opportunities through lack of material opportunity.

Some of these criticisms are directed at particular types of rules, others at the manner in which rules are enforced. In particular, there is an assumption that rules go along with the liberal idea that rules are 'neutral' and therefore produce justice. However, LEP makes no such assumption and is compatible with the view that rules should, for instance, include gendered terms if this is necessary to address gender bias or gendered interests.[40] A second line of defence is to point out that rules need not embody selfish individualism. Not only can rules relate to the conduct of groups, but they can reward beneficence and punish uncaringness. The image of society as a body that pursues individual self-interest controlled only by rules which forbid injuring others is a purely contingent utilisation of rules. Not only can the area of negative freedom left by rules be utilised in beneficent as well as selfish ways, but the rules themselves can require action which runs counter to the self-interest of the subjects.[41] Third, it must be agreed that the capacity of rule change in itself to produce significant social change is highly limited. The prospect of solving social problems in this way alone is clearly ephemeral. This does not show, however, that rules are not an essential part of successful and enduring social change. Similarly, while a system of rules must be conservative in ideology, in that the rules stand until they are changed, and in any unjust system the rules will therefore perpetuate injustice, this does not mean that rules as such support hierarchy or exploitation.[42]

Finally, it should be noted that some criticisms of rules are based on the assumption that this term covers all the various standards and norms of current law, with their existing vagueness, ambiguity and abstraction. The argument is that such 'rules' function poorly in the control and coordination of human conduct. Within LEP, however, a good rule is a norm which is sufficiently clear, unambiguous and specific to enable distinctions to be drawn between descriptively different modes of conduct that enable us to recognise without controversy whether actual conduct does or does not conform to the rule.[43] Critiques of bad rules do not undermine arguments for the utility of good ones.

Conclusion

This chapter has set out to emphasise the social and political significance of rules in order to provide a context in which the arguments for Ethical Positivism can be appreciated. In particular, it has shown that rules have social significance prior to and independently of the role of government. Indeed, government can be seen as in the main an extension or refinement of the regulative dimension of social structure. This sets the scene for the important contention that, other things being equal, government should not act so as to undermine the effectiveness of the pervasive underlying social order.

It has also demonstrated that the distinctive features of centralised political authority give rise to further significant arguments in favour of government through rules, particularly where a democratic system with built-in safeguards for minorities are concerned. In sum, there would appear to be sufficient positive arguments in favour of government through rules to render plausible the contention we started out with in Chapter 1, that government through rules is a precondition of political legitimacy.

Later chapters will take up again the more negative themes relating to the difficulties and disadvantages of operating via rules, especially precise rules of the sort which can be applied by judiciaries without the exercise of independent moral judgment. As far as this chapter goes, it is sufficient if we have made a prima facie case for dismay and regret should it turn out that these disadvantages are sufficient to outweigh the considerable benefits that are available through the effective operation of a system of formally and sociologically good rules.

Notes

1 Positivists vary in the terminology used (norm, rule, command and so on) and in their analyses of these fundamental terms. Hart (1961, pp.8–13) identifies the concept of a social rule as one of the central puzzles of legal philosophy. All concur that what we are dealing with is more or less general 'ought' statements which function as setting standards or acceptable patterns of conduct within particular groups or societies. Those who use 'rule' as the preferred term do not necessarily imply that rules are distinguished from other norms by their greater precision or particular role in legal reasoning (contra Dworkin, 1977, Chapter 2).

2 One alternative approach is an explanation in terms of rights, but the analysis of legal rights itself involves rules. See Campbell (1983, pp.27–32).

3 Hart (1961, pp.79–88).

4 Ibid., p.85: 'The rules supported by this serious pressure are thought important because they are believed to be necessary to the maintenance of social life or some highly prized feature of it.'

5 Austin (1954, Lecture I).

6 *Collins English Dictionary* gives as one meaning of 'rule': 'the common order of things; normal condition'. The *Macquarie Dictionary* has 'that which customarily or normally occurs or holds good: the rule rather than the exception'. Interestingly, such empirical generalisations as are held to be universal are often referred to as scientific 'laws'. Schauer argues that we have two species of the genus rule, the descriptive and the prescriptive, which have in common that they both deal in generalisations. He then proceeds to draw lessons about the generalisation aspect of prescriptive rules from the way that generalisation operates in descriptive rules. It would appear that the parallels break down, for empirical generalisations are only regarded as rules if they fit the formula 'as a rule'; that is, where the generali-

sations relate to strong but not conclusive correlations. There seems no reason to transfer this feature to prescriptive rules.

7 All this is part of Austin's scheme and is clearly set out in Schauer (1991). 'Do not ever sit down in that puddle' is an interesting borderline case which was suggested to me by Jonathan Woodger. This becomes an important point when it comes to the critique of rules as indeterminate, since the indeterminacy of classification applies routinely to the expression of the only normative alternative to rules, particular instructions. It should be noted that the universality of the terms involved in rules is not a matter of applying to all persons or being general in the sense of vague. Classifications and hence rules can be narrow and precise. Hayek (1960, pp.153–4) starts its equivalent analysis of law with 'general abstract rules': 'a true law should not name any particulars, so it should not single out any specific persons or groups'. However, Hayek notes that 'The requirement that the rules of true law be general does not mean that sometimes special rules may not apply to different classes of people if they refer to properties that only some people possess'. In fact, nearly all rules do this. As Hayek concedes, what matters is that these distinctions are justified rather than whether they delineate a limited group of persons.

8 The scope of a rule is determined by what is variously called the operative facts or factual predicate (Shauer, 1991, p.23) which identify the type of situation which triggers the imperitival force of the norm. Compare Gottlieb's 'protasis', Twining and Miers' 'operative facts'. The generality of rules is not equivalent either to generalising to all members of the class, or being general in the sense of vague. Indeed classifications can be narrow and precise. Certainly they need not be abstract, in that they do not refer to empirically determinable classes of entity.

9 For moral universalisability, see Kant (1948) and Hare (1963 pp.7–50).

10 Knowledge of the descriptive element enables us in principle to tell when a rule has been observed as far as external conduct is concerned.

11 See Campbell (1990, pp.125–8).

12 Warnock (1971, p.65).

13 Raz (1975, pp.35–45, 73–6). Implicitly it is accepted that rules have 'let out' clauses along the lines of 'other things being equal'. Thus we may drive on the wrong side of the road to avoid an accident. However, this can be construed as a justified act of rule breaking. No such justification is required for a 'rule of thumb' which is no more than advice as to how to act to gain our objectives. Alexander and Sherwin (1994) see this as involving an element of deceit on the part of rule makers as they do not really mean that it is always wrong to act in the way prohibited by a rule. However, no such deceit is strictly necessary as the citizen can accept that she is not to follow her own judgment even though the rule may be unjustified in a particular circumstance. Nevertheless, it is correct to say that exclusionary force is a matter of degree and that this is not always made clear.

14 Schauer (1991, p.11).

15 Ibid., pp.4–82).

16 Schauer would appear to disagree to the extent that he assumes that all regulative rules exercise 'normative pressure', which is associated with their 'strength', a characteristic which relates to 'the sanctions (whether positive or negative) that attach to following or violating rules, or from attitudes about rules held by addressees of those rules'. On the other hand, 'the strength of a rules resides not so much in a rule's logical status or linguistic meaning as in the conditions surrounding its applicability, acceptability and enforcement' (Schauer, 1991, p.8). 'Weight' is what Dworkin (1977, Chapter 2) ascribes to principles but not rules, which follows from the reason-giving nature of what he defines as principles which enables us to estimate the moral or other significance of the rationale of the principle. The idea of force is not so closely tied to content as is weight and can be seen as

an independent variable which simply ascribes the priority of a rule in relation to other rules or in its power to override non-rule considerations, such as utility.

17 Schauer (1991, p.4), following Mill (1910).

18 For this reason, Positivists need not explicate positive norms in terms of sanctions simply to avoid relating legal obligation to the content of the rules in question.

19 This point is not easily admitted by Positivists. Thus Kelsen's 'Grundnorm' is presented as not just a presupposition of the logic of legal systems but as somehow grounding the system in a normativity which transcends positive law: see Beyleveld and Brownsword (1989).

20 For an account of the central functions of rules, see Postema (1982, p.185): 'Statutes, regulations and judicial precedents are often most valuable because they provide and are in part intended to provide, a focus for expectations of the parties engaged in complex patterns of social interaction.' It is tempting to claim that it is the basic function of law to facilitate and underwrite first-level coordination, but Durkheim (1933), for instance, gives solidarity a central role in sustaining unity in complex societies. Many theorists incorporate the symbolic function of condemnation in accounts of the social function of criminal law. More generally, see Aubert (1966).

21 See pp.30–2.

22 See p.31.

23 While it is possible to think of justice in relation to the treatment of one individual there is a distinct lack of intelligibility about associating any particular treatment with any particular type of conduct. Comparing conduct or qualities as being more or less meritorious and therefore deserving more or less of a scarce commodity is intellectually more manageable. For a general discussion of justice, see Campbell (1988b). This may be regarded as a gendered point but there are plenty of precepts which encourage caring conduct, and there need be no suggestion that in this context there is a commitment to legalism in the sense of conformity to rules for its own sake. Nor is there force to the view that prohibitions are more susceptible to rule format than are exhortations to benevolence, since both types of consequence can be specified in more or less detail and, in any case, we are not arguing in this context that rules must be specific norms.

24 Genuine community membership requires an internal understanding of the significance of the rules rather than mere bodily conformity: See Schutz (1970).

25 In Schauer's terminology this is because rules are over- and under-inclusive in relation to their purposes: Schauer (1991, p.33).

26 This, the standard liberal rule of law argument, is most vulnerable to criticism as unrealisable. See Rawls (1972, p.231) and Shapiro (1994, esp. pp.297–327).

27 Much of this model emanates from Weber's ideal type of the rational–legal–bureacratic order: Weber (1947).

28 This definition runs together an analytical conception in terms of equal political power and certain justificatory rationales for equality of political rights in terms of the protection of interests and relatively uncoercive resolution of disagreements. See Dahl (1965) and Mayo (1960).

29 This need not be given substance in terms of government by referenda, particularly as referenda tend to lack specificity and do not therefore extend effective choice.

30 See Waldron (1991).

31 Democracy is, in one sense, simply a particular constitutional form of government, as all systems can be rule-governed, but in the case of democracy the ideal of constitutionality is a necessary requirement. It does not follow, however, that constitutional rules are not themselves democratically determined.

32 Despite this inconsistency of suppositions, many theorists use both approaches.

The classic criticisms were articulated by the American Legal Realists (see Llewellyn, 1960) and have been further developed within Critical Legal Studies: see Singer (1984), Kennedy (1976), Kairys (1984) and Boyle (1992).

33 Schauer (1991, p.33).

34 By looking to the past and not the future: Fuller (1944) and Aubert (1963).

35 See Sandel (1982) and Gutman (1985).

36 See Smart (1989, p.104).

37 See Graycar and Morgan (1990).

38 See Gilligan (1982).

39 Rifkin (1980, pp.85, 92).

40 This is the form in which arguments rage over affirmative discrimination. See Campbell, in Sadurski (1991).

41 But not as often as is sometimes assumed in, for instance, Nozick (1974). See Campbell (1983, Chapter 5).

42 A mistake made in Kerruish (1991); see Goldsworthy (1991, pp.548–70).

43 See Dworkin (1977) and Schlag (1985).

4 Positivist Ideals

The legal theory of Ethical Positivism (LEP) sets out a rule-based framework for mitigating the tragic dilemmas arising out of the paradox of politics. LEP suggests a feasible way of facilitating a form of democratic culture that serves both the moral and the material interests of minimally virtuous citizens. According to the theory, a defensible democratic polity should centre its political decision making on the choice of rules which approximate to the ideal of being applicable to specific circumstances without distortion by the unauthenticated viewpoints and values of those whose task it is to follow and apply the democratically preferred choices. These visionary possibilities underlie the further analysis presented in this chapter.

The Prescriptive Separation Thesis

Even well informed people are often surprised to discover that Positivists have moral views about law and legal process, and are even more surprised when they are told that many Positivists are objectivists in meta-ethics and make claims to moral knowledge with a clear philosophical conscience. Knowing that Legal Positivism is standardly defined as the theory that law is one thing and morality quite another, they miss the fact that Positivists give moral as well as conceptual reasons for holding to the separability thesis, as we now call the proposition that there is no logically necessary connection between law and morality.[1]

This separability thesis, according to which, in Austin's much quoted phrase, 'the existence of law is one thing, its goodness or badness another',[2] is generally cited as the central defining feature of Legal Positivism, even by those who are not overly fond of definitional straitjackets and tightly drawn conceptual boundaries. However, while the separability thesis may be seen as a distinguishing feature of Legal Positivism, it is to misunderstand its import if we take it to mean that Positivists do not have moral and political reasons for favouring the adoption and guiding the use of this analytic doctrine Nor does it involve the contention that law and morality are in fact entirely separate (the 'separation thesis'). Indeed, the conceptual point about the logical distinction between law and morals having been made in Positivist accounts of law, this is standardly followed by emphasising the many ways in which Positivists *do* relate law to morality, either empirically or prescriptively. Most theorists who are generally regarded as Positivist insist that laws do require to be justified morally, readily accept that social morality influences the content of law, and acknowledge that law cannot operate effectively without the support of a substantial moral consensus.[3] Often the separability thesis begins to look like a relatively marginal attribute of Legal Positivism, however handy it may be as an introductory identifier. Perhaps the contention that law is not necessarily moral is, as Coleman implies, no more than a minor analytical point to be noted as we pass to the substance of the theory.[4]

Marginalising the separability thesis enables us to escape some tedious and pedantic arguments about the 'real' meaning of 'law', particularly where it is assumed that this meaning can be culled by objective and culturally neutral conceptual analysis.[5] Instances of such terminological controversies arise in disputes over the notion of 'unjust law'. A common caricature of Natural Law makes it out to be the theory which holds that an unjust law is not really law at all.[6] This sets the scene for the Positivist's counter that, since our discourse permits us to speak of an unjust law, justice cannot be a prerequisite of the existence of a law. It is then concluded that law is conceptually distinct from morality.[7]

Such arguments usually convince only the converted. Unless we are already committed to the practical or theoretical importance of maintaining the conceptual means to talk about unjust laws, we will not be worried by the linguistic impoverishment brought about by a conceptual preference which locks law into morality, particularly if there are other benefits to be derived from so doing. One such benefit might be the ability to emphasise that it is morally suspect not to view an institution with such potential for both harm and benefit as subordinate to fundamental moral standards. Moreover, the acceptance of the idea of unjust laws may send the wrong signals to legislators and weaken the power of judges when confronted with grossly immoral regimes.[8]

Whatever we think of such arguments,[9] it is interesting to note that most Legal Positivists are not unduly worried by the fact that many legal systems do in fact involve moral criteria in the identification and interpretation of valid law. The truth of descriptive Positivism is an issue which preoccupies critics rather than advocates of Legal

Positivism.[10] All that most Positivists seem to require is that a legal system *need* not employ moral criteria in this context, the view Coleman dubs 'negative positivism'.[11] Looking for a more positive content to Positivism, Coleman fastens on the idea of law as a social convention, the thesis 'that the authority of law is a matter of its acceptance by officials'.[12] But first he rejects the theory of law as 'hard facts' according to which law can be identified uncontroversially in an objective manner which satisfies the tenets of logical positivism, namely that truth depends on empirical verifiability.[13] This is dismissed on the evidence offered by Dworkin that actual legal systems involve highly controversial judgments on questions of law. Evidence of this descriptive nature does not, however, undermine evaluative versions of positive positivism, such as that law and morals ought not to be identical in content, or the contention of LEP that a legal system ought to approximate as far as possible to hard-fact Positivism, however much actual systems may depart from this ideal. Assuming, in accordance with the separability thesis, that law does not *need* to be identified through moral spectacles, this opens the way for saying that what Legal Positivists in fact wish us to accept is that it is *undesirable* if there are such morally overt legal validity criteria. For such Positivists, the motivation behind the analytic point is to prepare the conceptual ground for the view that no legal system *ought* to permit morally explicit or other controversial standards being used to establish the existence of law or determine its implications. We may label this the 'prescriptive separation thesis'.

The prescriptive separation thesis – the view that law and morals ought to be separate at the point of application – is not, of course, established by conceptual analysis, any more than it is disproved by empirical evidence. It is, however, made possible by such analysis, for the separability thesis supplies a semantic scheme within which to state the prescriptive separation thesis. While we must be able to make sense of the idea of an unjust law and accept the meaningfulness of criticising certain validity criteria as inappropriate, the prescriptive separation thesis is primarily a moral contention, albeit one whose relevance presupposes certain sociological scenarios. Certainly, the logical possibility of a system which does separate the judicial identification and application of law from the assessment of its moral content must be more than a mere conceptual possibility if it is to have practical interest. For the prescriptive separation thesis to have much relevance it must identify an ideal to which actual systems can approximate to a significant degree.

This means that, subordinate within the prescriptive ideal of government through positive law, there are claims both about the analytical coherence of the prescription and about the practical feasibility of progressing towards such an objective. Indeed, as we have seen, many of the justificatory arguments in favour of rules and hence of LEP assume a fairly high attainability threshold of positivist rule instantiation and rule conformity without which the benefits of having specific positivist rules are not realised. Thus a relatively small number of deviations from rules which coordinate social activities can undermine whole systems of cooperative interactions. The contention of traditional descriptive Legal Positivism is that 'efficacy' (or general conformity to positive rules) is a precondition of the existence of a legal system. In LEP, however, efficacy is to be seen as the threshold level of conformity to law which is a prerequisite for obtaining the justifying benefits which derive from positivist systems of law, rather than as a criterion for the existence of a law or a legal system.[14]

On the prescriptive interpretation, the separability thesis moves back from the margins of legal theory and takes on the mantle of a potentially focal point within political philosophy. When we spell out the requirement that legal rules ought to be recognisable by their empirically identifiable sources and add that the acceptable content of formally good laws is such that they can be applied without recourse to the moral opinions of the judiciary, then prescriptive separatism may be taken to be the core feature of LEP. LEP thus combines the critical acceptance of certain forms of political authority with the insistence that the defensible deployment of political power requires the comprehensive mediation of efficacious rules, rules which are created by political choice, followed to a threshold point of conformity and, in cases of dispute, applied to particular circumstances without distorting recourse to the moral, class or gender assumptions of the adjudicators.

It should be noted that LEP is not to be confused with another prescriptive theory which MacCormick calls 'moral disestablishmentarianism'. MacCormick's thesis is centrally concerned with giving moral reasons for the view that substantive law should not embody a great deal of the dominant social morality. Moral disestablishmentarianism is the thesis that 'law and morality are not necessarily the same thing, and the claim that they should not be made so by legislation. Put even more simply: law and morality do not have to be identical, and should be kept distinct. Let that slogan indeed serve as my preliminary, admittedly crude, working definition of "legal amoralism".'[15]

While LEP can accommodate this partial prescriptive separation theory, it is not saddled with this particular line on the moral content of law. LEP, in its most general form, is concerned with the sources rather than the content of laws. There are, of course, a number of good reasons for restraint in legislating morality. Certainly, it is never a conclusive reason for a legal enactment to say that it prohibits morally bad conduct. The coercive nature of law, the existence of reasonable moral disagreement and the value of each moral agent making up her own mind about what is right are such that there is always a further step in the moral argument before legislation is justified, a step which serves to justify proscribing rather than simply condemning the immoral conduct in question. However, these further arguments are not of a different kind from those which bear on ordinary moral evaluation of conduct, but are generally simply moral reasons which are powerful enough to override the standing prima facie case against legislation. At least sometimes, when the purpose of law is to inhibit directly harmful conduct, precisely the same reasons which render conduct liable to moral criticism also serve to justify making it illegal. We have seen that many of the moral arguments for having laws relate to the value of having authoritative rules, but, as we have also seen, such considerations also feature in non-legal moral debate. The prescriptive separation thesis makes it easy to formulate the ideal of moral disestablishmentarianism, but the ideal is neither a necessary nor a sufficient element of LEP. LEP is in fact compatible with a prescriptive non-separation thesis which seeks to embody morality in law through legislation. LEP does not endorse, although it is compatible with, the view that moral and legislative rationales are discontinuous, and is relatively open as to how far law should go in requiring submission in controversial moral areas.

The Historical Associations

It is not argued in this book that LEP is the dominant form of Legal Positivism, either historically or contemporaneously. Historically, Legal Positivism has been identified with theories in which the separability doctrine is central.[16] On the whole, classical Legal Positivists seem to claim that Natural Lawyers are conceptually confused rather than morally wrong or factually in error.[17] However, there are grounds for holding that such conceptual theses are serving some further explanatory or prescriptive aim and that analytic Legal Positivism is always part of a larger enterprise, either sociological or normative. For the most part this larger enterprise is primarily a matter of description and explanation rather than evaluation.[18] Legal Positivists have always been keen to deny that their theory is morally deleterious,[19] but modern commentators are correct in assuming that the theory itself is standardly defended on conceptual and empirical rather than evaluative grounds. The moral arguments for Legal Positivism are, nevertheless, there in the tradition and are often openly declared. Moreover, the motivation of Legal Positivists is often more prescriptive than appears in the substance of their work. Indeed, it may well be the case that, consciously or unconsciously, Positivists, like so many legal theorists, feel it to be advantageous to present their views as objective fact or analytical truths rather than in the more debatable mode of moral and political value.

The founding father of Legal Positivism, Thomas Hobbes, with his commitment to peace and survival,[20] is hardly a detached analyst, while the Philosophical Radicals, such as Jeremy Bentham and John Austin, whose work provides the classical paradigms of Legal Positivism, treat law as an essential ingredient in their reformist utilitarian projects.[21] And, while the precise nature of the agenda-setting theories expounded in Hart's *Concept of Law* remain controversial, it is hard to think that his political liberalism is not responsible for much of his sociological insight.[22] Similarly, the analytical achievements of Raz, MacCormick and Schauer are not readily detachable from their prescriptive political philosophies. Perhaps Hans Kelsen represents a major counter-example, but if the rather obscure status of his 'Grundnorm' is interpreted in the light of its Kantian inspirations, a case for a moral foundation of even Kelsenian Positivism can be made out.[23]

While an historically grounded case for the evaluative basis of Legal Positivism could be mounted, particularly if a degree of deconstruction is permitted, it remains the case that, perhaps on tactical grounds, the standard Legal Positivist analysis of law in terms of the general commands or rules emanating from a sovereign or other social source is routinely presented and understood primarily either as a truth about the meaning of 'law' or as a key to the understanding of law as a social phenomenon, rather than as a particular type of moral position within political philosophy. In contrast, LEP interprets the positivist model as setting out a highly desirable but optional model of law, the beneficial effects of its adoption being no mere serendipitous spin-offs from a theory held on other grounds. As a theory, LEP does fit well enough with most ordinary understandings of the idea of law and it is often used to great explanatory effect, the more so as the system in question approximates to the positivist ideal. Nevertheless, the distinctiveness of LEP as a type of Legal Positivism depends on the way it centres on the notion of government through positive rules as an aspirational ideal which can play an important part within a range of more particular and complete political philosophies.

Examination of the frequently submerged moral grounds of Legal Positivism can be an illuminating way into gaining an understanding of what this tradition of legal theorising is all about. Bringing into the open what is often the hidden moral agenda of all Legal Positivisms can be more interesting than taking them at their conceptual or scientific face value. This is particularly so if we examine the ideological or legitimating functions of many Legal Positivisms which flourish on the perhaps disingenuous assumption that what ought to be the case about law actually is so as a matter of natural meaning or fact: a characteristic positivist example of arguing from ought to is, which may be called the normative fallacy.[24] In this way, the hidden agendas of Legal Positivists are readily viewed as malign, if not dishonest, devices through which the role of lawyers and legal academics, to say nothing of the absolute power of the state, is being falsely legitimated.[25]

Without denying that Legal Positivism has been and still is used as this sort of ideological tool, it remains feasible to detach our assessment of this tradition from this often persuasive critical approach and address the moral contentions of Positivism simply as moral and political arguments. For these reasons this book does not argue for Ethical Positivism as a matter of historical exegesis or even as an illuminating post facto reinterpretation of a great theoretical tradition. It certainly does not defend the standard ideological uses to which Legal Positivism has been put. Rather, the legal theory of Ethical Positivism is examined simply as a persuasive version of Legal Positivism which openly and argumentatively presents an aspirational ideal of what a 'good' legal system would be like, not directly in its specific content but in its form and functions.

This ethical interpretation of Legal Positivism runs counter to most contemporary accounts of the tradition. Thus Keekoh Lee[26] argues that Legal Positivism must be defined in terms of philosophical positivism as an affirmation of the epistemological priority of empirical evidence. However, his position becomes plausible only when it is tied in to his perception of the ideological role of Legal Positivism which relates law to order and reform. Lee cannot make out his case on purely historical grounds, as many Legal Positivists have had no problem with the idea of non-empirical truths. John Austin himself accepted Natural Law as well as positivist types of morality.[27] Lee's analytical argument is to the effect that without associating Legal Positivism with philosophical positivism – that is the view that all knowledge derives from empirical experience – Legal Positivism cannot be distinguished from Legal Realism.[28] Thus he dismisses S.I. Ago's definition of Legal Positivism in terms of the origin of all law in the exercise of human will, on the grounds that this would include the Realist view that law is the creation of judges. However, Realism can readily be distinguished from Legal Positivism either on the basis that Positivists hold that the existence of a legal system requires that the commands which are positive law must be general and emanate from a unitary sovereign, or/and the view that the processes of rule application and rule formation are distinguishable. Lee's thesis has merit, however, when we note that many Legal Positivists, in seeking to exclude moral judgment from the process of law application, commend that laws be formulated in terms which admit of empirical applicability, particularly when he goes on to note that all Positivists, legal and philosophical, associate their methodology with 'an ideology of order and reform'.[29] For LEP, of course, it is precisely some such ideology, rather than the exclusive use of empirically satisfactory adjudicatory methods for its own sake, that is the motivating force behind the adoption of the approach.

This riposte to Lee would be unacceptable to Jules Coleman who contends:

> The argument for law as hard facts that relies on the positivist program of knowable, ascertainable law is straightforwardly problematic. Legal positivism makes a conceptual or analytic claim about law, and that claim should not be confused with programmatic or normative interests certain positivists, especially Bentham, might have had. Ironically, to hold otherwise is to build into the conceptual account of law a particular normative theory of law; it is to infuse morality, or the way law ought to be, into the concept of law (or the account of the way law is). In other words, the argument for ascribing certain tenets to positivism in virtue of the positivist's normative ideal of law is to commit the very mistake positivism is so intent on drawing attention to and rectifying.[30]

This is a strong argument if the Positivist is committing the normative fallacy by passing from a statement about what law ought to be to a conclusion about how it is or has to be. It does not rule out, however, seeing the positivist conception of law as related to certain wider social and political ideals. When Bentham condemns the common law method, for instance, he is making more than semantic points: he is asserting the moral superiority of a different approach to, a different way of conceiving law, so that there are good and bad laws, not simply in their moral content, but in their form and nature.[31]

Another frequently proffered basis for the conceptual preference for one analysis of law over another is the legal discourse actually in use. Thus Raz argues that Positivism captures distinctions we make in practice, for instance the distinction between legal skills and other (say oral) skills.[32] Hart also appeals to conventions of language, although he hesitates to rely entirely on this base as 'we cannot grapple adequately with this issue if we see it as one regarding the proprieties of linguistic usage'.[33] Certainly, the classical Legal Positivists were more at home with stipulation than with reportive definitions.[34] Whether stipulative or not, fundamental distinctions, such as that between law and morality, require elucidation and refinement beyond the conflicting and often contradictory content of actual discourse. Hence the standard analytic move to separate out the primary and secondary uses of key terms such as 'law' and 'rights'.[35] While usage can point the way to useful distinctions it cannot vindicate particular usages except in relation to their helpfulness or otherwise in relation to further objectives, be they philosophical or empirical.

Equally, Natural Law contentions as to the necessary connection of law and morality are problematic as purely conceptual doctrines. Philip Soper argues that what we are dealing with in such controversies is a 'pre-analytic datum', which has ominous overtones of the discredited idea that there are primitive 'sense data' to be uncovered by phenomenological analysis. Ultimately his own appeal is to a particular view of the judge's moral duty.[36] He argues that '[a] judge's decision that something is my legal duty entails a claim about my moral duty, at least in the sense that in pronouncing a legal duty, the judge implies that he believes the duty is consistent with, or even required by, morality. This connector between law and the belief that law is just is precisely the connection I propose to defend as an essential feature of law.'[37] Soper concludes that legal officials 'claim what positivism denies – namely that there is a necessary connection between law and morality'.[38] Unfazed by counter-examples of judges who hold to positivist tenets on this matter and openly disapprove of laws they feel bound to apply, Soper contends that his theory is not a definition or an account of what judges believe, but rather that 'the system in which they operate assumes such a belief'.[39] His is not the historically more common Natural Law view that law must serve the common good, but the more sophisticated thesis that law must *claim* to serve the common good.

If we interpret Soper's thesis as saying that laws require moral justification, there is no conflict with classical Legal Positivism. However, the same Legal Positivists have argued that it is not for judges and citizens to evaluate the sovereign's rules before these are applied or complied with. This is not a view that is logically required by Positivism and some Legal Positivists hold to the view that judges and citizens have a moral duty to disregard laws which they believe to be seriously unjust, although if this were to result in widespread non-conformity to law then many of the benefits of legal systems would be lost. This is a possible moral position which both judge and citizen may respect. However, it is no more possible to claim that such morally based discretion is the presupposition of all legal systems than it is possible to exclude, as non-legal, systems in which judges have no moral commitments whatever. Detmold argues, in a stronger version of Soper's line, that legal rules are only prima facie binding and that judges must evaluate and endorse what they apply.[40] This is clearly a particular moral view, and one which misses the role of law in providing a means of making decisions in situations where there is no moral consensus and in which it is assumed that morally controversial decisions as to the laws which are to bind judges and citizens alike should be taken through democratic rather than judicial process.

Modern Positivisms

Legal Positivism is the presupposed orthodoxy which provides the standard background against which critical legal theories present themselves. As such, Legal Positivism is vulnerable to misrepresentations and caricatures which serve to highlight the claimed superiorities of its more daring competitors. Thus the view that law is 'neutral', as between competing interests, is repeatedly ascribed to Legal Positivism despite the latter's highly political account of law as the expression of dominant will.[41] Again it is often assumed that Positivism is to be identified with a conceptual formalism which deduces specific legal determinations from abstract concepts and repudiates all appeal to purpose, despite the fact that Positivism is centred on the recognition of the specific norms and highly purposive concept of the sovereign will.[42]

More specifically, the most powerful current critiques of Legal Positivism largely depend on the readily established claim that Positivism is descriptively inaccurate with respect to the ways in which modern legal systems operate. It is not difficult to demonstrate that judiciaries do not always, or even routinely, apply legal rules without recourse to personal, gender and class values.[43] Yet, however forceful such sociolegal evidence may be with respect to those forms of Legal Positivism which claim to represent and explain the realities of all existing legal process, LEP can actually draw on such critiques as condemnations of existing legislative and judicial practice which do not in themselves undermine their vision of what political and legal systems ought to be like. Indeed, something like LEP is often needed to formulate what judicial bias is and what is objectionable about it. While bias can be defined in terms of rule creation which unwarrantably favours specific groups, it can also involve departing from the authoritative rules in ways which systematically favour certain social and economic groups.

The critiques of Legal Positivism as descriptively false make the assumption that Legal Positivism must be taken to be a theory primarily within social science, the activity of identifying, describing and explaining the law of actual societies. Legal Positivism can, however, be taken as a citizen's, as contrasted with a social scientist's, theory of law, a theory about the way lawyers, and in particular judges, should identify and understand law, a theory, perhaps, which would have us view law as the general commands of a sovereign, not as a set of moral principles as perceived by the judiciary or as a creation of the judicial process. However social scientists may choose to identify and analyse the laws of societies, it is for citizens, lawyers and judges to help to make it the case that law is taken as originating in sovereign political authority.

The contrast of citizen's theory and scientist's theory is not undermined by the fact that few Legal Positivists now adopt the antiquated narrow empiricist theory of social science which reduces human conduct to material observables. Instead, following the likes of Dilthey, Weber and Schutz,[44] the appropriate scientific method to be deployed in the study of law is said to be the interpretative or hermeneutical method, in which the understanding of the participants is an essential part of the description and explanation of all social phenomena, including law.

According to Hart, for instance, study of ordinary legal and associated language from the participant viewpoint, particularly as it is used by legal officials, is what enables us to understand what law is really all about.[45] In MacCormick's variant, law is to be viewed as rooted in 'institutional' facts, a species of fact which cannot be simply observed since they presuppose knowledge of human institutions, a knowledge which can be obtained only by understanding what it is to participate in rule-governed social relationships and to have a cognitive grasp of the rules which enable us to speak of such social phenomena as contracts, wills and delicts.[46]

This 'new positivism' is sometimes called 'normative positivism' (thereby depriving the writer of a possible alternative to 'ethical positivism').[47] Following Kelsen, Normative Positivism holds that laws are a form of norm, a distinct type of entity which cannot be reduced to something else, particularly to any purely material phenomena, such as the predictable application of sanctions (as in Empiricist Positivism) or the decisions of courts (as in Legal Realism). According to the Normative Positivist, rules have an existence which is separate from these associated phenomena such that it makes sense to say that the predictable application of sanctions is justified by the relevant rules and that the decisions of courts are based on pre-existing legal norms.[48] More generally, law is seen as a system of practical reasoning, a process of decision making in accordance with certain norms, which is a distinctive part of a more general framework of practical reasoning. These legal norms are not held to exist in a purely ideal realm of mind but are ascertainable through the study of the conduct and expressed attitudes of those who operate and respond to conduct. This study enables it to be said, as a matter of fact (albeit institutional fact), that, for instance, within certain jurisdictions, contracts require consideration and citizens have a duty to vote.[49]

All this has great significance for the development of a viable form of social science. In this context MacCormick and Weinberger's institutional theory of law aims to prove 'an explanation of the nature and existence of law' within the positivist tradition. Their approach, which they call Institutional Positivism, builds on the philosophical distinction between 'brute facts' of a purely material nature and 'institutional facts' whose existence presupposes the social existence of rules which enable us to say, for instance, when a contract comes into existence and when it is extinguished.[50] Institutional facts are facts in so far as they are statable as true statements, 'but what is true is not true simply because of the condition of the material world and the causal relationship which obtains among its parts. On the contrary, it is true in virtue of an interpretation of what happens in the world, an interpretation of events in the light of human practices and normative rules.'[51] Parliaments, courts, contract, games, languages, marriage and friendship are all constituted by a collection of associated concepts and rules which enable us to interpret certain observable situations as instances of legislation, adjudication, contracts, football, Spanish, divorce and friendship. Law is explained largely in terms of the real existence of social rules, analysed along the lines which were outlined in the previous chapter: assertions of 'oughts' and 'mays' connected under general organising ideas. The implication of Institutional Positivism is that a narrow materialist empiricist form of scientific positivism is impossibly reductionist, and must be replaced by a hermeneutical method which enables us to utilise our insider understanding of what rules are and how they guide human action, that is conduct which is the result of conscious choice in the light of given information, including awareness of the requirements made upon us by the rules of our society.

LEP does require such a background ontology to explain the reality of social rules and an epistemology which enables us to know when institutional facts exist and when they do not. This much LEP has in common with the intellectual needs of the sociology of law, but the two areas of interest, sociological and philosophical, are unnecessarily and misleadingly blurred in this presentation of a 'new Legal Positivism'.[52] MacCormick and Weinberger argue that their theory provides a basis both for sociology of law, which renders law intelligible, and for legal dogmatics (or 'black letter law') wherein the law of a jurisdiction is expounded and clarified. This claim is not fully justified. Indeed, they do not directly address the crucial question of whether legal method is a form of sociological method. Weinberger, writing in the continental European tradition, speaks of legal dogmatics as 'legal science', but this is then expounded as a form of practical, not theoretical, reason. Throughout there is an ambiguity in their use of the words 'legal knowledge' to cover both sociological knowledge and lawyers' knowledge, the implication being that they can both be scientific in the same way, as if the sociologist and the judge are engaged in roughly the same enterprise.

LEP does eliminate personal moral assessment from legal reasoning but no claim need be made that this makes legal reasoning scientific. The activity of a social scientist saying what are the laws in a particular community and a judge determining what the law requires in a specific case are importantly different: the first must be scientific, the second may be very far from it (without therefore being bad judging in the sense that a non-scientific social scientist would be a bad social scientist). In fact, MacCormick and Weinberger are rather coy in disguising their underlying normative political philosophy. Their stated philosophical agenda[53] is ontological and epistemological: what law is and how we may know what laws there are. In fact, they are also concerned to show that there is a place for reasoning in law (not just about law) and implicitly that this role should be maximised. They note approvingly that law is more than rules and includes aspects of both logical evaluation and personal convictions (the latter presumably having no role in social science) and implicitly commend a balance of the two, taking reason as far as it can go, but being pleased with the flexibility that its inevitably limited role permits.

Thus, in his analysis of how institutions, such as contract, operate, with their associated rules for initiating and terminating and enforcing binding agreements, MacCormick points to the way in which it is possible to have a high degree of certainty as to whether a contract exists or not, and still allow the possibility that the relevant rules may be set aside or complemented in accordance with background principles that are brought in to modify or extend rules in an open-ended range of circumstances. Clearly, here MacCormick endorses the social utility of the routine certainty that conveyancing and marriage contracts normally provide, and at the same time welcomes the way in which rules can be overridden where they lead to patent injustice or supplemented when an abnormal situation arises.

Similarly, Weinberger, in expounding a non-cognitivist basis for a conception of justice which can be incorporated into a positivist theory of law, while primarily directing his analysis to show that it is feasible for a non-cognitivist account of justice to provide substantive guidelines for the evaluation and improvement of the content of law, goes on to commend consensual moral intuitions as a basis for justifying a legal system which conforms to the positivist model. It is clear that he has a neo-Kantian view of morality as involving the exercise of informed choice and regards the legal systems he analyses in positivistic terms as playing a part in promoting such a form of moral life and setting up standards for criticism of both legal content and legal procedure.

We can see that behind the use of the sociological version of Institutional Positivism there lie important ethical assumptions which help us to make sense of the way in which the hermeneutical social science method is assumed to be appropriate to legal dogmatics, and hence to legal reasoning, at least up to a point. Beyond that point the same values suggest what sort of consideration should inform our choice of interpretative methods: logic as far as possible, to give certainty and predictability, with an appeal to consensual ideas on justice to supplement and, where appropriate, to correct the formalised approach. MacCormick again:

> To be a so-called positivist in this mould [Hart's] is not to assert the superiority of law to moral considerations nor to treat it as a morally indifferent phenomenon. Rather, it is to present law as a form of social practice, a social institution which has to be subjected to permanent moral critique, a critique founded on principles of enlightened morality, principles which may be as radically at variance with the existing principles and values of law as Hart's brand of liberalism varies from the conservative moralism of a Lord Simonds or even a Lord Devlin.[54]

This is a version of Hart's claim that the separation of law and morals encourages a critical attitude to law and not, as critics such as Fuller suggest, passive subservience to existing laws. What is required to turn this into a genuine Ethical Positivism is an acknowledgement that this scene-setting for moral criticism of positive law is not just a happy side-effect of a sociologically correct theory, but an argument for adopting a particular conception of law, which then may be placed alongside all the other arguments (outlined in the previous chapter) which vindicate the positivist ideal of strong separation. MacCormick argues that seeing law as institutional fact is a highly 'credible' doctrine. The Ethical Positivist seeks to maintain that it is a highly creditable one.

What the Institutional Theory of Law does for Ethical Positivism is to give grounds for believing in the feasibility of its legal conception. The theory shows how we may believe in the existence of rules and how far we may hope to use them as part of a deontic logic. Its analyses make it clearer how we may frame non-moral criteria of legal validity which nevertheless make use of humanly created rules to identify laws as laws. Thus we may favour, on ethical positivist grounds, a rule of recognition which identifies valid laws according to their empirically determinable historical origins, rather than whether or not they accord with the moral opinions of the judge.

What then needs to be added, for a more substantial LEP, is a commitment to the formulation of rules which are conducive to this approach. MacCormick himself seems to be moving in this direction when he says, 'the great positivistic fallacy, which I for one have perpetrated or even perpetuated in my time, is to represent this view of law as though it were a simple description of a natural datum, or at least (in slightly less implausible versions) a social datum'.[55]

The distinction between a scientific approach to the study of law and the use of empirical technique in practical adjudication is, perhaps, not quite so obvious. It is nevertheless equally correct, with respect to that part of the legal process which consists of academic commentators seeking to provide systematic statements of the law of specific jurisdictions on the basis of their knowledge of statutes and cases. Such institutionalised legal writing seeks to make a systematic and coherent whole out of the relatively disorganised and inconsistent body of actual statutes and legal decisions.[56]

Even if we accept that the new Positivism is an impeccable exercise within the terms of social science, this does not establish that this is the method which must be recommended by Legal Positivists to be adopted in the activities of law making, law application and law enforcement. The methodology of social science, whether narrowly positivistic or broadly hermeneutical, does not dictate that the participants in actual legal systems do or should carry out their roles in this, or any other, scientific manner. That would be to confuse the methodology of the study with its subject matter. The fact that social scientists are (empirical or hermeneutical) Positivists does not establish that legislators, judges, police or citizens are, or ought to be, such. This seems evident, yet it is a common fallacy to move without argument from the premiss that, in social science terms, we must distinguish the law and (for instance) the morality of a society, and in general be careful not to confuse descriptions and evaluations, to the conclusion that legal reasoning (for example) is a scientific or quasi-scientific enterprise. Indeed, the scientific (sociological) study of law may provide us with empirical data showing that law as a process is a very unscientific business indeed, and this may be a matter of either relief or regret.

No doubt this confusion arises in part because it is correct to say that Legal Positivists hold to the view that those who apply and follow law should adopt certain methods which have scientific (or certainly non-moral) aspects or parallels. In particular, it is often contended by Positivists that judges ought to apply only those laws which have a certain historical origin or source, something which is in principle open to determination via publicly verifiable evidence. But this itself is an ethical contention, not a scientific description or a recommendation of a scientific methodology as such. It is a view of judicial ethics, based on moral grounds which are quite independent of the propriety of using preferred scientific methods in sociological studies.

This evident truth is, perhaps, not quite so obvious, although it is nevertheless equally correct, with respect to that part of the legal process which consists of academic commentators seeking to provide systematic statements of the law of specific jurisdictions on the basis of their knowledge of statutes and cases. This legal dogmatics, or black-letter academic law, is a valuable exercise where order, coherence and the communication of knowledge of law are seen as desirable objectives, but it is by no means simply a scientific endeavour of providing an empirically adequate description of actual legislation and legal decisions. Such systematic expositions of laws are directed as much at creating system as at describing it. In this regard, there is a constant, confusing and indefensible elision of 'legal science' as social science and 'legal science' as dogmatics.[57] A positivist social science is quite capable of coming up with evidence of a Realist or a Natural Law adjudicative process in actual societies. The separation of law and morality in scientific investigation involves no prejudging of their separation in the data that the social scientist gathers.

The point may be illustrated by reference to the contrast between the separation and the separability theses. If the separability thesis were to be taken to mean that the study of what law must be is separate from the study of what law ought to be, then it is an uncontroversial and relatively unimportant contention. But the separability thesis may also be taken to involve a conceptual truism to the effect that the morality of a society cannot be identified with its law. Thus, for instance, if there is no way for the social scientist to identify processes whereby certain persons in a society have the task of selecting those rules of conduct which are mandatory in that society then there is no strictly legal dimension to such a community. On the other hand, if there are such officials then the social scientist can observe the process whereby the non-legal becomes identified as the legal. However, this does not mean that those officials who identify the mandatory rules, as observed by the social scientist, do so in a scientific manner rather than by reference to their personal interest, their economic views or their moral opinions. Indeed, their conduct in this regard is precisely the phenomenon that the social scientist will wish to investigate.

The 'separability' thesis, on the other hand, in holding that adjudicators need not have reference to moral (or economic or political or private preference) criteria in their determination of law, does have the implication that a social scientist must be on the look-out in case this is indeed what takes place within particular legal systems. Yet the mere possibility that such empirical criteria may be all that particular participants require for their identification of law does not prove that this must be the case for there to be a legal system. The social scientist may observe, externally or internally, that the criteria in fact deployed in the adjudicative as well as the legislative activities are overt moral judgments, simple self-interest, economic rationality and so on. Further, no findings to that effect in themselves undermine the thesis of LEP that this ought not to be the case.

The separability thesis enables us to state neatly the essence of Ethical Positivism as the view that a good legal system is, inter alia, one in which adjudicators use only empirical or, more broadly, morally neutral criteria in their identification and interpretation of laws, and one in which legislators enact laws which can be so identified and interpreted. We may interpret Raz's 'sources thesis' along these lines. Raz contends that 'a jurisprudential theory is acceptable only if its test for identifying the content of the law and determining its existence depends exclusively on facts of human behaviour capable of being described in value-free terms, and applied without resort to moral argument'.[58] If a jurisprudential theory is one which judges should follow and legislators should facilitate, rather than one that is simply conceptually or descriptively accurate with respect to current practice, then Raz's sources thesis can be taken to encapsulate the possibilities which Ethical Positivism posits as an aspirational model.

The grand task of Ethical Positivism is to provide a moral justification for adopting this conception of law as the one on which to base our preferred legal systems. Clearly such a position presupposes the separability thesis, for it establishes that the Ethical Positivist's objective makes sense, but added to the conceptual feasibility of the enterprise is the justificatory task of establishing its desirability and gathering empirical evidence to demonstrate that it is, to a sufficient extent, a realisable ideal.

Legalism not Formalism

Many critiques of Positivism are in fact critiques of 'formalism' and it may be helpful to elucidate further the nature of the ideal put forward by LEP in terms of the analysis of formalism. In fact, 'formalism' is a label which is given to a number of different ideas, mostly with a pejorative connotation. One type of formalism is the view that law is a closed system in which legal answers can be read off from a combination of given rules and established facts,[59] usually with the rider that this impossible model denies the nature of the choices that have to be made in rule application and often masks the manipulative power of those who dominate the system to their own advantage.[60]

A second type of formalism is the idea that the rules of the closed system can themselves be deduced from general concepts within the system. Thus, according to Michael Moore, 'So construed, formalism asserts not only that there exists, in all or some cases, one unique result deducible from the rules and the facts, but also that the rules themselves may be derived from some more general theoretical statements.'[61] This more inclusive idea of a closed legal system is what Pound may have meant in his critique of 'mechanical jurisprudence'.[62] A more attractive variant of formalism is given by Schauer, who takes it to be 'the concept of decision-making according to *rule*',[63] a process to which he gives qualified endorsement: 'I do not argue that formalism is always good or that legal systems ought often or even ever be formalised.'[64] Here the contrast is with decision making which takes each case on its merits, unconstrained by pre-established limitations.

LEP can be substantially identified with formalism in Hart's third sense of rule-based decision making, although, in view of the ambiguity of the terminology, it is less confusing to call this position 'legalism'. This makes law a closed system only to the extent that it excludes certain matters from the decision-making process. Legalism emphasises rather than avoids the openness of law to change through political inputs beyond the adjudicative process, but suggests that it is right to avoid such inputs within legal process itself. In the words of MacCormick, legalism represents

> the stance in legal politics according to which matters of legal regulation and controversy ought so far as possible to be conducted in accordance with predetermined rules of considerable generality and clarity, in which legal relations comprise primarily rights, duties, powers and immunities reasonably clearly definable by reference to such rules, and in which acts of government however desirable teleologically must be subordinate to rules and rights.[65]

This, he notes, is 'an ethical and political stance about law, not an unimaginative attitude to its application nor an undue faith in the possibilities of literalism in legal interpretation'.[66] The language of generality used here raises the question of whether it is being assumed that highly abstract concepts can be used to yield determinate answers, as the conceptual variant of formalism suggests. If so, MacCormick's position is not to be equated with LEP which, to the contrary, holds that the process of rendering more specific highly general concepts requires political determinations at every stage. Hence the stress on rules which are as specific as possible in view of the purpose of the legislation and the moral or other distinctions that are being legitimated by the enactment. For instance, the analyses of freedom set out in Chapter 2 may be seen as providing a framework for rule formulation but cannot themselves lead to any specific outcome in terms of the extent of any particular freedom that ought to be permitted or protected.[67] This does not mean that particulars cannot be identified through universal terminology, but only that the legislative wording must be sufficiently specific to capture the political choice that is being made. The ideal of LEP is that all rules should be specific enough to be accurate expressions of the purpose of their creators. Where this is not achieved the system requires further inputs to enable a properly legal determination.

It is this reference to purpose that distinguishes LEP most clearly from formalisms of the first two types by suggesting that to understand a rule properly it is necessary to have some idea of the underlying purpose of the rules in question. This is not in order to vary the content of the rule according to its consequences when applied to particular cases, but in order to understand what it is that the rule requires. This understanding presupposes some awareness of the nature of the choices confronting the legislator and the way in which the language used signals a particular selection of options. Oddly, Positivism is usually lumped in with closed-system formalism as the orthodoxy to be undermined by, for instance, Critical Legal Studies or Feminist Jurisprudence. 'Oddly' because Positivism was born in a rejection of formalised models of the common law: the view (or pretence) that legal decisions could be determined by reference to basic principles, and by analogy reasoning, from decided cases. LEP must, however, take notice of those critiques which argue that the whole idea of rule-based decision making is mistaken, on the grounds that any rule, including the rules for identifying the authoritative rules, does not determine a specific outcome. Hart saw that rules may have uncontroversial applications in paradigm cases and controversial ones in marginal cases, and for this reason distanced himself from closed-system formalism. More radical critics, following in the Realist tradition, cast doubt on the allegedly uncontroversial paradigms which feature in Hart's partial formalism. They can do so, however, only by taking the language of particular rules out of the purposive contexts in which they are created and interpreted.

On close inspection, it is clear that there is a tension in such criticism between those who say that formalism is impossible and those who say that it is undesirable. Taking formalism (in its legalism version) to be the effort to decide cases solely by applying the relevant rules to the findings of fact in a particular situation, a repeated criticism is that this procedure fails to take note of the consequences of such decisions in the particular cases and unwarrantably ignores the instrumental purpose of the rules in question. Thus the mischief rule, whereby an unjust result should lead to the relevant rule not being applied on the grounds that this was not the mischief with which the rule is meant to deal, is taken as a better approach than a formalistic method which is blind to such consequent injustices. More generally, it is seen as the task of adjudicators to further the purposes which rules are enacted or created to serve. Particular decisions should be made in the light of what best serves these purposes in the case in question.

Such criticisms make sense only if they are taken as accepting that cases can be decided by more or less mechanical rule application but that they ought not to be. Here we can insert all the familiar criticisms of rule following: that it is subservient to the past, that it is insensitive to relevant aspects of particular situations, that it prevents adjudicators making just and efficient decisions. These criticisms can be countered with the standard ripostes in terms of the advantages of rule conformity discussed in Chapter 3. This is, however, a debate that assumes rule following to be a feasible activity.

Other critiques of formalism deny what the earlier ones take for granted. In a parade of 'hard cases' it is readily exemplified that often there is no one clear rule or consistent set of rules which apply to a particular fact situation and often no way of making a determination as to what facts are relevant. These examples often make very different points. Those made central to the debate by Dworkin often involve examples of the ways in which common law reasoning allows background and usually unspecific principles which embody moral-style terminology (such as 'justice') to override the outcome of applying specific rules when these outcomes are deemed unacceptable.[68] Evidently, these are hard cases, not because of the difficulty of working out the consequences of the relevant rules, but because of the content of the decision which uncontroversially follows from the rules. Such examples may serve to undermine the descriptive adequacy of the rule-following model and may point to its moral undesirability where there are no background principles which can be used to outweigh unacceptable outcomes. They do not, however, affect the viability, as distinct from the desirability, of legalism as a rule-following model of law.

If what is suggested is that the assumed purposes of rules should always override the consequences which would otherwise flow from their application then we have a repudiation of rule-based reasoning, not a critique of it.[69] As Schauer says, in this case, 'the view that rules should be interpreted to allow their purposes to trump their language in fact collapses the distinction between a rule and a reason, and thus loses the very concept of a rule'. However, there is no similar objection to a hierarchy of rules whereby routine rules are overridden by more fundamental ones, provided these more fundamental ones can be applied without recourse to subjective value judgments. Thus, for the situation in *Riggs* v. *Palmer*, we may have a rule which says that an inheritance will be void if the death in question results from the criminal action of the putative beneficiary.

Similar points may be made about those examples which cite situations where there are a multiplicity of rules which might be applied to the case in hand but which will produce different results. The problem here is not with the determinacy but with the multiplicity of rules, something for which there are possible solutions relating to the manner in which rules are selected and reconciled.[70]

Many of the critiques of legalism fasten on the de facto openness of the common law modes of argumentation, particularly precedent and analogy. Precedent is suspect because the process of arriving at the ratio decidendi of a case is inherently slippery. Analogy is question-begging in that it presupposes that we already have a rule to determine what is relevant and what is not. All that follows from these critiques, however, is that precedent is an inadequate form of legalistic reasoning unless it involves the identification and application of clear and specific rules. Analogy is similarly unacceptable unless what is being identified as relevantly similar comes within the terminology of such rules. From the point of view of legalism, rules should emanate from political decision and not from the determination of individual cases, and analogical reasoning is inappropriate where it expands or reduces the scope of a rule in a non-rule-governed way.

Many of the critiques of formalism are based on examples of very general rules which are so vague as to be open to a variety of incompatible readings. The legalist can, of course, reply that the rule is a bad one, but the problem of vagueness, as we shall see, applies in principle to relatively specific rules. 'Box' may be more specific than 'container', but there will be marginal cases of both boxes and containers. Here the legalist has to fall back on two claims. The first is that rules can exclude some possibilities, so that it is not the case that just any inferences can be drawn from any rule. The second is that precision is a matter of degree, and legalism represents a commitment to being as precise as possible in the context of the general purpose for which the rule is drawn up. This means that there is a preference for rules which are sufficiently specific to be uncontroversial, such as those which refer to natural kinds, and/or publicly observable recurrences.[71]

Many other critiques rely on the fact that judges often fail to follow the relevant specific rules. To this LEP has a predictable and decisive response, namely that, within the theory, the judge is acting unethically. Here we need to draw on the possibility of rule following to make points which are essentially the same as those of the critics of formalism: that judges pretend or erroneously believe they are following rules when they are drawing on their own preferences. These, and the more philosophical aspects of the indeterminacy critique, will be taken up again in the next two chapters, but, for the sake of providing an overview, it should be mentioned at this stage that legalism has to deal with the radical indeterminacy critique of rule following which points out that rules have to be interpreted in terms of the meaning that is ascribed to symbols according to the convention of a particular linguistic community. Since meanings are conventional, it is argued that we are free to ascribe such meaning as we like to the symbols which occur in the rules.

Briefly, this is a weak argument if it simply means that words could have different meanings. It is stronger if it is held that they often do have different if overlapping meanings in the same jurisdiction. In this case an appeal to a literal or plain meaning may be insufficient to obtain an uncontroversial reading. However, it is part of the art of good legisative drafting to take account of the conventional diversities of understanding that exist in a particular community, so that possible ambiguities are anticipated and explicitly dealt with by stipulated definitions. The possibility of approximating to legislation which is not open to ambiguity in the light of community diversity is not negated either by examples which show that judges choose to ignore plain meanings in order to achieve an interpretation which produces a result with which they can personally concur, or by examples of poor drafting.

Conclusion

This discussion does no more than sketch the parameters of LEP and indicate some of the moves that have to be taken in order to preserve its intelligibility and practicality as a legal ideal. That ideal may be summed up as securing a legal system in which conscious political judgments are formulated in specific rules at a level of generality sufficient to pick out the distinctions considered to be relevant by the legislature, enacted in a manner which makes their identification empirically determinable according to accepted constitutional rules and with a content which can be uncontroversially agreed by those to whom the rules apply.

Many of the defences outlined require the admission of the descriptive inadequacy of the theory and the assertion of its aspirational ideals. This means that LEP cannot avoid the problem of how judges and others should act where the model does not apply because there are no relevant rules of sufficient specificity, or where other judges are creating laws by the elastic use of precedent and analogy, or where the rules do lead to outrageous results that clearly no legislator intended. Of course it can always be argued that, if there is no suitable rule, no remedy can be given or no criminal charge may be proven. This seems unsatisfactory in that the losses in question are likely to fall unfairly on the weak and vulnerable members of society. In the case of rule conflict, sometimes non-formalist elements can be introduced which do not compromise the amoral, apolitical nature of the applicatory judgments, such as closure devices of a random sort, like the frequency of citation. Arbitrariness is not to be despised if it is a matter of luck rather than prejudice or whim, although it is far from satisfactory.

Other second-best strategies to deal with the positivist failures in actual legal systems involve adopting the role of a delegated legislature open to prospective legislative overruling. Provided that such devices are not used where they are not required, a second-best Positivist approach is to view the courts as giving effect to what they believe the legislature would enact if they had the opportunity to do so. In this they look to signs of political will as manifest through the sources and results of democratic decision process.

But prior to such departures from their normal role, courts should seek to provide techniques for giving effect to the purposive goals of the legal system in terms of the properly constructed decisions of the legislature. This will mean adopting devices which are not characteristic of the normal assumptions of legalism, which are to provide an answer which coheres with the total legal history. The political philosophy of LEP encourages the rejection of custom in favour of current authority.[72] However, where there is no clear political decision, Positivists will have regard to continuity and consistency as providing the most predictable mode of decision making in cases of uncertainty. Hence the proper limited regard for precedent in situations of rule deficiency. But neither consistency nor precedent can be used by the Ethical Positivist to override properly enacted and clear, relevant laws.[73] These are all topics which are taken further in subsequent chapters.

Notes

1 This section takes up and develops the discussion introduced in Chapter 1. See Coleman (1982a, p.140): 'I refer to the denial of a necessary constitutive relationship betwen law and morals as the separability thesis.' 'The contention that there is no necessary connection between law and morals, or law as it is and law as it ought to be is the second of five different characteristics of Positivism put forward in Hart (1982, pp.601–2, n.25). Rather confusingly, Shiner (1992, p.23) calls this the 'separation thesis', a term used here for descriptive claims about the negative relationship between law and morals.

2 Austin (1954, p.184).

3 See Austin (1954, Lecture V) and Hart (1961, Chapter 9).

4 Coleman (1982a, p.143): 'The form of positivism generated by commitment to the rule of recognition as constrained by the separability thesis I call negative positivism to draw attention both to the character and the weakness of the claim it makes.'

5 Glanville Williams (1945).

6 Aquinas (1966, Question 9). This is a standard view of the Natural Law position, although Finnis (1980, pp.19ff) claims that it is atypical.

7 Hart (1961, pp.206–7).

8 See Dyzenhaus (1991).

9 For example, Austin (1954, p.186):

> To prove by pertinent reasons that a law is pernicious is highly useful, because such process may lead to the abrogation of the pernicious law. To incite the public to resistance by determinate view of utility may be useful, for resistance, grounded on clear and definite prospects of good, is sometimes beneficial. But to proclaim generally that all laws which are pernicious or contrary to the will of God are void and not to be tolerated, is to present anarchy, hostile and perilous as much to wise and benign rule as to stupid and galling tyranny.

See also MacCormick (1981, p.24), Hart (1957–8), Fuller (1957, p.631), Hart (1961, p.204) and Beyleveld and Brownsword (1989, pp.49–50).

10 Contrast Dworkin (1986) and with Raz (1991).

11 Coleman (1982a, p.143).

12 Ibid., p.148.

13 Ibid., p.147.

14 Hart (1961, p.100–101), Shiner (1992, p.29), Kelsen (1967, pp.119–22) and Raz (1979, p.46).

15 MacCormick (1985, p.3) and Soper (1986, pp.31–7).

16 Lyons (1984, p.72): 'The tradition of legal theorising that we call "positivism" embraces two principal, related ideas: first, law is a species of empirical fact; second, law must be distinguished from morality – in particular, we must not confuse the law we actually have with the law as we would like it to be'. Shiner (1992) simply takes it for granted that Legal Positivism is a descriptive and explanatory theory.

17 Austin (1954, Lecture I).

18 Thus, Hart (1961, 2nd edn, 1994, p.240).

19 Hart (1961, pp.203–7).

20 Hobbes (1990, Chapter 20).

21 Both have an objectivist epistemology and an agenda for reform.

22 MacCormick (1981, Chapter 4).

23 As a non-cognitivist, Kelsen does not seem a promising candidate for LEP. But he had strong moral views, for example on relative justice (Kelsen, 1957, p.24): 'Since science is my profession, and hence the most important thing in my life, justice, to me, is that social order under whose protection the search for truth can prosper. "My" justice, then, is the justice of freedom, the justice of peace, the justice of democracy – the justice of tolerance.' But how far does this intrude into his science of law? The 'Grundnorm' is not a moral premiss, but then neither is the rule of recognition. It is a presupposition (while the rule of recognition is an actual social rule). If the motivation of his theory is ethical this seems to undercut his idea of social science as totally independent. But perhaps he has an ethical theory for not having moral argument in legal reasoning.

This would mean that he has a form of LEP in that his position is instrumentally related to anti-totalitarianism (a biographically strong interpretation). See Ebenstein (1971); also Raz (1979, pp.134ff). Raz argues that Kelsen's basic norm establishes 'justified normativity' (actually justified) not simply 'social normativity' (upheld as binding standards in a society), but that the legal point of view from which this judgment is made does not commit the legal professional to regarding the laws as just. However, so great is Kelsen's hostility to the intrusion of ideology into legal science and his emphasis on cognition of the essence of law as the essence of his pure theory, that it seems best to categorise his approach as that of a transcendental conceptualist. Yet it could equally be argued that his efforts to exclude legal policy from the study of law were an attempt to establish a general justified framework within which competing ideologies could express themselves. See Kelsen (1992, p.3): 'The required separation of legal science from politics does have political consequences, negative ones, and it is understandable that opponents are hardly inclined to be fair to a theory that calls on legal science to exercise self-restraint, which many regard as self-demotion. In order to be able to resist such a theory its opponents must disallow its pure nature... In a word, the *Pure Theory of Law* has been suspected of every single political persuasion there is. Nothing could attest better to its purity'; and p.18: 'The Pure Theory aims to depict the law as it is, without legitimizing it as just or disqualifying it as unjust; the Pure Theory enquires into actual and possible law, not into "right" law.' Given that 'all ideology has its roots in will not cognition', it would appear that his theory, as a cognitive exercise in pursuit of truth, cannot adopt an evaluative position on the value of law as opposed to other forms of political control.

24 Campbell (1990).

25 Kerruish (1991).

26 Lee (1989, Chapter 1). Also Postema (1986, p.165): 'Any adequate general theory of law must give a satisfactory account of law as a social phenomenon.'

27 Austin (1954, pp.9–12).

28 Lee (1989, Chapter 1). Interestingly, this involves virtually excluding Kelsen from the pantheon of Legal Positivists on the grounds that he abandoned the positivist's belief in the possibility of objectively verifiable empirical propositions.

29 Ibid., p.183.

30 Coleman (1982a, p.147).

31 Postema (1986, pp.328–30).

32 Raz (1979, p.48).

33 Hart (1961, p 204).

34 Thus Austin (1954, Lecture I).

35 Austin (1954, p.7: 'laws properly so called'; Hohfeld (1919, p.53): rights 'strictu sensu'.

36 Soper (1986, p.44).

37 Soper (1984, p.34).

38 Soper (1988, p.209).

39 Ibid., pp. 232f. See also Beyleveld and Brownsword (1986).

40 Detmold (1984, p.23).

41 Kelman (1987, pp.262–3), Klare (1979, p.123), Stubbs (1986, pp.65–7) and Mensch (1980, pp. 23–6).

42 Douzinas and Warrington (1991, pp.21–8) and Goodrich (1987, pp.35–44). For an excellent discussion, see Schauer (1988).

43 For instance, Griffith (1977).

44 MacCormick and Weinberger (1984, pp.134–9), Dilthey (1970), Weber (1968) and Schutz (1970).

45 MacCormick (1981).

46 MacCormick and Weinberger (1984).

47 Tur (1985).

48 MacCormick and Weinberger (1984, pp.1–24).

49 Ibid., Chapter 6.

50 Anscombe (1958, pp.69–72) and Searle (1969, pp.50–53).

51 MacCormick and Weinberger (1984, p.10).
52 Ibid., title.
53 Ibid., p.27:

> Our institutional theory of law aims to provide a sound ontological and epistemological foundation for the equally valid and mutually complementary disciplines: legal dogmatics and the sociology of law. It aims accordingly to make a contribution to the understanding of legal structures and to the methods proper to legal study. And it aims finally to show the place (and limits) of practical reason in law and on human social life. These are matters with which any comprehensive theory of law must deal.

Note that they write of the methods *proper* to legal study.
54 Ibid., p.139.
55 MacCormick (1989, p.188).
56 Thus MacCormick and Summers (1992, p.19): 'Legal Scholarship calls for the experience of a disciplined and intelligent imagination in order to reconstruct the fragmentary material issued by decision-makers into a rational coherent and systematic whole.'
57 MacCormick (1989, p.184).
58 Raz (1985, pp.39–40).
59 Hart (1961, pp.124–30).
60 Schauer (1988, p.510).
61 Moore (1981, p.159).
62 Pound (1908, p.605).
63 See Schauer (1988, p.534).
64 Ibid., p.540.
65 MacCormick (1989, p.184)
66 Ibid., p.188.
67 See pp.21–6.
68 Dworkin (1977).
69 Schauer (1988, p.534).
70 Singer (1984, pp.17–18).
71 See Chapter 6.
72 Schauer (1988, p.514).
73 Postema (1986, p.9).

5 The Ethics of Positivism

Introduction

Positivist ideals relate directly to the political justification of prescriptive Positivism. The ethics of Positivism has to do with the conduct of those who fill the various roles within a system of government through rules: principally legislators, citizens, lawyers and judges. Questions of ethics cannot be resolved without reference to the ideals of the institution within which these roles have meaning and the justifications which support that system. The objective of this chapter is to explore the ethics of LEP in this context.

Ethics is a matter both of the moral standards of conduct which ought to govern the performance of the various legal roles and of the required commitment and conformity to these standards, typically where there are no legal sanctions involved.[1] This is partly a matter of devising and seeking conformity to appropriate rules of conduct, but also involves the choice of alternative performances when the rules do not or cannot adequately cover the situations in question.

'Ethics' is the appropriate term here, not simply because much of the normative substance relates to role performance rather than personal behaviour, but also because the rules and standards are not in themselves laws, although some of them may be administered in a quasi-legal manner by the professional groups involved and their determinations may be challenged and adjudicated at law.[2] If ethics is reduced to a legal-style enforcement of professional rules then it becomes in effect a matter of regulation rather than morality and, given that the professional sanctions are enforceable at law, is in many ways indistinguishable from law itself. In such circumstances the 'ethical' tag is justified, if at all, by the fact that the moral standards required by the offical rules of the role are 'higher' than those which are expected of other people. In fact, much of the content of what is taken to be a matter of 'professional ethics' involves standards which merely put some limits to the apparent immoralities that are licensed by the role of lawyers in protecting the interests of clients. In general, lawyers' ethics may be perceived as rather 'lower' than average in the scale of morally admirable conduct. Moreover, there are aspects of professional codes which are directed towards protecting the interests of the profession and regulating internal competition between lawyers. To the extent that such matters are central to codes of professional 'ethics', there is little that is ethical about them.[3]

It is part of the paradox of politics that no legal system can adequately deal with the problem of controlling the controllers.[4] Whatever the division of powers involved in a polity, one or more parts of the constitutionally defined political system has to be trusted to act appropriately with respect to the foundational rules and goals of the constitution. Thus, for constitutional government to exist, it is arguable that some body other than the legislature must decide whether or not the legislature is acting within its powers. There is no evident constitutional manner in which the power to make such decisions can be reviewed by the legislature without rendering them vacuous. In this case courts in their constitutional rulings with respect to the validity of legislation must simply be trusted. Alternatively, the legislature may be left to act within its constitutional powers with no external legal controls. It then has to be trusted to remain within the conventions which govern the propriety of its proceedings. Whichever body is given the final decision on such matters has an ethical choice, in that there can be no immediate sanction involved and no legal remedy readily available. This trust is diluted rather than avoided by a Madisonian system which takes the separation of powers to the point where the effectiveness of government is in doubt.[5] This means that some role occupants, individually or jointly, can get away with whatever they decide, short of unconstitutional political moves being made against them. This does not mean that there are no rules involved. The ethics of roles are governed by social or political conventions as well as by explicitly enacted constitutions. However, it is characteristic of such situations that they are underdetermined by the rules and conventions involved which, in the absence of readily available mechanisms for overt change, are subject to flexible interpretations and gradual changes to accommodate the political pressures of the time.

These factors arise most evidently in the case of high constitutional roles such those occupied by Supreme Court justices, presidents and parliaments, but they also have application to lesser roles within a legal system even though the rules may be more available and far more readily changed at hierarchically lower levels. Here also problems of enforcement often mean that it is not easy to police and assure conformity with the proprieties of role performance. Indeed, it is a sociological truism that legal systems require most citizens to obey the law other than from a fear of legal sanctions. Similarly, no legal system can operate without a degree of conscientious conformity to the role standards by lawyers and judges.[6]

In addition, there is another ethical aspect of all role fulfilment in relation to rules which is particularly relevant to LEP. However sound the rules may be from a positivist viewpoint, it is possible to adopt attitudes towards rules which represent either a good faith attempt to understand the rules and follow them conscientiously or a bad faith avoidance of this objective or, somewhere in between, an endeavour to read the rules in the way which best suits the individual concerned and follow them only to the extent that is necessary to avoid sanctions. It is trite to say that it is morally preferable to follow the spirit rather than the letter of the law. If by the 'spirit' of the law we mean the purposes of the rule makers rather than the meaning – or 'letter' – of the law, then this is not part of the ideal of LEP, which subscribes to the view that rules exclude such considerations. But following the spirit of the law can also be taken to imply that rules should be read and followed in good faith, that is by taking an impartial view of their meaning and conscientiously endeavouring to follow the rule so read. 'Impartiality' here means no more than bracketing off the consequences for the individual concerned from the factors which are allowed to influence the decisions made, except in so far as these consequences have a moral relevance which can be appreciated from the point of view of those not directly involved. In other words, impartiality involves viewing the situation as you would if you were not one of those principally affected: the point of view which is suggested by the principle of universalisability.[7]

It is contended that the ideals of LEP are not realisable unless the majority of participants in a legal system take such an 'ethical' attitude towards their role enactment, whether as legislator, citizen, lawyer or judge. We shall see that this runs counter to the idea that it is the duty of a lawyer to do whatever serves the interests of a client even if this means suppressing evidence, intentionally distorting the otherwise clear meanings of rules and seeking to frustrate and delay the legal process, to mention a cross-section of the practices which give lawyers and lawyering a bad name.

First, we need to review the general argument that law as an institution is amoral, an argument which would destroy the foundation of the whole idea that Positivism has a legal ethic.

Legal Positivism and the Alleged Amorality of Law

We have seen that the separability thesis, according to which law and morality are conceptually distinct, often gives rise to the mistaken view that Legal Positivism cannot be based on an affirmative moral or ethical view of law and politics.[8] We have also noted that it is necessary to distinguish LEP from the more specific thesis of moral disestablishmentarianism according to which the extent to which the morality of a society is reflected in the content of law ought to be minimised.[9] Moreover, LEP does not take the view that laws can be neutral with respect to the morality of different ways of life, but only in the sense that they be identifiable and applicable without the exercise of autonomous first order moral judgments.[10]

On the other hand, it has been acknowledged that there is basis for the contention that some Positivists are amoral (that is, non-moral rather than immoral), in that Legal Positivism has historical connections with 'positivism' as a hard-nosed empiricist theory of science which has no place for questions which involve critical moral evaluation.[11] Versions of such amoral Legal Positivism have been espoused by Logical Positivists and others who hold that moral judgments are non-cognitivist, in that they are ultimately a matter of personal preference rather than intellectually or empirically testable belief. Logical Positivists, and some Legal Positivists, are dismissive of any objectivity or epistemology which is not based either in empirically falsifiable propositions or in analytical truths derived from morally contingent definitions.[12]

These philosophical views with respect to the subjectivity of moral opinion are often associated with Legal Positivism and linked in with the fact that many classical Legal Positivists have tended to come out firmly for unconditional obedience to law, whether substantively good or bad. Before commenting on these associations, we should note that, while Positivists, like everyone else, cannot without contradiction deny that there is a *legal* obligation to obey or respect all positive laws, modern Positivists take it to be a virtue of their theory that the sharp distinction between what law is and what law ought to be makes it a visibly open question whether citizens are morally bound to carry out their legal obligations.[13] The classic Positivists tend to Bentham's view that the citizen is under a moral duty to obey punctually, to censure freely,[14] but modern Positivists are keen to emphasise that the censure may involve recommending legal non-conformity. Certainly Austin, amongst others, invokes the spectre of anarchy as grounds for condemning the use of individual judgment in the making of decisions about whether or not to obey law,[15] although he does so on the basis of a cognitivist epistemology. Further, these Positivists argue that Natural Law has the disadvantage with respect to social order that those who accept the theory will tend to make up their own mind about the morality and hence – in accordance with Natural Law theory – the legality of what is required of them by courts or statutes. This argument has little force unless it is assumed that, under Positivism, disobedience on the grounds that the law is believed to be immoral is not a moral option. In this case it might appear that the Positivist is renouncing a moral approach to law and this may be the basis for the view that Positivism is an amoral theory.

This conclusion fails to take account of the fact that an absolutist theory of political obligation must be based on moral reasons for the suspension of individual judgment concerning the morality of a law when it comes to the point of deciding whether to abide by it. These moral reasons are second order ones in that they do not engage directly with the morality or immorality of particular laws and focus instead on the reasons for having laws. Such second order moral reasons are aptly called 'ethical' as distinct from moral. At this point LEP feeds on all the varied arguments that have been presented in earlier chapters for the utility and morality of government through rules. Convenience conventions and organisational institutional arrangements do not work without general conformity; deterrence requires that we in general disallow individuals' conscientious objections; while democracy and justice require the general acceptance of those majority decisions which are expressed in the form of rules. All these considerations morally ground arguments for conformity without immediate regard to substance. However, we have seen that none of these rule rationales justify total suspension of individual moral judgment.[16] Not only do most of them involve some assessment of the efficacy and benefits of conformity to rules in accordance with some view of their type and purpose, but all of them require us to accept the possibility that, in particular instances, the harm done by conformity so clearly outweighs the possible benefits as to make the conformity morally unacceptable. While there is a danger of self-partiality in anyone acting from such assessments of their own conduct where this enables them to avoid a burden which would otherwise fall on them, Positivists may accept that it is sometimes morally correct to act in accordance with such assessments despite the danger of self-interested delusion and the prospect of undermining the generally beneficial habits of obedience on which social order depends.

A great deal in the debate about the moral defeasibility of legal obedience depends on the extent to which there is moral disagreement in a society, particularly moral disagreement on this very topic, namely how far the individuals should follow their own conscience in practical reasoning about the force of specific legal obligations. Where it is known that a significant number of citizens have strong moral reservations about enacted laws and hold to the belief that conformity to such laws is either not morally required or actually morally unacceptable, then those rule rationales which depend upon the assumption of general conformity are potentially undermined. Conformity may, of course, be obtained by deterrence and incentive means, but this may not be effective and has moral costs in its impact on the significant liberties and moral dignity of the disaffected citizens.

In such situations the moral question to be addressed is whether the cost in terms of liberty and moral dignity which result from requiring people to act against their first order moral convictions are worth paying for the (perhaps reduced) benefits obtainable through the set of rules in question. It is hard to come to a position on such matters without paying attention to the moral views of the dissenters. Where their views have some plausibility, moral or empirical, this would appear to weaken the case for enforcing conformity, something which may cause few moral qualms where the dissenters hold what are regarded as outrageous beliefs about, for instance, a fundamental human right. There can ultimately be no defensible line drawing with respect to morally permissible or required disobedience without reference to the moral substance of the laws in question.

Yet to give weight to the differential acceptability of the divergent moral opinions which threaten legal conformity does seem to presuppose a cognitivist meta-ethic, for we require to have some confidence in the universalisability of our own moral judgement if we are to treat the views of others as unreasonable or outrageous.[17] Here we do come to a logical connection between the issue of political obligation and at least some forms of Legal Positivism, for many Positivists adopt a non-cognitivist view of ethics which would appear to preclude their taking the sort of moral stand that is required to justify disobedience to valid law. Conversely, denying that there is such a thing as moral truth gives them one reason for rejecting the Natural Lawyer's commitment to disobeying unjust laws, namely that we have no way of knowing what is substantively just. Since LEP involves a cognitive moral epistemology, it looks as if it cannot rely on this particular argument against individual moral discretion in the face of morally questionable law, but, if the version of cognitivism held by the Legal Positivist is such that it is very difficult to arrive at moral truth, at least on certain matters, and if it is allowed that the selfishness and ignorance of human beings means that there is a weak correlation between such knowledge of moral truth as they possess and their actual conduct, then the implications for moral discretion of the admission of an objectivist meta-ethics is greatly reduced; but then so is the scope for condemning particular laws as outrageously immoral.

It is clear, then, that LEP does not take an amoral view towards the question of our moral obligation to obey or disobey laws, although other Legal Positivists may do so. In general, LEP presents an array of ethical reasons for legal conformity: significant liberty, fairness, the efficient pursuit of public goods and the general happiness and, where applicable, respect for democratic power. What LEP does is to point up a number of arguments in favour of adherence to positivistic rules which provide defeasible rationales for conformity to positive law which are sufficiently specific for us to work out a moral position in relation to our response to grossly immoral rules and regimes. This is not an amoral position, although it is one which morally requires that we, as citizen, lawyer or judge, routinely subordinate our own first order moral views as to the substance of a piece of legislation to our second order or ethical views about the legitimacy and value of the system as a whole. If it is the case that subordination to valid law is not always morally overriding, it must be the case that a moral judgment has to be made in each case, not about the validity of the law, but about whether to conform with it. If the decision is taken simply in terms of the content of the rule then that is never compatible with the role of a citizen or judge, but it is always a moral option to override the moral reasons in favour of rule conformity because of the gross immorality of the rule in question. The choice of whether or not to conform in these cases is not a legal judgment but an ethical one, and it is an ethical one which is compatible with the moral foundations of LEP. This means that, potentially, any judgment as to role performance is a matter of ethics. It follows that the way such a decision should be reached must conform to the requirements of impartiality and good faith that were outlined in the introduction to this chapter. This is a long way from regarding legal systems from an amoral point of view.

Lawyers' Ethics

Defending Positivism against amoralism is to confront only the lesser charge, for it is often argued that Positivism is an ideology which seeks to legitimise not only the amorality of law but the immorality of lawyers.[18] We shall consider shortly the plausibility of associating Positivism, the dominant theory of many Civil Law jurisdictions, with the alleged shortcomings of the adversarial method, which is a feature of Common Law systems, but first we must examine the substance of the charge that lawyering is no job for a morally good person.[19]

In accordance with the popular jibe, the difference between lawyers and rats is that there are some things that rats just will not do.[20] In contrast to rats, lawyers are perceived, no doubt unfairly, as being willing to lie, conceal, manipulate and do down anyone other than their client. In their more defensible forms these actions are regarded as a matter of the lawyers' duty to their clients within an adversarial system. In their less palatable form they are regarded as part and parcel of the purely pragmatic conduct of lawyers in the pay of the wealthy and unprincipled clients on whom they depend for their livelihood. Such criticisms, particularly the latter, draw indignant repudiations from a profession which regards itself as having a high calling and a position in society which is justified by professional standards of integrity and trustworthiness: it is simply a matter of public misunderstanding that single-mindedness in the protection of a client's interest is anything but a particular commitment to seeing that justice is done. Here we seem to have uncovered another paradox, to the effect that the self-image of the lawyer as having higher than average ethical standards, and thus being especially worthy of public trust, is grounded in much the same conduct as gives rise to the public perception of lawyers as unworthy of respect.

Something in this mismatch between the internal and external views of the legal professional is due to difficulty in appreciating the nature of role morality, that is the rights and duties which attach to a position within a social institution rather than as ordinary persons.[21] These difficulties in understanding role morality as instrumental within larger social organisations are exacerbated by the nature of the lawyers' task in advising and representing clients in a legal system which culminates in an adversarial process in which the just outcome is held to depend on two conflicting parties doing their best to discredit the contentions of the other side, with the gladiatorial contest being adjudicated by an impartial umpire, perhaps with the assistance of a jury that takes no active part in the proceedings. Once the subtleties of role morality in general and the adversarial legal role in particular are appreciated then, it is argued, it will be seen that good lawyers are indeed good persons because they are striving to do their best for someone else in a situation where that person's important interests are under attack and vulnerable to coercive and detrimental intervention, and the lawyers have the skills necessary to protect those vulnerable interests. Lawyers' duty is to subordinate their own views and interests to those of the clients in whose service they must deploy their legal and other skills and knowledge: hence the twin ideas of neutrality with respect to the moral goals and character of the client and zealous partisanship in furthering the interests identified by the autonomous client.[22]

As we will see when we come to the role of the judge, it is easy to appreciate that persons with special responsibilities must have higher standards of ethical conduct than others. Thus, judges, like most officials, have a duty to impartiality which does not apply to the individual citizen. But, the example of soldiers in war notwithstanding, it is nothing like so easy to assimilate the idea that special responsibilities may require exemptions from the ordinary standards of moral conduct. We therefore find it hard to accept that lawyers are entitled to lie for their clients or withhold evidence which would clearly establish that their client is guilty or legally liable. While an element of partisanship may be admirable, especially in defence of an accused or an underprivileged civil litigant, we are less likely to warm to the delaying tactics, manipulations and try-ons which lawyers may adopt in the service of wealthy corporate clients.

Despite an extensive literature on these matters, there is little agreement on the precise parameters of the lawyers' role. There are certainly difficult lines to draw in such matters. Even if lawyers should subordinate their own interests to those of the client, may they sacrifice the interests of others by withholding evidence, or destroying the credibility of witnesses they know to be telling the truth? Is permitting the presentation of perjured evidence simply the price to be paid for the assurances of confidentiality which encourage the disclosure by clients of information which may be necessary for lawyers to carry out their appointed task or representative role? The challenge is to discover a principled way in which lines can be drawn between acceptable partiality and unacceptable partisanship. It is uncontroversial that the lawyer may do only that which is within the law, but that does not help us answer questions about what the law should be in these matters. In any case, we are concerned with professional standards which go beyond the legal minimum. Nor can we settle for the neat thesis that the lawyer may do only what the client may do for himself, for the client's morality may diverge from that of the lawyer, and this formulation does not enable us to arrive at a specific service role which involves doing things for clients which the clients cannot do for themselves.

Unavoidably, therefore, we have to confront the nature of court process in relation to its functions and the ways in which it carries out those functions. The standard thesis put forward by practitioners is that justice is served if court proceedings are adversarial, with each party's legal representative putting forward the best legal and evidential arguments on each side with a judge whose duty is to enforce rules of procedure and choose between the two cases as presented, perhaps with the assistance of a jury for the determination of matters of fact. Thus it is often asserted that the prime purpose of a trial is to arrive at the truth regarding disputed claims or accusations, and to apply the relevant legal rules to the court's view of what actually occurred. It is in the determination of factual disputes that courts are mainly concerned and to which the adversarial system seems particularly germane. If, it is argued, there is an open debate between parties who are striving to establish or to disprove a particular allegation of fact then we are most likely to have before the tribunal all the evidence which is relevant to its determinations. The specialist role of looking for evidence either for or against a factual contention is said to be particularly effective in establishing the truth. Hence also the importance of eye witnesses and the need to test their recollections by vigorous questioning.[23]

In relation to the purposes of law, all this would be highly persuasive if it were true that unfettered adversarialism produces factual accuracy better than any practical alternative. In particular, it would fit neatly with a positivist model according to which the idea is to apply rules accurately, which must require reliable fact finding above all else. It is less persuasive on a Realist view in terms of which we can look for favourable or predictable decisions but not of accurate or correct ones.

The effectiveness of the adversarial system with respect to fact finding cannot be explored here, although we may note that there is little evidence to support its effectiveness as against Civil Law methods.[24] But the argument does have the merit of making the question of professional ethics dependent on empirical claims about the workings and outcomes of alternative legal systems. The principle we are looking for in relation to ethical line drawing in professional practice becomes at least in part a matter of testing alternative court procedures in the light of desired results. It then becomes a matter of empirical investigation to discover what role conduct is best adapted to the systems objectives. This immediately frees us from a dogmatic commitment to serving a client's interests come what may, for the professional role becomes that of doing for the client only that which maximises the effectiveness of the system. Given this approach, it is likely that we will be able to come to some conclusions about such matters as the ethics of destroying the credibility of a witness whom the lawyer knows to be telling to truth, failing to reveal relevant evidence to the other side or telling and supporting lies.[25]

The prospects of agreement on lawyers' advocacy roles may be disputed as resting on naive beliefs about the possibility of knowing what is in fact true or false, as distinct from seeking to prove one or the other.[26] It may be that the lawyers' zealous partisanship is justified by the fact that consensual factual beliefs rest on common prejudices rather than sound evidence, prejudices which are shared by the individuals who act as lawyers. The role of lawyers is to appreciate that such consensus is an inadequate empirical basis for important determinations of truth or falsity and to force themselves to try and see the alleged facts from a different perspective, and in particular to see the events in question from the perspective of the client. Thus, whatever the lawyer believes to the contrary, the client may in fact be innocent; therefore it is right for lawyers to pretend that they believe this so as to give that client's point of view proper representation.

This may even apply where the defendant shares the common prejudices and so has what might be regarded as a distorted view of his own conduct. In such cases the lawyer's duty is to challenge even the client's perceptions if it is in that client's interests to do so.

Similar points may be made about the lawyer's role in arguing questions of law. The Positivist's ideal of respecting the plain meaning of legal rules is countered by the lawyer's duty to argue for that reading of the rules which most favours her client's case. Hence the motivation, perhaps the duty, to undermine the Positivist goal of achieving rules which can command consensus as to their meaning as well as their content. It might seem odd that a lawyer's duty is to render plain meanings obscure but audience understandings of the same words and sentences can vary enormously within a given society. Some such process may be seen as the best way of arriving at an agreed meaning for a rule in social situations where communication is a problem and rules are not plain in relation to the diverse criteria of meaning actually in operation. Certainly, this approach is appropriate when we are seeking to improve legislation by removing obscurities and ambiguities. It may be thought to be equally helpful in arriving at an authoritative sense of relevant law.[27]

This is difficult terrain, but solutions can be sought by examining how court lawyers' roles contribute to the role which the judge is expected to play. If, in brief, judges are enjoined to exercise considerable imagination as to putative fact situations and considerable open-mindedness as to how rules may have been understood by those to whom they are addressed, then we believe that their role performance would not be assisted by suppression of relevant evidence or deliberate deceit, or by placing witnesses and litigants in situations where they are pressured in a way which makes it less likely that they will give honest and accurate accounts. But it does allow for a considerable effort on behalf of lawyer and judge to see the matters in dispute from the points of view of both parties.

We may argue that the parameters of the court lawyers' duties are set by the ideal of the accurate application of law in situations of dispute and the particular way in which the system in question seeks to attain that objective. Commitment to clients' interests thereby becomes secondary in theory but may be all but paramount in practice. Much the same can be said about other lawyer functions, such as advising and mediating. But not all lawyering has to be seen in the context of possible litigation, and not all litigation is motivated by narrow self-interest. Law is for the good man as well as the bad man, and legal advice may be sought, and perhaps should be routinely assumed to be sought, with a view to determining legal rights and duties for the purpose of enabling the enquirer to conform to the requirements of the law. Indeed, we can say that, from the point of view of LEP, while it is the lawyer's duty to advise the client in terms of what he may and may not do legally, this does not mean concentrating on how closely a person can get to breaking the law in the pursuit of his personal objectives without actually violating or going beyond the law.[28]

In an influential article on the failure of Legal Positivism and other theories of law to justify the adversarial system, William H. Simon both castigates Legal Positivism for endorsing what he calls the ideology of advocacy and argues that it in fact fails to provide an adequate defence of the system.[29] Simon's analysis is unhelpful in its caricature of Positivism as an extreme manifestation of egoistic liberalism which has not developed since the time of Hobbes, except to take on board a measure of American Legal Realism.[30] He fails to notice that most Legal Positivists have not supported the adversarial system. Simon does treat Legal Positivism prescriptively, although he assumes that social order in the interests of individual autonomy is its sole supporting value, ignoring altogether such matters as Hart's focus on facilitative rules. The substance of his argument is to the effect that the existing legal system does not produce the certainty and predictability that is the Positivist's raison d'être for law. This is because Legal Positivists, having introduced procedural rules to control the power of the state, take justice to be a matter of sticking to these adjectival rules rather than seeing to the accurate application of first order law. Further, lawyers are said to fail to treat their clients as autonomous beings by erroneously attributing to them the egoistic rationalism of the theory itself.[31]

Simon marshals a great deal of evidence which demonstrates that, in the United States at least, procedural rules are used to thwart the discovery of truth, that litigation is undertaken for reasons other than enforcing the arbitrary will of the sovereign, and settlements are routinely made which ignore substantive law. His persuasive conclusion is that the procedural discretion given by the Common Law in civil cases to litigants (and so in effect their lawyers) means that the law is in the hands of private power and is used by the wealthy as a form of legalised blackmail so that 'the threat to the citizen from the sovereign has been alleviated only at the cost of aggravating the threat from his fellow citizens'.[32] Simon argues that Positivism can offer no help in restoring the credibility of the adversarial model because it lacks any notion of shared values on which to reassert substantive justice or render accessible the non-egoistic ends of clients.

In fact, however, there are plenty of positivist sources beyond Simon's simplistic caricature on which we can draw for these tasks. In particular, the approach to the procedural complexities of the Common Law adopted by Bentham coincide with Simon's own critique of the fetishism of process. It is precisely in the attempt to reform procedure in a way which makes it serve the end of accurate rule application that Positivism can make a contribution to clarifying the issues of legal ethics. Bentham's argument is that the system should be flexible in the admission of evidence so that the court can make its own evaluations of its worth.[33] This goes with a move to debunk the mythological complexities in the law of evidence, a matter in which Simon echoes Bentham by identifying it as a source of the commercial value. Indeed, Bentham's recommendation that each person be his own lawyer is remarkably similar to Simon's own idea of non-professional advocacy.[34]

Simon's empirical evidence cannot lightly be put to one side when contemplating the prospects for realising a positivist system of adjudication. In particular, there is an enormous problem in the incompatibility of lawyering as a private business designed to generate income for the lawyer by serving the interests of the consumer and the role of lawyer as a servant of the court with a public function which has to do with ensuring justice for all. While this problem may be less acute in those jurisdictions where the lawyer is more of a civil servant than a business person, this has its own disadvantages in so far as government through rules is intended to distance the government from the implementation of its enactments. Here we are up against another dilemma arising out of the paradox of politics: whether to view the role of lawyers and judges as part of or independent of government.[35] If it is accepted that an independent bar is the better option as a system of defending accused persons and enforcing legal obligations, then we have to put great weight on the private monopoly of legal services being entrusted to a group of specialists with a powerful public morality which puts the interests of formal justice above those of their clients. This must apply particularly within an adversarial system that enjoins strict confidentiality and specialist partisanship. If these values are not combined with a real commitment to honesty, and a total repudiation of misusing protective procedures to manipulate legal process in the service of illegalities, then the justification for the privileged access of the lawyer to clients and court is without foundation.

There is much else that can be said about the ethics of lawyering, and a great deal of it concerns nothing peculiar to role morality except that it is heightened by the monopoly privileges of lawyers that render them open to temptations with respect to overcharging and other abuses of privilege. These matters are secondary to the overall picture which is rooted in the instrumental role of the lawyer as the mediator between the citizen and the legal process. In relation to the court-centred matters on which we have concentrated, this means seeing the lawyer as contributing to a process of accurate first order rule implementation in a way which takes into account the difficulties of establishing truth and meanings and the need to do this in a way which is not biassed against the parties involved. In other words, lawyers' ethics are subordinate to the adjudicative process which, as we shall now see, is equally dependent for its functioning on respect for its ethical rationales.

The Ethics of Adjudication

It is the arguments for government through rules which serve to explain the need to separate rule application from rule making. If rules are to fulfil their functions, they must be applied as well as promulgated. Legal systems presume that most initial rule application is done by the persons to whom they are addressed, the rule followers, whose conformity is the prerequisite of government via rules. However, a measure of non-conformity and inevitable disputes about conformity or non-conformity render self-application insufficient, hence the need for systems of rule enforcement, principally (a) in the detection, proof and punishment/rectification of non-conformity and (b) in the settlement of disputes between individuals as to their mutual conduct in relation to the rules.

In both aspects disagreement about the meaning and scope of the rules may require resolution in the light of circumstances which are not clearly defined by the applicable rules. In principle, such determinations or clarifications might be done by those who create the rules in the first place. This would at least have the advantage that rule makers would be required to provide the necessary specification and interpretation of the rules which have been legitimated by their enactments. However, there are many powerful arguments for making the enforcement of rules and the settlement of disputes in relation to rules a specialist and distinct activity of a specially trained set of officials:[36]

1 the advantages of requiring governments to govern via rules is dissipated if governments have power over the application of rules. The interpretative element in rule application, which is considered in the next chapter, gives scope for varying the application of rules in ways which violate their purported universalisation, to the detriment of both fairness and efficiency;
2 the processes of accurate fact finding in relation to rules is a complex and time-consuming activity requiring specialist application and skills and removed from the political pressures which would lead to differential rule application according to the political affiliations and significance of those involved;

3 the task of selecting and interpreting rules as expressions of political choice, while holding to the generality of their form, is a complex process requiring a distinctive professional skill and ethic. This is the central topic of the rest of this chapter and the next.

In sum, such arguments present an overwhelming case for a distinct judicial role which institutionalises the conceptual distinction between rule creation and rule application. Exactly how the judicial role should be carried out is a central preoccupation of LEP. The models adopted follow in large measure from the reasons given for having separate adjudication, particularly the avoidance of political bias in the application of rules to concrete circumstances.

The analysis here centres on the fact, agreed by all legal theorists, that rules do not apply themselves. There is always a fallible human activity involved in taking a general rule and applying it to particular circumstances. There is the problem of identifying which rules to apply in the first place. Then there is the task of seeing whether the situation defined in the rule as required or permissible has occurred in the case in point. This requires knowledge of the meaning of the rule and evidence about the historical event in question. The first is rendered problematic by the fact that rules are always general, referring to types of situation, whereas fact situations are particular and involve an infinite specificity of existences only some of which are to be selected as relevant to the issue. The fact situation will include many facets not covered by the rule which may have relevance to the specification of what has occurred. The second is rendered problematic by the difficulty of reconstructing the past on the basis of second-hand evidence rather than direct inspection.

Given that it will often be a very difficult task to apply rules with any accuracy to past events, it is easy to see how those who apply the rules could be influenced by their personal preferences for a certain type of outcome. This would mean, however, that power is then being exercised by the person applying the rule rather than by the rule creator, thus defeating the objectives for which rule governance is established. For its completion, LEP requires, therefore, to provide an account of how judges ought to go about their task, a technique and an ethic of judging. The professional ethic of judging involves a number of elements which are summarised here and developed further in the next chapter:

1 reading the rules in some appropriate register of the ordinary natural language of the society in which they are adopted and to which they apply;
2 understanding the rules as expressions of political choices se-

lected from amongst the alternatives known to be available in that culture at that time; but

3 limiting that understanding to the rule-formulated versions of such political choices rather than the further objectives of the legislature; thus, while it is proper to see the rule as a purposive attempt to control or facilitate human activities so as to achieve certain objectives, it is improper to vary the rule in ways not specified or evidently implied in the rule on the grounds that this might better promote these background purposes;

4 minimising bias by reducing as far as is possible the effects on the processes of fact finding and rule interpretation of the personal value assumptions of the judges;

5 maximising impartiality in judgment by disqualifying judges with a personal interest in the outcome of the case and utilising techniques to give scope for the appreciation of the disparate points of view of those who are directly involved;

6 giving priority to the recent decisions of legislative authority over the implications of previous legislation or past judicial decisions; but

7 subordinate to (6), having regard to the rationales for adopting the ideal of government through rules, especially the liberty advantage and moral form advantage, and being sensitive to the distinction between types of rules, particularly cooperative and control rules, in the extent to which they may be modified in the light of particular circumstances; and

8 accepting the duty to make exceptions in the application of rules when the results are unexpected and clearly contrary to uncontroversial consensual values.

Such objectives and maxims must be multiplied and extended in the form of techniques of interpretation and precise rules of procedural and natural justice, but, however well formed, they will always be manipulable by those who have the interest and de facto power to so. Ultimately, therefore, the attainment of rule through law depends greatly on the integrity of the judiciary in its commitment to Positivism and its awareness of the insistent and insidious effects of social prejudices and powerful self-interests.

Central to this sketch of judicial ethics are the concepts of impartiality and bias.[37] Both can be explicated in terms of instrumental values which contribute to accurate rule selection and application. In its weaker form, impartiality is a formal matter which requires that no-one is a judge in their own case or, more widely, in a case the outcome of which has direct relevance to their own material interests. The marginal problems with such a principle relate to cases where the judge is a member of a social group that may benefit differentially from a precedent-establishing decision. In its stronger form, impartiality is a matter of giving equal weight to the same considerations without regard to the individuals or classes of person involved, unless the latter is specified in the rule. This is axiomatic where the considerations are identified in the rules themselves, but there are always many factors which have to be taken as understood or implied and which therefore give scope for arbitrariness. The techniques applicable here involve a combination utilising assumed background rules which are designed to deal with partiality and psychological devices related to imagination and sympathy which help to bring to bear the interests of all parties, even those socially and economically distant from that of the judge.

Bias, on the other hand, has more to do with tendencies to view situations and meanings from a social and cultural viewpoint which favours one party above others. This may be regarded as a source of strong partiality which is less visible and explicit. Since all perceptions and readings are affected by background cultural assumptions, there is a sense in which bias is ineliminable, but the effect of bias can be reduced by paying attention to the cultural positions of the parties involved so as to bring to the fore perceptions of social circumstances which are particularly relevant to the parties involved.

The idea of continuing judicial education is not therefore necessarily a product of Realist assumptions according to which it is the judges who are the actual law makers in that it is their particular decisions which actually determine the legal outcome in any particular case. In accordance with the tenets of Legal Realism, it is evident that good judges must be schooled in all aspects of the impact of their decisions on the interests and values of those involved and the wider society. They must be economists, psychologists, sociologists, to say nothing of moral and political 'experts'. Something of these requirements may also hold within LEP in so far as it is accepted that often judges must make decisions where there is insufficient guidance from existing law but a decision cannot or should not wait on a political determination. In such circumstances judges must be as able and informed as the best law makers. But even when adequate legislation is available it cannot be argued that judicial skill is as simple as purely legal expertise in terms of knowledge as to which are the relevant rules and how they relate to each other. The processes of interpretation in hard cases involve an extensive knowledge of the social and political context of the creation and continued use of the rule. And even in relatively easy cases judges have to be sufficiently aware of the social sources of moral and political bias and the ways in which these can affect the way rules are read and understood in order to avoid the danger of being affected by the values and assumptions of their own particular socioeconomic group. These are matters which are taken further in the next chapter.

At the core of the judicial ethic is the unenforceable ideal of self-restraint in relation to the use of the de facto power to influence the outcome in a way which is pleasing to the judge's personal predelictions. The temptations here are hard to resist, for many reasons, including the fact that many theories of adjudication actually encourage the exercise of moral judgment in the course of legal reasoning. Indeed, the whole tradition of Common Law reasoning is so loose as to invite moral reflection in terms of the similarities and differences between fact situations on which the analogical development of the Common Law is said to take place.

There are two further debates which are particularly relevant to these matters. The first is the argument we have already touched on as to the ultimate moral responsibility of everyone, lawyer and judge included, for their actions. The second is the particular difficulties which arise for judges in relation to the rule of recognition. Both may be illustrated by reference to Hart's difficulty in distinguishing between an internal attitude which is required to understand a rule and an internal attitude which involves endorsement of the rule. Hart appears to argue that, for a legal system to exist, the judges and other officials must endorse its substance.[38] In fact, all he requires to claim is that officials are sufficiently inside the system to understand the rules in question. However, others have filled this theme out by saying that, as a moral agent, a judge must approve of what she is doing, that this involves approving of the substance of her decision and that this in turn involves making moral judgments about the correctness of the valid law she is applying.

It is surely correct as an analytical truth that a moral agent must make all significant practical choices as moral choices, for which she can be praised or blamed. It does not follow, however, that the proper criterion for every choice must be moral, only that the activity in question must pass moral scrutiny. Thus, as a moral agent, I must morally justify my action of playing golf every week when I might be working, but this does not mean that my choice of club is a moral choice. The same reasoning applies, according to Positivism, in relation to judging, which calls for legal reasoning, not moral reasoning. Of course participating in moral reasoning needs justification in moral terms, and taking on paid employment as a judge or lawyer is particularly in need of moral justification. This does not mean, however, that judgments within the activities of judging or presenting cases are themselves moral judgments.[39]

Somehow it is thought that law must be different. Must judges not morally endorse the decisions they make? Law is not simply a technical matter because its outcomes have impact on people's interests. This ignores the possibility that it is not the duty of judges to apply what they think to be right, but to apply the law. If judges consider this is an immoral activity, they ought to resign from their position. Here the judge is not in any position different in principle from the citizen of a democratic country who accepts the moral obligation to abide by the outcome of the democratic process.

Perhaps there is a particular problem with the rule of recognition. Thus Postema notes how Hart responds when confronted with the fact that judges may be challenged about the rule of recognition they use.[40] Postema is unhappy with Hart saying they just note current practice in the judiciary with respect to the acceptance and rejection of possible sources of law. Surely judges must justify the rule or recognition they use, either individually or collectively? Perhaps the assumption is that judges are free to choose the rule of recognition in a way that they are not free to adopt other rules. But this is clearly not the case, for such rules are the result of political determination over who has the power to make law. The question of who has this power is something which calls for moral justification, but not by judges in particular.

Postema's line is to argue that by pointing to the conventional rules judges are offering a form of normative justification based on the same grounds as any other convention. 'At bottom his [Hart's] claim is that the authority of criteria of validity ultimately rest not on the justice, correctness, or truth of the criteria as a matter of critical morality but, rather, on convention.'[41] His argument is that conventions are grounded in the social benefits of practices which embody some generally recognised ways of securing mutually beneficial coordination:

> the rule of recognition, then, is best understood as involving a convention, that is, a regularity in the behaviour of law-applying officials and citizens in situations calling for the identification of valid legal standards, such that part of the reason why most officials conform to the regularity is that it is common knowledge that most officials and citizens conform to the regularity and that most officials and citizens expect most other officials and citizens to conform.[42]

In other words, the coordination benefits that we have noted apply to rules in general are particularly appropriate to the rule of recognition. This is understandable, given that the whole system of law cannot function in a predictable way without a mutually agreed rule of recognition. This is clearly pivotal in providing the benefits of coordination and order generally.

It seems to follow that, qua judge, a judge should adopt the rule of recognition in common use, but this is only in default of a higher political determination as to the foundation of the constitution. The convention argument is sound from a positivist point of view if judges have to make up their own minds which rule to use, but this does not mean that they have the right to make such a choice, otherwise we would have to concede that judges are the creators of constitutions, whereas, within any democratic ideology, the origin of valid law is a matter for political determination. The fact that it is difficult to control judges who usurp this power is one of the main reasons for insisting upon the need for a powerful judicial ethic.

The general argument here is similar to that which must be deployed to interpret the undoubted fact that the day-to-day legal reality is that it is the judiciary which decides what is or is not a good or acceptable legal argument.[43] What counts as an acceptable argument depends on what is acceptable to 'a particular group, the legal audience'.[44] If this is correct then there is considerable responsibility on this group to maintain the approach legitimated in their system for the sort of reasons that Postema gives in relation to the rule of recognition. Realists such as Llewellyn see the importance of the judicial traditions and have their own recommendations to make as to which method is desirable.[45] Most Realists prefer the grand style of flexibility in the light of perceived purpose and social utility, for they see the opportunity for judges to solve social problems by enlightened decision making. Positivists clearly provide a more rule-governed approach. Given that such decision making can never be tightly deductive, there is always the capacity of the individual and the group to move towards a partiality of power. Here there is some tension in LEP between those who would advocate a rational reconstruction of decided law in order to enhance coherence and consistency, and those who see this as a way of diluting or thwarting the contemporary political decisions which should be given authority over and above their compatibility with the outcomes of prior political process.

Looking ahead to the discussion of interpretation in the next chapter, we will see there that there is a convergence of those who take legal reasoning to be a broad matter of practical reason merging with general moral reasoning and those who wish to keep a separation between the two, but accept that in some circumstances recourse must be had to second-best approaches where the law is unclear or in some other way inadequate for the circumstances in hand. These second-best approaches can be similar to the preferred methods of others in ideal conditions.

Traditionally, the central Common Law method of legal reasoning centres on precedent and analogy. Precedent uses decided cases as a flexible basis for deriving, through a formulation of the ratio of a case by examining the facts which were crucial in the reported decision, a rule or principle to apply to the case in hand.[46] Analogy comes in when comparing decided cases with other sets of facts to determine whether the situations are relevantly similar.[47] This approach has the feature of merging reasoning about whether an existing rule of law covers a particular set of facts (are the facts of the situations from which the ratios that contribute to the formulation of a legal rule derive sufficiently similar to the case in point?) with reasoning about the formulation of the content of the legal rules which emerge from Common Law reasoning (what are the relevant similarities between the decided cases that contribute to the formulation of the legal rule?) and involves the variation of existing legal rules to take in situations which have not hitherto been regarded as relevantly similar but are now held to be so. In other words, Common Law precedent and analogy merges rule application, rule formulation and rule change. This is starkly clear in those many cases which determine the scope and generality of ratios and rules which is a matter of how broadly the rule or principle behind a series of decisions is to be formulated.[48]

At the same time this form of reasoning can be placed in a wider context by looking on it as part of a more general process of establishing a set of coherent rules and principles. Thus where a novel fact situation is confronted a number of precedents and analogies can be brought to bear with the constraint that the process of reasoning should seek to render their application to the novel situation consistent with maintaining and developing the compatibility between the diverse pieces of the mosaic of accepted law. The coherence goal can, of course, be used both to guide decision in the case in point and to affect the interpretation of a decided case or rule of Statute Law to render it more consistent with decided cases.

Positivism has problems with the way in which traditional method merges the task of rule creation and rule application, and seeks to make a distinction between the analogies that are involved in the application of rules (what are the relevant similarities in terms of the rule?) and the analogies which are involved in varying a rule (for instance by extending it to cover fact situations not originally encompassed by the rule as at present formulated). LEP in particular has at least three worries about the confusion that this generates. One is the ease with which statutory rules can be altered by the judiciary. A second is the tendency to dilute legal changes by ironing out their novelties in the process of seeking coherence with existing law. A third is that, as the method of adapting existing law to deal with such problems as gaps in the law, it is unduly restrictive. Where rule creation or significant rule variation is involved, some loose analogical similarities which may further the coherence of laws may be helpful, but it is important that what is in effect a legislative decision should be undertaken, if it has to be, in the light of a wider range of factors, such as social policy, political morality and economic consequences. For such reasons, LEP seeks a sharper distinction between legislative and adjudicative modes of judicial activity, the latter being the prime purpose of the courts and the former being more in the nature of a regrettable second-best process designed to deal with defects in the form and coverage of existing positive law.

The relevance of this discussion to judicial ethics is that judges ought in general to refrain from variation and creation of Statute Law and, where they do cross the boundary from application to creation of law, they should do so overtly and in the light of the full range of factors relevant to the legislative task. Making these distinctions clearly not only improves the manner in which the innovations deriving from judicial discretion are determined but clearly signals to the political process what is going on so that the uses of judicial discretion which, through the impact of precedent, have legislative force can be reviewed and, if necessary, amended by the prime legislative process.[49]

If we entrust to the judiciary for one reason or another the task of filling out the laws as a matter, perhaps, of delegated legislative power, then this does provide scope for opening up this aspect of judicial activity to the full impact of preferred methods of political and legislative reasoning. In this context it makes sense and is ethically proper to call in the methods of Rawlsian equilibrium,[50] of the discourse ethics of Habermas[51] or the empirical application of utilitarian or economic principles.[52] In general, these are to be preferred to methods which purport to restrict judicial legislation to methods which circumscribe its scope by insisting on a peculiarly legal dimension, such as Alexy's theory of legal argumentation[53] or Dworkin's Herculean method which allows us to draw on principles but not on policy.[54] Such approaches not only are unduly limited in the scope of judicial reasoning in legislative mode but blur the distinction with the prime applicatory function of courts, thus encouraging every case to be approached in terms of what is a legislative challenge, albeit one that has to be met with an apparently and perhaps actually limited range of factors. Particularly when such methods are deployed in relation to Bills of Rights or fundamental principles of Common Law, they provide courts with the opportunity to revisit every legislative enactment to see whether or not they agree with the political judgments involved.[55]

For some legal theorists this is a welcome tendency. This may be openly argued by saying that courts are above some of the immediate political pressures to which politicians are subject and are therefore in a better position to argue clearly as a matter of principle and long-term policy, taking in the interests of the citizenry as a whole. Court-centred legislation is in this way preferable, particularly on matters that legislatures have difficulty in coping with because, for instance, intense minorities can block important legislation and indifferent majorities are denying the significance of minority interests. Courts, in their impartial role freed from the morally irrelevant pressures of electoral considerations, are the morally preferred legislators, at least on certain matters.[56]

This approach greatly exaggerates the significance of the impartiality of courts which is suited more to the adjudicating of particular fact situations than to the choice of legislative alternatives. The impartiality of non-involvement does not enable decisions to be made between competing political values and the capacities of courts for arriving at well formulated policies are meagre compared with the policy-making resources available to the modern state. These claims cannot be substantiated adequately here. The former in particular would require us to offer a full critique of the limitations of the methods of Rawls[57] and Habermas[58] if they are claimed to be anything more than pointers towards how political discourse should be guided. The gist of the critique must be that no methods of this sort can be used to generate a consensus, for none of them can avoid the selection and prioritising of fundamental values, and all of them underestimate the intractable nature of the moral choices that have to be made to arrive at just and efficient legislation in relation to morally justified goals. It is perhaps easier to be brisk on the matter of the policy competence of courts, in that it is evident that, if courts are to be legislators in competition with the legislative branch of government with the backing of the administrative resources of modern government departments, then they will in large measure have to become indistinguishable in resources and accountability from the executive and legislative branches of government combined. This serves as a vivid reminder as to what is involved in collapsing the boundary between legal and political argumentation.

The Legislative Ethic and the Role of the Citizen

The ideal of the judicial professional ethic which requires that its prime mode and area of expertise is strictly adjudicative is dependent for its realisation on the raw material with which it is provided. This means that prior to judicial ethics there is legislative ethics, particularly the requirement that laws be enacted which are capable of being interpreted in positivist terms.[59] Other legislative norms (which are often erroneously taken to be primarily adjudicative norms) are consistency and comprehensiveness in legislation, prospectivity in relation to conduct and practicability in requiring only conduct with which citizens are able to comply.

These familiar aspects of the governance of rules can be fleshed out in a number of ways. One important dimension is the degree of specificity which a rule should embody. In the interests of clarifying a clear exclusionary force, rules should be as specific as possible congruent with their objective. This is necessary also for maximising the liberty advantage and refining effectively the means for reaching the goal of legislation.[60] However, the moral-form advantage requires that such generalisations as are involved do not involve unfairness, with morally irrelevant distinctions being drawn in a way which makes some groups bear inequitable burden or enjoy unfair advantages.[61] There is therefore some tension between the need for precision and the need for fairness.

There is a continuing argument about whether it is in the nature of rules to be precise, as distinct from principles, which are general. Some theorists take 'rule' to be a generic term to cover all norms specifying conduct, approved and permitted. Others see them as having a specific role, which differentiates them from principles and standards, for instance.[62] Principles may be simply more general than rules, or they may be rules (whether general or not) that embody an evidently moral or normative rationale (such as reasonableness). These may also be referred to as standards.

Initially the positivist contention that law is or ought to be a system of rules may be taken as utilising a purely general concept of a rule to cover all behaviour-stipulating norms, but within more specific analyses of the functions of rules it becomes clear that some norms are better than others in securing these functions. Controlling conduct, coordinating activities and distributing fairly may be done more effectively by way of clear, concise, unambiguous, intelligible rules which are within the capacities of those addressed than by way of general principles or standards, even if these do point to certain background values.

In the context of this discussion, a 'good' rule is a rule which is good not in substance but in the characteristics which enable it to do its job. Of course these characteristics will vary with the job in question. Symbolic functions may often be served by vague and obscure but fine-sounding rules. Power allocative functions may be served by general rules or rules with moral terms, for these enhance the power of those who administer them. However, if we take the dominant social and political function of rules to be action guiding, conduct coordinating and power controlling, then good rules will tend to fall into the categories of clear and specific.

This is not uncontentious. There is a problem over highly specific rules that they approximate to particular commands. Some generality is required for efficacy and moral form, and yet generality which takes in substantial groups of individuals breeds vagueness. Nevertheless, rules may retain sufficient generality to be useful, and still be clear enough, if they do not use terms whose application is controversial or not open to public verification, and if they are pitched at a level of generality which takes in classes of conduct that are readily recognisable: either natural kinds or uncontroversial socially recognised categories.[63] It is also important, of course, that the level of the categorisation fits the nature of the objective of the rule. Thus if it is dangerous animals that are in question, then that is the best categorisation, provided we can give empirical content to the concept of 'dangerous'. Simply specifying a list of dangerous animals has the drawback that some dangerous animals may be missed out. On the other hand, a list of readily identifiable animals is more precise and more capable of generating agreement.

There are problems in the inclusion of vague moral judgment-inviting terms like 'just' and 'reasonable' which encourage extensive judicial discretion. But while it may not be possible to exclude these altogether, they can usually be interpreted as disguised references to accepted standards of conduct in the rules of society at the time, thus incorporating current practice into the law. This may be seen as acceptable if there is no significant controversy about these practices. Alternatively, such terminology may be read as an invitation to a judge and jury to express an opinion which is then taken as a sample of positive morality, but this is a doubtful procedure in a pluralistic or inegalitarian society. Or it may be taken as an invitation to investigate the state of public opinion or some section of it at the time.[64] But, in general, such legislation is undesirably vague and ambiguous in purpose and insufficiently restrictive of judicial legislation. It represents an understandable but regrettable passing of the legislative burden from governments to courts.

Considerations of this sort also apply to such matters as the promulgation and availability of rules, as there is little possibility of a conduct-guiding rule doing its job if the rules ar not known and discoverable by those to whom they are addressed. Lon Fuller created a procedural version of Natural Law theory out of such ingredients, inferring the desirability of such qualities as clarity, prospectivity and publicity from the idea of law as 'the enterprise of subjecting human conduct to the governance of rules'.[65] The force of these points is dissipated by his concurrent insistence that such qualities not only are means of efficiently ensuring that rules serve their purposes but also have some validity as moral criteria in that a system which respects his eight ways of failing to make law will tend also to manifest respect for its subjects as moral agents. He concluded, rather too hastily, that law is in this sense an essentially moral enterprise. Neverthless, Fuller seems to be on the verge of explicating the moral-form advantage which makes rule governance a necessary but not a sufficient condition of moral acceptability.

Hart decisively criticised this aspect of Fuller's move from the sound premiss that government by rules protects a measure of liberty for the subjects by enabling them to avoid the consequences of violating such rules to the exaggerated conclusion that, in such a system, the content of the rules will tend to justice and efficiency. Unfortunately for Fuller's scheme, 'good' rules can very effectively serve awful purposes.[66] However, this wayward claim, which constitutes the Natural Law aspect of Fuller's theory, is not essential to its enduring contribution, namely to trace the significance of law to human purpose and in particular to the purpose of morally acceptable forms of governing. This is, of course, a characteristically positivist theme.

Conclusion

In an ideal Positivist world there would be no such thing as judicial legislation, although there would always be a legislative element in rendering general terms more precise in relation to the complexities of concrete situations. In the non-ideal world we actually inhabit judicial legislation may be the lesser of the two evils. Particular aspects of the judicial ethic apply to situations where judicial legislation is required: for instance, where there are gaps in legislation and we have nothing but highly general principles to go by and some decision is required to avoid injustice or waste.[67] Most Positivists urge courts, in these second-best circumstances, to draw on the positive morality of existing social opinion. Where there is no clear positive morality or convention it might be expected that LEP should commend devices to discourage judges from drawing on their own moral views. Indeed, in some cases even lottery methods may be preferred to moral adjudication, for randomness is preferable to systematic bias.[68] Indeed, some Common Law techniques, charitably interpreted, can be viewed as lotteries in relation to the competing interests at stake.

However, it is congruent with Positivism to argue that, provided judicial legislation is subject to legislative overruling, as it normally is, what matters is that judicial legislation be conducted in accordance with ideal legislative method. This means going beyond consistency with existing law, although this certainly has merits where the outcome is non-controversial and decisive. It means going beyond arguments of principle in Dworkin's sense to include utilitarian aspects of the morality of legislation, provided that this is done overtly and after informed discussion and relevant expert evidence. One reason for taking this approach is that there are aspects of the judicial role that overlap with reasonable moral methodology. In particular, the impartiality of the judiciary may be thought to be an advantage, provided that matters of social class and intellectual elitism are not at issue. At this point, the methods of Rawls and Habermas may perhaps be followed through in courts to advantage, on the grounds that they approximate to an approach which is compatible with judicial neutrality. However, impartiality of form and effort, while it may iron out certain partialities and unfairnesses, is no substitute for making the moral choices which do not follow from adopting an impartial viewpoint alone. On the other hand, it is admitted that there may be good reason to eschew this as inviting this second-best approach to encroach into judicial practice in situations where it is not absolutely necessary.

We thus have a framework for deriving an ethics of LEP according to which it is the duty of the legislature to enact formally good law that makes it possible for the citizen to understand and obey or fairly utilise enacted law and for judges to confine themselves to its interpretation and application in an adjudicative manner when there is dispute about legally relevant conduct either between private legal persons or between such persons and the state. In this context we can work out the ethics of lawyers as deriving largely from their roles in the processes of adjudication that are appropriately used to determine disputes and in advising and assisting clients with their affairs in the light of the ideal of the governance of rules.

All this will fall apart if it is not possible to make the relevant distinctions between legislation and adjudication. It is to this potentially damaging but actually supportive topic of post-modern legal philosophy that the next chapter is addressed.

Notes

1 In a broader sense, 'ethics' is used for the philosophy of morals: see Ewing (1953), Williams (1985) and Brink (1989).

2 Examples of professional codes of conduct include the American Bar Association *Model Rules of Professional Conduct* (1983) and the *Solicitors' Professional Conduct and Practice Rules* (1994) promulgated by the Council of the Law Society of New South Wales.

3 Shaffer (1987, p.297): 'Most of what American lawyers and law teachers call legal ethics is not ethics. Most of what is called legal ethics is similar to rules made by administrative agencies. It is regulatory. Its appeal is not to conscience, but to sanction. It seeks mandate rather than insight.'

4 See Chapter 2.

5 The locus classicus is James Madison, *The Federalist Papers*, no. 51.

6 For a helpful introductory discussion, see Waldron (1990, Chapter 4).

7 This limited sociological conception of impartiality is central to the moral and legal theory of Adam Smith. See Smith (1976).

8 See pp.2–5.

9 See p.11, n.12.
10 See p.5.
11 See pp.73–6.
12 See p.75.
13 See pp.7–8.
14 See Postema (1986, pp.318–19); Bentham (1970a, Chapter 2).
15 Austin (1954, Lecture VI).
16 See p.61.
17 This is a controversial philosophical view which may be said to mix up ethics and meta-ethics; however, I would argue strongly that meta-ethics does have implications for the degree of seriousness it is rational to invest in moral judgment/opinion. For the opposing view, see Mackie (1977).
18 See Simon (1978).
19 For the provocative phraseology, see Fried (1976).
20 For this and other quips, see Luban (1994, pp.xiff).
21 Thus Wasserstrom (1975).
22 See Pepper (1986).
23 See Freedman (1978).
24 For critiques of the accuracy of the adversarial method in relation to the assessment of evidence, see Simon (1978, pp.119–30).
25 The standard examples of so-called 'moral dilemmas' whose mere formulation can be seen as the basis for moral criticism are those discussed in Freedman (1966). They all relate the criminal defence advocacy: attempting to discredit an adverse witness whom the lawyer knows to be telling the truth, putting a witness on the stand whom the lawyer knows will commit perjury, and counselling a client in a way which will encourage him to commit perjury. Examples which may be thought to be nearer to real dilemmas often relate to the duty of client confidentiality in situations where innocent persons will suffer unless that confidence is breached.
26 'Sir, you do not know [a cause] to be good or bad untill the Judge determines it....An argument which does not convince yourself, may convince the Judge to whom you urge it: [A]nd if it does convince him, why then, Sir, you are wrong and he is right' (Boswell, *The Life of Johnson*, 1987, pp.47f). Rhode (1985, p.619) takes this to be a positivist view, although it smacks more of Legal Realism.
27 The recognition of the distinction between a possible interpretation and a manipulative try-on may, of course, be difficult to institutionalise, but it is a characteristic of many moral distinctions that they fall to be made by the agent in question.
28 Simon (1978, p.30) argues that Positivists assume their clients to be egoistic individualists when in fact they may not be so at all. While it is true that this strand is an element within the utilitarian individualism of Hobbes and some later utilitarian Positivists, it is unclear why this legal viewpoint is particularly tied to contemporary Legal Positivism.
29 Simon (1978).
30 Ibid., pp.39–42.
31 Ibid., p.58: 'The Positivist lawyer is not an advisor, but a lobbyist for a peculiar theory of human nature.'
32 Ibid., p.48, and Pepper (1986).
33 Postema (1986, pp.347–50).
34 Simon (1978, pp.130–44).
35 For the contrast between civil and common lawyers in this respect, see Abel and Lewis (1988–9).
36 For a more detailed summary, see Wroblewski (1992).
37 For helpful analyses of impartiality and bias, see Leader, 'Impartiality, Bias and the Judiciary', in Hunt (1992, pp.241–68).

38 Hart (1961, p.56).
39 Beyleveld and Brownsword (1986).
40 Postema (1986).
41 Ibid., p.171.
42 Ibid., p.198.
43 See Bell (1986, p.45–65).
44 Ibid., p.46. See also Aarnio (1981), Peczenick (1982) and Alexy (1989a) for legal argument as a form of social activity which is part of a way of life, with specific rules and practices and important conventions and understandings. Note also Simpson (1973, p.94) who speaks of law as a set of social practices observed and ideas received by a caste of lawyers.
45 Principally, Llewellyn (1960).
46 See Harris (1980, Chapter 13) and Simpson (1973).
47 See Cardozo (1921).
48 As in *Donaghue* v. *Stevenson* [1932] A.C. 562.
49 See Waldron (1990, p.147). Contrast Dworkin (1986).
50 Rawls (1972, 1994).
51 Habermas (1987, 1989).
52 For instance, Posner (1977).
53 Alexy (1989a).
54 Dworkin (1977).
55 See Campbell (1994b).
56 This is argued lucidly in Dworkin (1990).
57 Daniels (1975).
58 Raz (1979, p.212).
59 One aspect of this demand is manifest in the 'plain language' movement.
60 See p.59.
61 See pp.54–6.
62 For a discussion of rules and principles, see Campbell (1988a, pp.45–55).
63 For the concept of 'natural kinds' in a different context, see Moore (1981).
64 As proposed in Collins (1986, p.71): 'given that the legislative lacks credibility as a pure system of democratic control, it becomes acceptable to recognize that other institutions of government, like the courts, may equally claim authority derived from a democratic input even though that input is weak and incomplete'.
65 Fuller (1969, Chapter 2).
66 See Hart (1957–8).
67 See Chapter 6.
68 Thus Goodwin (1992).

6 Ethical Interpretations

Introduction

'Legal Reasoning' might serve as the title of this chapter which concerns the relationship between law making and law application. However, the modest term 'interpretation' focusses more effectively on the issues of rule identification and rule application which constitute the positivist view of what legal reasoning ought to be all about.

The selection and application of relevant valid rules to disputes and allegations involves a variety of skills, both in relation to the determination of matters of fact and with respect to the understanding of rules, including rules for selecting valid laws. While the realities of ill-formed legal systems make a degree of judicial innovation and creativity inevitable, a central purpose of Positivism is to circumscribe the pretensions of judging and judges which are fostered by the more grandiose term 'legal reasoning', with its implied invitation to expansive styles of open-ended practical reason. To this end, LEP involves the articulation of a normative model of judicial application which establishes the rules and procedures that ought to be adopted in the identification, interpretation and application of laws.[1] In the case of LEP, this normative model rests on the presupposed political ideal of a system of rules which are identifiable, discrete, clear, comprehensive, consistent and applicable without recourse to disputed value judgments or untestable factual assumptions. Such an ideal system does not routinely require complex or innovative interpretations in the procedures for identifying and applying valid law.[2]

No actual legal system comes close to the positivist ideal, hence the normative model of judicial application must include rules for dealing with problems of interpretation which arise as a result of such defects as poor drafting, inadequate coverage and internal inconsistencies. Further, on current philosophical assumptions, it cannot be taken for granted that interpretation ever denotes a limited and manageable activity which has to do with techniques for settling non-standard cases which involve, for instance, abnormally vague, ambiguous or incoherent rules. It is sometimes contended that every reading of every rule involves some 'interpretation'. The fact that words and sentences do not carry their meanings with them but require to be understood by their users and audiences in terms of existing conventional linguistic practices is taken to mean that every case of rule application is a process which has all the ingredients that have more traditionally been regarded as limited to non-standard cases. At the same time, the idea that interpretation is simply a matter of settling on an appropriate meaning in cases of uncertainty has been expanded to take in the moral or other reasons which may justify a departure the 'plain meaning' of the text. On this view, there is no meaningful line between rule interpretation and rule creation.[3]

Against these trends, I argue that, despite all the practical difficulties involved, there are important lines to be drawn between understanding, interpretation and innovation and, more particularly, that there is a politically important distinction to be made between 'interpretation' in its traditional narrower use in which it connotes approaches to unclear texts and the more characteristically postmodern, broader use of 'interpretation' which assumes that all communications are necessarily of open and uncertain meaning, a use which carries the implication that rules cannot serve to alter conduct in the manner specified in the rule.[4]

These reaffirmations enable us to give sense to the prescription of LEP that formally good laws are those which do not routinely raise problems of interpretation because they are clear, unambiguous, consistent and applicable without recourse to controversial postulates or undecidable affirmation conditions. Good systems of law enable us to identify uncontroversially the relevant authoritative rules, understand them and know how they ought to be applied to different situations. This then puts us in a position to deal with questions about what judges (and indeed lawyers and citizens) should do when confronted – as they often are – with formally bad laws, that is laws which do require complex and innovative interpretations or creative supplementation before they can be utilised for regulative purposes.

The propriety of limiting the role of interpretation in judicial process does not require the refutation of any philosophical consensus in theory of meaning and epistemology. Indeed, theories of meaning which rely on intersubjective agreement sustained by shared cultural understandings are philosophically preferable as the basis for a theory of language to the more individualistic epistemological assumptions derived from Locke and other pioneers of modern theories of meaning which build on purely subjective images or thoughts.[5] Concentration on the pragmatics of social practices holds out more hope of achieving successful communication than the refinement of subjective images through increasingly subtle private languages. Whatever theoretical approach we adopt in the theory of language, provided we do not repudiate the workaday tests of the communicability of meanings without which no dialogue, even those about legal reasoning, can get off the ground, we can make the crucial initial distinction between comprehending a sentence and interpreting it. We start this process with the assurance that, when people disagree about the proper interpretation of a text, they can only do so on the basis of some shared understanding of the words and sentences about whose interpretation they disagree. However difficult it may be philosophically to explicate this shared understanding, it is a presumption within which it makes sense to raise points of disagreement and communicative failure. Moreover, even if the articulation of the meaning of a rule is difficult, this does not mean that the rule is necessarily unclear in practice: 'there is a way of grasping a rule which is not an interpretation, but which is exhibited in what we call "obeying a rule" and "going against it" in actual cases'.[6] At the same time, some philosophical debates alert us to the multifarious ways in which communication can fail and may suggest procedures which may be adopted to minimise such failures and deal with their consequences.

The assertion that the laws of a society can have clear literal meanings for members of that society involves no denial either that meanings are human creations dependent on human conventions or stipulations, or that knowledge is in large part a creation of the categories of the human mind in the pursuit of human concerns. What we do require is an acceptance of the possibility of sufficient local agreement on meaning rules and shared assumptions on the acquisition of knowledge to achieve effectual communication between legislators, judges and citizens.[7] LEP holds that, in the interests of achieving a good polity, it is worthwhile working at improving the communication of authoritative rules.

The presupposition of the possibility of communication is not itself something which has to be debated in detached and purely philosophical contexts. We are dealing here with the very practical question as to how far government through rules can be an effective means for attaining chosen political objectives and how far such a process can serve to limit government within acceptable democratic bounds. The failures of communication – intentional and unintentional – which matter are those that affect these two entangled functions of law: the implementation and limitation of political power. In this context, short of paralysing scepticism as to communicability, theories of meaning and theories of knowledge are relevant to such concerns in so far as they indicate how these particular uses of language can be thwarted or furthered. Of course, radical scepticism, whether novel or ancient, can undermine any claims to such consensual possibilities, however localised and convention-dependent they may be. It is beyond the scope of this book to deal with critiques of cognitive solipsism and we must be content here with the common and perhaps rather feeble refutation of such despairing philosophies by drawing attention to their ex hypothesi incommunicability and pointing, in a regrettably ad hominem manner, to the apparently successful communication of the very sophisticated philosophical views on such matters around which considerable discourse flourishes.

On the other hand, LEP makes no claim that actual legal systems approximate to the standards of law making and the ethics of law application which are required to make interpretation a marginal and limited activity. Moreover, there are particular interpretative problems concerning legal discourse which derive from its high communicative ambitions, the combative dispute resolution procedures which are involved in Common Law systems and the coercive consequences of the outcomes. And yet defending the notion that, even in legal contexts, some meanings can be clear and uncontroversial is not difficult as a practical matter since there are endless examples about which, even after extensive reflection, we are so certain that we can be said to know that we know that they have been successfully communicated. Of course, it is equally easy to bring forward counter-examples, particularly from the corpus of controversial cases which reach appellate court level in jurisdictions which license the application of unspecific rights and principles, often of some antiquity, by judicial organs. It is apparent that even the clearest laws can be rendered obscure by removing them from their standard contexts or bringing them into juxtaposition with other parts of the legal corpus. Faced with this range of phenomena, the interesting question is whether progress can be made towards achieving clarity in legislation to a degree which makes it reasonable to aspire to creating a legal system which operates substantially on positivist lines. Obscure drafting, the politically irresolvable disagreements which lie behind fudged legislative enactments, the effects of undemocratic political theories of adjudication, the existence of a plurality of linguistic communities within a jurisdiction and the abuse of professional legal roles are only some of the enemies of positivistically good legal systems. It is in this confusing and contested context that this chapter offers some directional points on the approach to adjudication which an Ethical Positivist can recommend to participants in an imperfect legal world.

In summary, the position adopted here is that, in a system of law which approximates to the ideals of LEP, it is the duty of a judge to identify appropriate legal rules in accordance with the politically authoritative rule of recognition and apply them as the legitimate human sources of the law intend, the defeasible assumption being that the legislative intent is that laws should be read in terms of the conventional understandings of the language involved within the appropriate community of subjects in standard contexts, that is, in terms of their literal or evident meanings as understood by participants in the relevant social situations. As an alternative to what is traditionally referred to as the 'plain meaning' approach, I signal a somewhat more sociological perspective by using the phrase 'evident contextual meaning' to indicate the prime standard of positivist adjudicative practice.

These assumptions regarding legislative intent may be overridden by stipulative definitions given in the authoritative text or by conventions of interpretation standardly followed by the judiciary and known to the legislatures in question, legal professionals and, so far as is practicable, even to those who are expected to follow the rules in question. Where the laws are imperfect in terms of the positivist ideals of generality, specificity, clarity and internal consistency, predictable techniques to ameliorate these defects should be adopted, having particular regard to such matters as consistency with existing clear law, evidence of particular legislative intent with respect to meanings and, if necessary, knowledge or assumptions about legislative purpose to the extent that this is compatible with the policies publicly defended or uncontroversially assumed by the political sources of the legislation in question. In other words, LEP gives priority to readings which facilitate the objectives of legislation while seeking to preserve the limitations on power which government through rules is intended to achieve.[8] Finally, in actual legal systems, there is defensible scope for a measure of interstitial judicial creativity as a matter of delegated legislation, provided that this is kept within clear and explicit bounds and the outcomes of this limited discretionary power are subject to routine legislative review.

Interpretations

We may distinguish three overlapping but rival views on the scope of interpretation which have relevance to LEP.[9] The first, *interpretation as comprehension*, takes interpretation to cover everything that is involved in giving a meaning to signs and symbols and their syntactic relationships and all the further ways in which we can understand a text in one way rather than another.[10] The second, *interpretation as bounded selection*, takes interpretation to be a matter of selecting one from a limited number of different possible meanings of a text in situations when this is required owing to lack of evident contextual meaning.[11] The third, *interpretation as innovation,* takes interpretation to consist of (or perhaps encompass) a wide range of more creative activities which take their starting point from a text but involve a measure of development, such as making the text more consistent with other texts or adapting it to render it more applicable to novel circumstances, or simply more acceptable to the interpreter or her audience.[12]

According to the interpretation as comprehension view, to understand the meaning of even a simple sentence like 'the cow is brown' we must interpret each word or sentence in the light of ill-defined meaning conventions we bring to the task and adopt or ascribe meaning to the sentence in the light of our implicit conventions relating to syntax and sentence construction and our own particular viewpoint and interests. A word or sentence does not in itself have any meaning whatsoever and any sentence can with propriety be read in an infinite variety of ways. Written or spoken symbols do not in themselves have any correct meanings, or certainly any one correct meaning. Meaning is given to rather than derived from what is written and spoken.[13]

The second view, interpretation as bounded selection, does not dispute that mere noises or marks have no meaning in themselves, but assumes that, in normal communicative contexts involving ordinary members of the linguistic community, the relevant meaning, grammar and syntax rules make it unproblematic to speak of 'the' meaning of a sentence which is used in any standard context in the way of life they share since meanings are effectively determined by the the commonly accepted meaning rules, conventions or linguisitic understandings within the group. In such circumstances interpretation is not necessarily involved in understanding or construing a sentence.[14]

For a variety of reasons there may be no evident meaning, or a range of equally obvious or not so obvious ones. This may be due to obscurity in the conjunction of terms or the assumed context or simply the lack of clear and agreed assumptions for the proper (that is, shared) use of the terms involved. Choices then have to be made on criteria which will vary with the aims of the reader and the audience. This effortful activity is standardly called interpretation. Often the object of such bounded interpretation will be to discern what the speaker intended to convey. Thus, in the assumed absence of blue cows, 'the cow is blue' will cause puzzlement which may raise doubt about whether it is being meant literally or is intended to indicate that the cow is cold. Knowing whether the speaker is describing a painting or conducting a veterinary examination may clarify the matter and enable us to make an interpretation based on our assessment of what the speaker intended. However, there are a variety of ways of approaching uncertainty of meaning, some of which seek to steer clear of speculation about speakers' intentions. Precisely what techniques should be used in such circumstances is a fundamental issue for legal reasoning in LEP. At this point we may simply note again that interpretation is not involved in standard deployment of meaning conventions and is required if and only if there are significant choices to be made between readings which are alternatives within such relevant conventions as are available and generally utilised. Hence the term 'bounded selection'.[15]

Interpretation as innovation is best exemplified by a novel rendering of a piece of music without any claim that this is how the composer intended it to be performed or that this is the correct way to do it. It is assumed that there are lots of different renderings from which we may, without impropriety, select or which we may create according to what pleases us most. In legal contexts it may include filling in gaps in the law by the use of analogical reasoning which radically extends the scope of a rule, or departing from the literal meaning of a rule in order to make it more consistent with other rules or just more appropriate to the issues that fall to be decided in a particular case. Interpretation as innovation is not restricted by any alleged correctness of an interpretation in relation to shared linguistic understandings but is determined by its utility in relation to the ideas of what should be done when legal reasoning is no longer tightly fettered by such conventions. Such a creative process may still be regarded as a species of intepretation rather than actual rule making if it is a matter of developing a meaning for a rule rather than introducing a new rule. This is often a difficult line to draw, in part because of the problem of individuating rules and so being able to distinguish them one from the other.[16] Ultimately, there will always be an arbitrary element in choosing at what point in the gradation of differences between an original and a variant rule to start speaking of a new rule.

While those who take interpretation to be bounded selection tend to deprecate the use of the term to cover the looser usages in relation to either the bare ascription of meaning or creative innovation from texts, there are those who contend that all interpretation is innovative. Thus Stanley Fish argues that there is no significant difference between interpretation which is innovation and interpretation which is not: in every case there are prior understandings of the interpreter and her community which make a reading innovative with respect to other people with different understandings.[17] However, the fact that audiences have different meaning assumptions does not entail that their understandings or interpretations are or are not innovative. Innovation is relative to the presuppositions of the audience in question. What can be questioned is the extent to which bounded interpretation is sufficient for communicative success in a community with a plurality of distinct understandings due to cultural, educational, gender and social class differences.

A different sort of attack on the idea of interpretation as innovation can be taken from Ronald Dworkin's expansive view of the interpretative process. His position is that going beyond interpretations within the bounds of ambiguities and unclarities need not be innovative since it may and should be a matter of drawing out what is already there in the given rules and legal tradition. 'Interpretation' here involves in effect creating a coherent view from the existing frequently incoherent legal material. However, given that the same legal materials can be rendered coherent in a variety of ways, Dworkinian interpretation requires coming to a view as to which of the coherent readings of the tradition is to be preferred in the light of the critical morality of the interpreter. This process of adopting an 'interpretation' which takes a reading that 'fits' existing law in a way that makes it 'the best that it can be' must count as innovative because of the element of moral judgment involved, even though it is based on the assumption that there are some legal materials which are relatively clear and unproblematic with which a 'fit' must be made.[18] This is a matter of bounded innovation rather than bounded interpretation. Indeed, since it may involve rejecting a clear rule on the grounds that it is inconsistent with the rest of the legal system, particularly its underlying principles, it is openly both legally creative and legally destructive.

In this chapter I argue against both the idea of interpretation as comprehension and the idea of intepretation as innovation. The former effectively vitiates the objectivity of the search for evident contextual meanings and thus makes routine governance through rules impossible. The latter enables judicial authorities to bypass legislative enactments at will and is a confusing and tendentious extension of the term to cover a range of activities which are more accurately described as rule extension, variation or creation. This serves to legitimate an extensive political authority of judges by making out that their rule extension activities are really a matter of mere interpetation. An objective is to render meaningful the positivist assumption that we can distinguish formally good laws, which are framed in a way which minimises the need for interpretation because their meanings are clear in the contexts to which they are applicable, and formally bad laws, which lack evident contextual meaning and have to be interpreted by selecting the meaning which, with certain qualifications, is most likely to reflect the intention of the legislators qua legislators.

Contextually Evident Meanings

From the viewpoint of Ethical Positivism, discussions of interpretation which start with the judicial role, particularly in appellate courts, start in the wrong place. Kelsen notwithstanding,[19] the base relationship in law is between the sovereign law maker and the legal subject. Legal norms are primarily for the guidance of those whose conduct is regulated. Judicial interpretation is secondary to this primary communication nexus, which it is its function to facilitate. In other words, adjectival law is secondary to laws which regulate the conduct of non-judicial persons. This obvious point is neglected to the extent that legislating in terms which are intelligible to those citizens to whom the legislation applies is very often subordinated to the traditional imperatives of technical legalese. The ethics of legislation require that subjects' liberties and opportunities be specified in language they can understand and which makes clear and straightforward what is required of them or what they are empowered to do.[20]

It follows from this that, for judicial interpretation, it should be assumed that communication with the public, or that section of it likely to be affected by the law, is part of the legislative intent. Contextually evident meaning is, from the citizen's standpoint, the starting point of positivist interpretation. This means that legislation and interpretation have to focus on a shared understanding of the language of citizens as it functions in the sort of contexts to which the legislation applies. This literalist approach enjoins the judiciary to use only what is usually referred to as the 'ordinary and natural' meaning of the words which appear in the legislation, as distinct from the technical, specialist or contrived meanings which can be attributed to the same words.[21] Nothing here hangs on this naive use of 'natural' to label that which is instinctive and effortless as distinct from learned and striven for. It can be assumed that, in human society, while shared conventions are cultural creations they are experienced as spontaneous understandings.[22] This is not the sort of 'literalism' that attempts to read a text without an understanding of its contexts of origin and application. LEP does not involve a context-independent formalism. It does assume that a rule can have a meaning which licenses its application over a range of relevantly similar circumstances.[23]

On a narrow view, there should be exceptions to the contextually evident meaning rule only where there is an evident absurdity that can be put down to an error in drafting.[24] On a somewhat broader view, it is legitimate to select from a range of possible meanings one of the less evident ones if this avoids what looks like a highly unsatisfactory result. On a broader view still, if there are 'absurdities' which arise from contextually evident meaning this may be used as a justification for disregarding even strained interpretations of the text. Such absurdities relate to the highly undesirable consequences of applying a rule in its evident meaning which were clearly not contemplated by legislators and seem to be uncontroversially idiotic or unjust.[25] Frequent recourse to this sort of let-out principle would enable judges to put legislation aside when they do not like its implications. Ultimately, it could be used to denote any case as 'hard', that is not obvious with respect to the understanding or application of the rules involved,[26] when a judge finds the results of applying the rules unwelcome, thus opening the way to expansive judicial power. In the positivist scheme, the consequences of applying the rules should normally be assessed and altered legislatively through the political process and it is part of judicial ethics to have recourse to consequential absurdity in order to amend evident meanings only when the consequences are uncontroversially senseless or harmful. Restraint in this regard is a fundamental aspect of judicial ethics.[27]

While, strictly speaking, no philosophical theory of meaning is requisite to make sense of the idea of contextually evident meaning, Positivists have in general been impressed by the capacity of truth-conditional theories of meaning, according to which knowledge of what must be the case for a sentence to be true is equated with understanding its meaning.[28] Although this approach does not cover the full gamut of meanings, it is particularly appropriate, especially when combined with an empiricist view of the sources of knowledge, for enabling us to make progress towards achieving the legislative ideal that laws should enable us to identify the observable conditions that must be met for compliance with them. Without denying either that there is a role for other types of meaning, be they metaphysical, religious, aesthetic or moral, or that there are situations when these meanings are readily communicable, the Positivist confidence in the role of regulation by way of contextually evident meanings rests heavily on the prospect of framing most laws within the ambit of what can be coped with by an empiricist epistemology in conjunction with a truth-conditional theory of meaning. This ideal generates difficulties in framing rules of conduct, owing to the subjective elements of intention and motive involved in human action, so that good positivist law will often be unsatisfactory for the purposes of direct moral assessment of conduct. But that is not its purpose.

The LEP approach to interpretation appears to assume that ambiguities and other unclarities can be recognised from a standpoint which is neutral or objective, at least with respect to the range of views competing for legitimacy at any particular time and place. This is not always so, for ambiguity, like meaning, is relative to the understandings of the audience. Conventional meaning rules are inadequate guides without a well defined context and a viewpoint which is shared by speaker and audience. These are significant problems, which we address later, but if the evident meaning in a specific context is not accepted because of the moral implications of its applications or because it does not suit the interests of a contending party this is not to be blamed on the indeterminacy of contextless rules. It is usually possible to go for non-evident meanings to avoid the undesirable consequences. Because of the conventional nature of language, citizens, lawyers and judges can always find ambiguities if they put their minds to it, but this may be self-serving or dishonest. Such 'try-ons' are the stock in trade of those citizens and lawyers who lack a commitment to positivist justice. The fact that contextually evident meaning can be ignored does not undermine the claim that it can be a social reality and therefore part of a realisable ideal.[29]

The same argument applies to all attempts at communication, in that the decision as to what is 'plain' or contextually evident is itself a matter of evaluation since all literal readings as made from a standpoint which involves certain values or attitudes. Meaning rules cannot be detached from the way of life within which they operate and ways of life are value-oriented. However, the sociological truism of the purpose-oriented nature of human language systems does not mean that those who share a way of life cannot also share a set of meaning rules which transcend the evaluative differences between them and so make moral choice possible within that community.[30] In times of social change a community's language may be inadequate to express its emerging moral options and its language requires development to permit the prospect of articulating novel possibilities. New distinctions require to be drawn, new terminology introduced. However, if political choices as to mandatory regulation are in prospect, then that language must achieve the relative value neutrality of facilitating the clear expression of the choices confronting decision makers. It is in the adjustment that courts have to make when utilising old laws to address such changed linguistic circumstances that much 'interpretation' takes place. Positivists argue that the interpretative techniques used do not need to involve taking sides in the evaluative disputes at work in the political and legislative process. Of course, the choice of rules of interpretation themselves is also an evaluative matter, for they are not selected arbitrarily but with a view to certain objectives, such as their power to settle issues definitively. As with ordinary first order rules, the fact that evaluations are involved in their creation does not mean that they cannot be framed in such a way that they themselves can be applied without reference to the objectives which led to their adoption.[31]

Critics of bounded interpretation can point to the immense range of social forces which combine to destabilise such meanings as are agreed in local social contexts. Self-interests, class-interests, gender biases, nationalist commitments, racial prejudices and religious affiliations all in one way or another have language as one of their battlegrounds – territory to be conquered, adapted and deployed to serve the partialities of the contending parties. Equally, coalescences of these partisan viewpoints can serve to provide a consensus on agreed interpretations within different communities, a phenomenon which provides the sort of predictability sought by Legal Realists, a predictability which depends more on the interpersonal subjective agreement of individuals or a coalescence of interests than on any constraint deriving from the 'neutral' meaning of the texts in question. The nub of the Critical Legal Studies (CLS) critique, following the model of the Marxist analyses of ideology, false consciousness and reification, is that this shared prejudice is falsely presented as, and believed to be, objectively true, thereby conferring a legitimacy on the process which it would not otherwise possess.[32] Evidence of this process, in particular case studies, is strong and in itself a powerful falsification of many of the claims of descriptive Legal Positivism. On this basis, it is plausible to regard Positivism as part of the ideological process of bourgeois legitimation.[33]

LEP is not undermined by such studies, unless they can establish that its ideal model for a legal system could not be realised in the systems under scrutiny. Indeed, it is against the background of a positivist model that the critiques have their greatest intelligibility and force. A criticism of bias requires a conception of the unbiased, otherwise it is an assertion of mere difference. Because we have some idea of what a positivist scheme of law might be like and because we appreciate its virtues, we can take on board the evidence that it is not attained in specific cases and systems and present this as a matter for regret and criticism. Indeed, LEP can accept the general line of argument that the exposure of the biases of existing systems features as a delegitimation of their status quo. Ethical Positivists can share in the outrage and condemnation of systems which claim to rise above group partialities but in practice fail to do so. Thus LEP critiques of bad drafting, ineffective political decision making and shoddy rule application have common ground with much CLS analysis.

Ethical Positivists also point out the indeterminacy, contradictoriness and bias of existing legal systems. It is precisely such departures from the positivist ideal in actual systems of government that provide the basis for delegitimations of many of the actual uses of power. LEP does not assume the same homogeneity of forces at work behind false claims to objectivity in actual and particular systems, but readily accepts many of the insights of critical and feminist theorists relating to the inadequacies of existing law and legal processes. In particular, LEP can recognise the process of reification, whereby human creations are falsely assumed to be pre-existing entities which limit the options of their creators. The ontology of this exposure of reification fits the positivist doctrine that law is made, not discovered, and is at our disposal to change at will. The 'pseudo-objectivity' associated with misguided beliefs in the 'naturalness' of laws is a critical view which brings LEP and CLS together. False claims to objectivity deny the capacity of the law maker and misdescribes the role of the courts. This is the thrust of many a positivist critique of both Natural and Common Law.

Radical CLS views deny that any adequate move towards objectivity in rule application is possible. Ironically, this takes away the moral force of any implied critique of existing practice since, on this extreme view, nothing is possible besides delegitimation and ad hoc engagements to protect the interests of those who are oppressed by the existing system. This may mean a CLS practitioner can only join in the process of rendering the law less certain, and argue for any meaning which is likely to benefit his (ex hypothesi oppressed) client. An Ethical Positivist takes the view that our response to the failings of legal systems should be to seek improvement through the pursuit of more determinate laws, better interpretative practices, relevant legal ethics and the extralegal creations of the social circumstances necessary to attain some community of meaning which is not incurably distorted in favour of powerful groups.

Stipulations

When giving instructions and permissions through legislation, careful expression is required beyond that which applies in everyday discourse. The communication is not face-to-face and cannot readily be clarified through the process of question and answer. Moreover, there are lots of pitfalls in the way of successful communication even in quite straightforward regulatory situations. Avoidance of these pitfalls is a complex matter which requires great sensitivity to the different ways in which the same set of words and sentences may be taken by different individuals and various contexts, and within different groups in the same jurisdiction.

A central locus of these problems remains Hart's helpful distinction between core and penumbra uses of terminology with respect to classificatory terms which has been subject to much irrelevant criticism. For core meaning we have no problem in communicating our meaning since the words are used in relation to standard examples with which the communicating parties are familiar. Given the nature of language as a set of conventional signs, and the often shifting forms of natural phenomena, there will be many cases where there is no agreement about how to classify certain types of thing in relation to a chosen category or observed situation. On this analysis, any concept *can* be vague in certain applications; that is, there is always the possibility of marginal cases in which it is not clear whether or not the term is appropriate.[34] Boundary vagueness of this sort is not to be confused with mere generality. Very general terms can have sharp edges and quite specific ones can have fuzzy ones. Nor is it the same as straightforward vacuity, which arises with highly abstract terms with no determinate reference into which we pour what content we please. It is possible to have legislation which contains general terms with relatively sharp boundaries which are not in the least vague in relation to the standard cases to which they have routinely to be applied. Not many parking tickets are disputed on the grounds that the offending object is not a vehicle. This need not and probably cannot routinely be the case, for concepts are not vague in relation to the standard examples which make possible shared understanding.[35]

There are many ways out of the difficulties in penumbral and other marginal cases. One is to look to the purpose of the legislation, and we consider this below.[36] Another is to provide artificial meaning determinations by way of stipulations which are suited to the cases in point. It is possible to provide as many stipulative definitions as are required to reduce ambiguities which are foreseeable given the variety of audiences addressed and the nature of the regulatory matter. Wherever possible this should be done by selecting an alternative within everyday discourse, but often the objectives of the legislation in question require that distinctions be drawn which are not standard, in which case specifically legal stipulations are necessary. These then become technical legal terms with distinctive legal meanings. This can be particularly helpful when the legislator hopes to capture an important moral distinction in terms of observable conduct rather than subjective meaning, a recurrent positivist project which seeks to take moral assessment out of the process of rule application.

Where possible, such stipulations should be clearly identified as such, although it is often the case that ordinary words are adopted and given specialist meanings, thus introducing ambiguity into legislation which was not in the language in the first place. It is the duty of the legislator to signal such legally created ambiguities as clearly as possible and to stick with them consistently. Evidently, it is unhelpful if legal stipulations are multiplied beyond necessity and this creates pressures to adopt pre-existing legal stipulations in new enactments, a tendency that leads to the perpetuation of what is pejoratively called 'legalese', a term which may be used to describe stipulations which are not necessary or lead to complexities which remove the language of legislation so far from ordinary discourse that it becomes inaccessible to all but a few specialists and hence useless as regulation. In general, from the positivist viewpoint, there is an overemphasis in courts on rendering new legislation 'consistent' with existing legal stipulations rather than addressing the intention of legislation, which is to deal with contemporary objectives and political determinations without the encumbrance of past political enactments. Where possible, to further the aim of effective political control, the objective of communication of political purpose via contextually evident meanings should take priority over consistency with previous legal terminology.

Legislative Purpose

LEP points us, in the first place, to socially plain or literal contextual meanings and, where necessary for the avoidance of unclarities, legislative stipulations. When these do not produce unambiguous clear outcomes, a theory which is committed to the idea of governance through rules may choose between refraining to make a judgment on the ground that no determinations should be made in the absence of clear rules, which is usually appropriate in criminal law, and the recommendation of second-best solutions to a situation which calls for some judicial remedy, pending legislative resolution.

Stipulation is itself one such remedial tactic when it is employed by precedent-setting judicial ruling. A similar role is played by many conventional assumptions of judicial interpretation known to legislatures and perhaps also to citizens. Thus the presumption, not in itself attractive for democratic reasons, that legislation does not alter Common Law doctrines or invade Common Law rights, unless it is clearly shown that this was intended by the legislature, functions as a way of dealing with ambiguities as well as a device for protecting existing rights.[37] If abused, such intepretative rules make it difficult to overturn unacceptable Common Law precedents, thus thwarting the decisions of legislature. This can be avoided with legislative care and judicial integrity.

A prevalent remedial tactic is to appeal to the intentions or even the purposes of the legislature beyond those that are evident from reading the text itself. Such appeals will often seem simple-minded to those who share the common view that the notion of legislative intent, whether or not embodied in the meaning of a text, is a fantasy and that the idea of there being a further sense of legislative purpose underlying texts is equally fantastic. Certainly, there is no doubt that appeal is routinely made to an empirically indeterminable 'legislative purpose' simply to find a phoney legitimation for the political or personal objectives of those in a position of judicial or executive power. It is also true that nothing much follows from purposes which are stated so broadly that almost anything follows. Usually, it is only in the choice of specific rules that selection of priority purposes is actually made.[38] This does not mean, however, that the notions of intention and purpose in the context of legislation have no intelligible content or useful role. Quite apart from what can be inferred from the text, often such intentions and purposes can be discovered or construed, given the legislative context or history, or even just a basic knowledge of the alternative political positions which were current at the time of the legislation.

In the first place, sense can be given to the distinction between 'utterer's meaning', that is what the speaker intended to say, as opposed to 'actual' meaning, that is what the existing conventions entitle the audience to understand by what was said.[39] We can meaningfully contend that the actual meaning may not be the speaker's meaning. More generally, it is a familiar fact that we regard others as having purposes, including linguistic purposes, some of which are only partially revealed in what is said, and may indeed be deliberately concealed in the language used but knowledge of which may help us get at a speaker's intended meaning. It makes sense therefore to raise questions about whether the words of an Act accurately convey legislators' intentions, in the sense of how they intended the words to be understood.[40] Legislators may succeed in making their intended meaning identical with the actual meaning and they may or may not achieve thereby the purpose for which they enacted the law. Equally, legislators may fail actually to say what they mean and in this way fail to communicate with their audience. This is not the same as failing to achieve their purpose in enacting the legislation. Rules may be understood as intended and punctiliously followed without this producing the further results hoped for by their authors. And they may, fortuitously, fail to convey their meaning but nevertheless succeed in their objectives.[41]

By and large, LEP holds to the view that actual meaning has priority and legislators have the duty to ensure that their intentions are accurately captured in the enacted text.[42] Without this, many of the positivist advantages of law, such as certainty, democratic control and moral form, are lost. There is little point in arguing over the words of a bill unless actual meaning is adjudicatively prior. When dealing with the activity of legislation as distinct from crude models of imperitival theory which focus on the idea of an individual legislator giving general orders, we can take it that there is no significant gap between meaning as the speakers intend and meaning as it is understood by applying the rules of standard use which give us the meaning of the utterance detached from speakers' intent. Because the activity is that of legislating it can be assumed that the intent of the legislators is to enact rules which should be understood as relatively detached utterances rather than in terms of the largely undiscoverable information as to what the speakers intended to convey. In other words, *legislative* speakers ought to intend to enact rules which can be read in terms of the publicly ascertainable meanings derivable by the application of the meaning rules of that community. To this we can add the legislators' knowledge of the rules of statutory interpretation which enable them to anticipate how their enactments will be understood, and modified if they are disputed in courts.[43]

Now it may be that some of those who vote within a legislature will not even have read the Act in question or seek to understand it in any detail, but from the meaning of the words of the enactment in the given context it is proper for those subject to that legislation to assume that they intended to produce rules for the guidance of the population or some section of it. This means that, within normal understanding of what legislation in general is all about, it is proper to assume that legislators intend the contextually evident meanings of their enactment as it would be anticipated in the contexts to which the legislation applies. This assumption may be overturned if, for instance, it turns out that there was no opportunity to propose and consider amendments during the legislative process. This may be a fiction but, within the confines of democratic legitimacy, it is an acceptable fiction provided that the legislators have had the opportunity to read and debate the bill. It is this that gives structure and point to legislative debate and decision making.

When actual meaning is unclear then LEP, in its endorsement of law as the expression of a (it is hoped democratic) will, readily turns for interpretative guidance to whatever it was that the legislator intended to convey. Legislators' intent in this sense is not to be confused with legislators' purpose, that is, what their further intention was in enacting the statute (for example, the policy goal) as distinct from how they intended the words of the statute to be understood. Rather, what is involved is an examination of legislative history which is confined to investigating what it was that the legislators were trying to convey.[44] This may be assisted by a knowledge of the policy purposes underlying the legislation but it is a common mistake to think that we must understand the background policy purpose before we can begin to understand the rules themselves.[45] This mistake is exposed when we note that the words of the text can be used to arrive at a view on legislative purpose. Moreover, as MacCallum notes, 'until he [the legislator] forms opinions about the "meaning" of the words, he cannot consider that they will serve his purpose'.[46]

Beyond legislative intent is legislative purpose: the objectives that legislation is intended to achieve. With simple prohibitions of evidently harmful acts this purpose may not be in doubt, but instrumentally tailored legislation may have a variety of 'further' objectives. By and large, LEP holds that such further intentions or purposes are not relevant to adjudication. However, they may be introduced in various second-best situations, as when law contains significant gaps, or major ambiguities are unresolvable by other means. The idea of legislative purpose may enable a judge to ask what a legislature might have enacted had they considered the case. This can serve the positivist goal of furthering the aims of government, although it runs against the positivist norm of rule governance. This process is suspect from the point of view of many of the underlying values of Positivism, but it may be the preferred second-best option where these values are not seriously compromised, as when a general knowledge of legislators' purpose is available to the citizen as well as the judge so that the former is able to anticipate the determinations of the latter. The problem is also mitigated when the purpose is not morally controversial in that community.

What may be objected to in the idea of legislative intent and the notion of the purpose (of further intent) behind legislation is that a *group* of people can have intentions and purposes. Again, it is not open to serious contention that human beings can have shared intentions and purposes around which they organise their conduct and about which they communicate. The difficulty is in ascribing such intentions and purposes to a large group of individuals who have disparate objectives within the social setting that counts: legislative enactments. If the legislation is the product of a unified political party that dominates the legislature then the problem may be reduced, but in normal circumstances it is usually wrong to say that a legislature has a shared intention or purpose. Interestingly, such a criticism has force precisely because we can make sense of the idea of what it is for a large group to have a shared purpose. It is also interesting that the same considerations give us reason to fasten on actual rather than intended meanings.

Nevertheless, it is evident that there are especially grave difficulties in divining legislative intentions or purposes speculatively or by selective use of legislative history. One possible solution is to have purposes explicitly stated in legislation. The dangers of this practice for the positivist model are considerable. Purposes are in general unspecific and the crucial political decisions are often focussed on creating the rules which give effect to them. Further, once we allow judicial use of legislative purpose, even if narrowly defined, there is a considerable danger that such purposes will be used to displace contextually evident meaning, thus undercutting the rule of rules. Whether or not this happens will depend on the quality of the legislation, the narrowness and specification of the authoritative interpretative rules and the ethical conduct of the judiciary in adhering to those norms in good faith. However, if it is possible to state with some specificity the purpose of an enactment it seems reasonable to refer to this in cases which require interpretation.

Many critiques of legislative intent and legislative purpose are based on crude misunderstandings of what is involved. The critiques concentrate on what is best referred to as ulterior purposes, or the motives of the legislators, whereas the Positivist's notion of legislative intent is centred on the purpose as stated in the legislation or the politically authenticated statement of the legitimating purpose of the law in question.[47] The reasons why legislators support a piece of legislation may vary from a desire to be re-elected or gain promotion to or within the government, to pleasing their spouse or satisfying their consciences. Their understanding of what it is that they are voting for is quite another matter. That is determined by what meanings they think will be given to the words of the bill by citizens and judges. Legislators who have grossly divergent motives may all agree as to what they are voting for, what they intend to enact.

With these distinctions in mind it is possible to consider further the extent to which it may be appropriate for judges to look behind obscure or incomplete actual meanings to legislative intent or purpose. Thus, where legislative intention is at issue, we may allow judges to look into the processes of drafting, committee discussion, administrative preparation and so on. Where purpose is in question we may permit investigation as to the publicly stated views of leading proponents of the legislation in question and the situations which gave rise to the policies behind the laws.

Here we may contrast approaches which focus on subjective meaning as the actual purposes envisaged by those involved rather than on objective meaning as some sort of fictional purpose of a rational legislator. On the 'rational reconstruction' approach, there is the 'subjective purpose', namely, 'that which is conceived as being the very purpose or end actually embraced by the members of the legislature in the process of the legislation'. And there is 'objective purpose', that is 'the purpose imputed to the legislature as an ideally rational legislator responsible for enacting that set of provisions in those historical and political circumstances'.[48] For LEP the rational reconstruction approach gives far too much leeway to judicial reasoning and effectively invites the judiciary to revisit the political determination of controversial issues. Rather, the prime aim of looking at such legislative history should be to establish the legislators' intended meanings. On the other hand, when such intended meanings are unclear or inadequate or hard to determine, as they frequently are, it may be proper further to examine the same materials to determine what legislative purpose may have been at work, either to clarify the actual meaning or to rectify some other formal deficiency in the legislation. In this regard we may readily take in knowledge of the publicly stated purpose of the legislation to the extent that this makes the context of the application clear. Allegedly unclear intent may become clear when we view the legislation in purposive terms relative to the social or economic context addressed in the legislation, rather than detached free-floating terminology. This is particularly so if we have some awareness of the range of intentions that could have been adopted in such legislation at such a time.

Often ordinary meaning or standard techniques, such as following precedent in the interpretation of certain words and phrases, are put aside by considering the context in more detail, for instance the fact that an enactment took place in time of war. Thus in a UK wartime regulation, *Liverside* v. *Anderson*,[49] 'reasonable cause to believe that a person is of hostile origins or otherwise threatened national security' was taken subjectively rather than objectively in relation to the conception of reasonableness enshrined in precedent. On appeal, Lord Atkin held there was no ambiguity here as 'reasonable' had come to be interpreted objectively in such enactments. He went on to argue that to interpret it subjectively, and so rely on the minister's discretion, however unreasonably exercised, would be to manifest an ethics of judicial deference to the executive. On the other hand, Lord Macmillan took the purpose of the legislation to be protecting public safety. He was also able to appeal to the wording elsewhere in the Emergency Powers (Defence) Act, 1939, which appears to contemplate wide ministerial discretion. Certainly, 'the detention of such persons whose detention appears to the Secretary of State to be expedient' looks subjective enough and explicit enough to overrule any interpretation based on stipulative precedent. He then argues that those responsible for national security must make the judgment, for Parliament would not have accepted it as an emergency measure if the court had to decide on the reasonableness of the minister's decision.[50] In other words, by looking to the context of the legislation, a wartime emergency dealing with national security, we can come to a clearer meaning of what must have been intended. We may, of course, regard Lord Atkin's approach here as an expression of Positivism: 'I protest, even if I do it alone, against a strained construction put on words with the effect of giving an uncontrolled power of imprisonment to the minister. To recapitulate: The words have only one meaning. They are used with that meaning in statements of the common law and in statutes.' However, while he may have been right as to the general precedents for interpreting such terminology, he may have been wrong in his assessment of the evident meaning of the Act when read in its context. Indeed, Lord Atkin's real objection to the Act may be the perceived violation of basic Common Law rights rather than his commitment to positivist interpretative principle.[51]

More generally, awareness of the 'purpose' of an area of law may be enough to help with appropriate readings of decided cases for determination of their ratio. Thus a knowledge of the central purposes of tort law may enable judges to move to higher and lower levels of generality in determining what factors are relevant in novel situations.[52] Similarly, a sense of whether rules are intended to coordinate or control activity may be decisive for their interpretation in doubtful cases. However, where the judgments of relevant similarities are controversial this is precisely the point at which it is for legislatures to concretise their preferred values with respect to the categorical distinctions that capture the moral boundary which they wish to draw. This illustrates that there is a sense of legislative purpose, beyond legislative intent in relation to meaning, the limited use of which can be defended within LEP. The publicly given and defended purpose of an enactment as distinct from the further purposes (or motive) of the legislators is a relevant part of the context of understanding. Legislative purpose in this sense cannot be a routine first and overriding resort for a rule-governed system, but it is appropriate in second-best situations in which a decision is needed to avoid a failure to execute the legislative decision. It is congruent with the idea that law is an expression of the will of the legislator but in tension with the idea that power be exercised through rules. It is a matter of judicial ethics that the latter should not be overwhelmed by the former. The legislative ideal is one of clarity and comprehensiveness, but where this is lacking it is acceptable to look behind the words, not to the motives of the legislators, but to the officially legitimated purpose of the legislation as exemplified in manifestos, debates, reports and ministerial statements. Such purpose might include the reduction of accidents in a cost-effective way, promotion of material equality in society, or the stimulus of trade.

From our discussion of rules it is clear that it is not the citizens' or adjudicators' duty simply to act in a way which best furthers such purposes. In this case rules would be superfluous. But, if the question is about what meaning should be ascribed to a rule in the absence of an evident meaning, the politically authorised purpose of the enactment has relevance, provided this is not thought to license changing the evident meaning of a rule according to its specific consequences on specific occasions. As Schauer points out, while a justification is not part of a rule, when its meaning is in doubt it seems 'unimpeachable to look initially at the justification lying behind the rule'.[53]

It is, however, a violation of the ethics of interpretation when judges strive to unearth an ambiguity in the language of an Act because they think that the outcome of the case would otherwise be unacceptable. According to Griffith C.J., when confronted with alternative meanings 'one of whose constructions will do injustice and the other avoid injustice, then it is the bounden duty of the Court ... to adopt the second'[54] but this will do only where the meanings have equal plausibility from the viewpoint of literal contextualism. If ambiguities are in effect created to avoid a perceived injustice by opting for an otherwise odd interpretation, then what we have is judicial legislation. These practices may be relatively uncontroversial if there is a shared sense of justice, but when extended to controversial matters they become an illegitimate tactic which is fostered and disguised by those interpretative rules and practices which encourage appeal to such wide purposes as 'justice'.

LEP generates general reservations about putting aside contextually evident meanings simply because the supposed purpose of the legislation is not being achieved. These reservations are heightened by the overt encouragement to use purpose found in some legislative developments concerning the norms of interpretation. One example of such an unacceptable line is Section 15AA of the Australian Acts Interpretation Act 1901 (Cth): 'In the interpretation of a provision of an Act, a construction that would promote the purpose or object underlying the Act (whether that purpose or object is expressly stated in the Act or not) shall be preferred to a construction that would not promote that purpose or object.' In many jurisdictions with such provisions they are, in fact, rarely used, or the purposes may be stated so broadly as to be interpretatively useless. Indeed, they may be no more than a statement that the purpose of the Act is to amend and improve the existing legislation.[55] However, where specific purposes are given in the statute it becomes imperative to know which takes precedence if there is conflict: the evident meaning of the rule or the stated purpose? Thus the Cattle Compensation Act (Amendment) Act 1991 s. 1 says that 'The purpose of this act is to increase the maximum amount of compensation payable under the Cattle Compensation Act 1967', but it is clear that some sections might produce a decrease in the amount paid. Are they then to be disregarded?[56] If so, then the rules have ceased to be sticky or sufficiently exclusionary to count as anything more than rules of thumb.

Having regard to legislative purpose fits readily within LEP if this is done to resolve issues of bounded interpretation, but it becomes wholly unacceptable if it involves the mere fact of perceived failure to promote that purpose in particular circumstances being used to modify the application of a rule of law. The latter practice evades the limits on power that rule governance is intended to impose. Such ad hoc appeals to legitimating purposes, whether authorised or not, are unacceptable because they seek to go behind the rule format through which governments must operate in terms of the political philosophy outlined in Chapter 2. Governments require to be limited as well as empowered by mechanisms of governance through law. The legitimating force of the imperative to operate via specific rules is, as we have seen, in part for protecting minorities and ensuring a minimal form of equality of citizenship, while promoting signficant liberties, but it is equally a matter of facilitating effective democratic process and enabling working systems of cooperation. It is politically illegitimate to evade the specified generality of rules by routine direct appeal to political purposes. Governments should in general be held to what they can achieve within governance mediated by law and it is not up to administrators and judiciaries to help them avoid what may often seem to be an annoying straitjacket but is in fact a condition of the legitimate exercise of coercive power. Within these paramaters, LEP can endorse many more particular systems of intepretation but the rationales for such pragmatic strategies remain the same and in general suggest that agreement on conventions that enable us to predict how courts will approach problems of interpretation is more important than the precise nature of these conventions.

This broadly sketched position constitutes a partial positivist endorsement of Lon Fuller's contention that all rules must be understood in the light of a background context of purposeful activity,[57] with respect to both the activities being regulated and the act of legislation itself. However, LEP seeks to emphasise the significance of legislative selection of words and sentences and the structuring of clauses within an Act taken as a whole, for the purpose of controlling and guiding conduct by utilising the relative trans-contextual aspects of discourse which flow from the abstraction and generalisation which makes language, and thought, possible. Within this relationship, contextually evident meaning takes priority. Only when there is a failure of communication between legislator and subject is a direct use of legislative purpose relevant to the regulatory process.

Similarly, despite the positivist base presupposed by Dworkin's approach to legal reasoning, which seeks to incorporate the inherited mass of legal decisions and legislative outputs within an integrated whole, LEP stops short of endorsing the later stages of the Herculean model as a variant of LEP. Dworkin's so-called 'interpretative' approach to law ultimately substitutes the adjudicator's purposes and values for those of the legislators.[58] On the other hand, a narrow commitment to literal meanings which takes no account of the context of the legislation may block legislative purpose in ways which are not required by a commitment to governance through rules. Here judicial use of narrow plain meanings can be compared to citizens looking for ways round the law in order, for instance, to minimise their tax liability. Just as the advocacy of possible but strained acontextual literal meanings which serve to minimise the legal duties of the subject can generally be construed as a form of dishonesty, so contextually blind judicial literalism is often an unethical use of judicial power in much the same way as expansive purposive interpretative practices; it is a device for avoiding the legitimate political directive which it is the court's duty to implement.[59]

Recognising Rules

Seen as an attempt to constrain governments within the rule format of governance and judges within the authorised rules, discussions of the interpretation of rules may seem beside the point if, as Legal Realists contend and is widely accepted, judges can pick and choose which rules to apply.[60]

Much can be achieved quickly here by allowing that it is often in the de facto capacity of judges to ignore some rules and utilise others, in that they cannot effectively be prevented from so doing, but denying that this is unavoidable and ethically correct or legally legitimate. The ethical case against Legal Realism is that it encourages the further politicisation of legal process and disempowers democratic process. Further, although some positivist rationales, such as certainty, argue for the incorporation into a legal system of invalid judicial decisions, other positivist rationales, such as political efficacy, reject the view that precedent is sufficiently powerful to make such de facto exercises of power binding on subsequent adjudicators.

However, there are problems in establishing how citizens, lawyers and judges are de jure able to know which rules are authorised as laws and relevant to a case in hand. How can the proper criteria of legal validity be determined? LEP does not have anything like the same problem with this issue as a descriptive Positivist, who has to take into account the diverse sources of law in particular jurisdictions.[61] An Ethical Positivist can draw on the prescriptive separation thesis[62] to stipulate that there ought to be a rule of recognition such that citizens and adjudicators can be in no reasonable doubt as to the authorised sources of law. This would mean excluding rules of recognition that are not clear, internally consistent, decisive, impartially applicable and which actually produce routine agreement when used as selection criteria. In this regard it is easy to appreciate positivist qualms about case law systems which embody tortuous ways of determining ratio decidendi from decided cases, themselves somewhat randomly selected, as a method of developing rather than interpreting law. Such a system enables adjudicators to act as largely unbounded legislators, and fails to bring them back to relevant legislation or to generate institutional demands for legislative reform.

This still leaves us with the theoretically ultimate problem of identifying and interpreting the rule of recognition itself. Rules of recognition can be seen as descriptions of social practice or as norms binding on judges. In between, as we have noted, is the idea that they are conventions which both describe and prescribe, or whose prescriptive power derives from their social facticity. We have seen that this can be unpacked consistently with LEP as meaning that there is reason to follow existing practice where having a practice is useful for your chosen objective, such as the furtherance of social cooperation.[63] The line adopted by the descriptive Positivist is that the rule of recognition is to be discerned in the actual practice of judiciaries. This is one of its weakest doctrines, for it seems to assume the implausible thesis that all significant judicial actors adopt the same rule of recognition. There are no a priori or empirical grounds for believing that the practice of judges is uniform in this regard. Nor, it may be said, can such a method of identification account for the prescriptive force of a rule of recognition beyond the argument from conventional acceptance, which in itself gives no grounds for selecting one convention over another.

In contrast, LEP takes rules of recognition to be prescriptions and makes recommendations as to the acceptable content of such rules. It requires that the rule of recognition be derived from a political constitution outside the legal system itself. This is partly a philosophical matter of the sort discussed in Chapter 2, as anything else will produce an infinite regress of basic authorising rules. But it is more centrally an ethical point about morally legitimate power. Judges cannot be the source of a rule of recognition because they lack accountability and credibility as constitution makers. Electorally accountable legislatures are stronger candidates as sources of constitutional authority, but there is still something unsatisfactory in legislatures authorising the rule of recognition that makes them the source of valid law. Validity may be a legal concept and legitimacy a political one but it is not one which an institutionalised political authority can readily bestow on itself. Ethical Positivism is a political philosophy that seeks to avoid giving judges the right to determine the content of their rule of recognition, but does not eagerly ascribe this right to legislatures. Here we are back with a vengeance at the tragic paradox of politics. On balance it seems right that the articulation of the foundation principles of government, including the rule of recognition, should be primarily within the scope of legislative power, assuming that this legislature is electorally accountable to some threshold degree of political legitimacy. Moreover, the articulation and enactment of matters relating to the authoritative rule of recognition in a jurisdiction cannot be subject to judicial review with respect to its substance without transferring the foundational power. Given that the choice of a rule of recognition is a matter in which the legislature has what may be described as an intense private interest, the political choices made in this regard are ones which require a powerful ethical commitment. This being so it is unlikely that a polity can attain or retain a democratic and rule-governed political system without a degree of effective electoral accountability together with a vibrant political culture which is sensitive to the requirements of democratic legitimacy.[64]

Jurisdictions with a comprehensive written constitution may appear to have an edge in the tortured logic of legitimation, but, with respect to the constitution itself, it appears necessary to take refuge in unique moments of political legitimation.[65] In fact, these foundational experiences may also feature centrally in constitutional histories which have not produced a definitive constitutional text. Further, the interpretation of constitutions is far more problematic than the interpretation of statutes or cases as the context of their origins fades into distant and increasingly irrelevant history, especially when, as is usually the case, constitutional amendment is very difficult to achieve in normal times.[66] Nevertheless, the fabrications of creative pseudo-interpretation may still appear preferable to relying on fuzzy conceptions of the will of the people or popular conceptions of democracy, neither of which can be very helpfully articulated through the crudities of constitutional referenda or satisfactorily identified by courts. The discussion of these issues is taken further in the next chapter.

Conclusion

The discussion of this chapter deals mainly with the role of interpretation in the ideal positivist model, with occasional asides on interpretation in far from ideal conditions, together with a brief flight into the realm of constitutional philosophy, which will be taken up again in the next chapter. It concludes with some further thoughts about what to do when this model has not been achieved, the point at which judiciaries have to adopt second-best approaches to their adjudicatory task.

While the line between interpretation and innovation is imprecise, it is evident that some rules are so unspecific or ambiguous as to lie beyond the resources of mere interpretation. Similar problems arise where there are equally valid but inconsistent laws. Also, of course, courts are sometimes faced with a situation where there is no valid applicable law, when there is said to be a 'gap' in the system.[67] A first line of approach to such eventualities is to make no decision, on the grounds that there is no law applying to the situation in question.[68] A closure rule of this sort makes every case decidable. We have said that this is usually the proper positivist response when dealing with criminal charges, especially where significant liberties are at stake. The idea that courts have a residual discretionary power[69] to add to criminal law, even by appeal to basic principles, may be regarded as stemming from pre-democratic eras. It is no longer appropriate for courts to make the assumption that there is a shared acceptance of a pre-legal 'natural law' even in the area of criminal law. In civil matters it is more appealing to let matters, and hence losses, lie, but this means a partiality for the status quo, and hence for the socially and economically powerful. Such a policy may favour able but immoral members of society to obtain unjust advantages until such time as legislatures get round to improving the law to deal with such situations. Positivists could accept that in such situations it may be right to give delegated legislative powers to courts so that they may create new rules to solve novel disputes. Nevertheless, the positivist advantages to which we have so frequently referred suggest that remedies here be provided by prospective legislation or, as a second best, prospective overruling of prior case law.

A second approach is to impute a legislative intent on the basis of a calculation of what the legislature would have enacted if they had considered the matter.[70] This may, of course, be arrived at through reflection on the purposes of recent relevant legislation. But it is in general too arbitrary in the selection of which legislature we are to consider, and too speculative in its pursuit of volatile counter-factuals. Of which legislature at what time and in what circumstances are we to conjecture?

A third approach is to require judges to fill gaps by drawing on positive morality, or popular opinion, as to the matter under dispute.[71] Advantages of this view include its apparent recognition of the bounded nature of judicial legislation, and it has a pleasing democratic ring. It also accords with those traditional areas of the Common Law which have been left largely to judicial development or in which the legislation invites courts to apply existing community standards. Unfortunately, it is a decisive approach only in those matters which are politically uncontroversial and therefore generally unproblematic. In a pluralist society with powerful competing interest groups it is all but useless. Inevitably, therefore, it is left to the judiciary to decide which or whose positive morality to draw on. The 'reasonable person' yields few results as a description of shared moral responses and gives plenty of scope for the sort of judicial discretion that runs counter to the positivist ideal.

A further way of filling gaps and curing other deficiencies in actual legal systems is to legitimate open judicial legislation by pointing to the moral authority of judges.[72] The idea is that judges are well situated to 'legislate', in that they have an impartiality which is absent in partisan politics and a capacity to argue from principle according to testable maxims which makes them superior as moral reasoners. The impartiality of the judiciary imparts to them a certain moral authority. To this may be added a situational view of ethics to the effect that moral issues ultimately relate to particular cases and cannot be finally decided without an openness to the novel detail of the individual situations. Thus the ordinary courts may be seen as providing impartiality with respect to the determination of matters of fact, while the higher appellate courts are fitted to carry on principled moral debate on the grand issues confronting a polity.

There are major weaknesses in this approach, one being that impartiality, in the sense of non-involvement in the case at hand or in the activities of party politics, is not sufficient to ensure impartiality in the selection of values.[73] Indeed, it is not clear that impartiality is relevant to value selection which goes beyond identification of personal desires. Additionally, judges are not in a position to undertake the empirical work that is required to enact legislation which seeks to formulate adequate social and economic policies. It may be that, in certain areas of individual justice which are unconnected with class and gender bias and do not require extensive policy research, judges may be thought to be suited to making acceptable moral and hence legislative judgments. Maybe some issues, where long-term consequences are not at stake, and particularities are all important, should be left for judicial legislation. Candidates might be such personal issues as euthanasia or many other aspects of medical law, although such matters are inherently controversial. It is difficult to find areas where controversial and empirically complex policy matters do not arise, in that the further consequences of individual determinations have long-term social impacts. Further, the matters which are often left to judiciaries are in practice ones which are just too complex and sensitive for legislatures, rather than those to which wise impartiality can find an answer. Courts have no claim to special moral authority in such matters as abortion and euthanasia, concerning which there are insoluble clashes of incompatible and incommensurate values.

Giving even such limited legislative power to judiciaries seems to open up the possibility of just too many different ways in which such powers may be exercised. Possibilities range from the development of Common Law methods involving, for instance, fairly remote analogies or the application of very general principles, which is unlikely to find favour with LEP, to an effort to mimic the activities of an actual or imaginary legislature, using, perhaps, utilitarian reasoning, maybe in conjunction with some limitations imposed by assumed human rights prohibitions.[74] The Common Law tradition which utilises the idea of consistency with general principle and analogies drawn from not entirely dissimilar situations may serve to keep judicially initiated change incremental, but is as unsatisfactory as any from the point of view of predictability and certainty, and has the added disadvantage of using past political decisions to determine contemporary issues. Second-guessing legislatures is apparently the most evidently democratic approach, but not one which is always feasible in view of the vicissitudes of political life, assuming that actual rather than fictional legislatures are the starting point of the exercise. Appeal to what a reasonable legislature would have enacted if they had considered the matter can be little more than an exercise in personal moral reflection, since 'reasonableness' cannot determine which of the political alternatives is to be preferred. The variety of possible methodologies remains, therefore, a principal difficulty with making judiciaries into reserve legislatures. Perhaps this is one reason why there is attraction in limiting judicial legislation to the 'interpretation' of fundamental rights, as Dworkin in effect recommends. Is there the prospect of a Positivism of human rights to fill the gaps in actual legislative provision which might also help to solve the paradox of politics by enabling legislatures to be overruled in this limited range of basic principle? The argument of the next chapter will indicate why this may not be such a good idea.

Notes

1 Wrobleski (1992, p. 26): 'a normative model does not refer to the judicial application of law either though generalizing or by using a theory of a higher level of generalities. The model in question indicates how the judge has to apply the law, that is, sets standards for proper application of the law by judges.' Also see Honore (1973).

2 Thus, from a critical standpoint, Collins (1986, p.67):

> 'When we consider modern theories of legal reasoning and adjudication ... we discover that the rival schools share much common ground. The objective is to present a description of the procedure for answering questions of law which claims implicitly the legitimacy of this procedure by reference to a general theory of the state. This general theory asserts the natural division of responsibilities between the various organs of government. In particular, the duty of the democratic legislature is to enact laws designed to further the common good, and the duty of the judiciary is to uphold those laws, and more generally to uphold the constitutional framework of the Rule of Law'.

3 This is indisputable as a description of much appellate judicial practice. Whether or not the nature of language makes this inevitable is a question within the philosophy of language and in particular the neo-relativism of radical pragmatism and deconstructionism: see Kramer (1991) and Bix (1993).

4 See Kripke (1982), Yablon (1985), Norris (1988), Greenawalt (1991) and Drahos and Parker (1992).

5 Locke (1689 3.2.2).

6 Wittgenstein (1968, sect.201).

7 See Wittgenstein (1968) and Radin (1989).

8 This approximates to Wroblewski's legalistic model of legal reasoning. See Wroblewski (1992, p.26): 'the legalistic normative model ... constructed according to the binding rules of law which regulate the administration of justice as distinct from the extra-legal model which draws on extra-legal ideology of judicial application of the law, that is 'bound judicial decision' rather than free judicial decision'. According to this model, 'the court ought to justify its decisions by valid legal rules, which constitute the normative basis for the decision and determine the legal consequences of the proven facts of the case' (p.75).

9 For useful discussions of interpretation, see Marmor (1992); also Barnes (1988).

10 Wroblewski's interpretation, 'sensu largo'; MacCormick and Summers (1992), pp.120–21.

11 Wroblewski's interpretation 'sensu stricto'. See Wroblewski (1992, p.88): '"interpretation" in a strict meaning refers to the situation in which there are doubts concerning the proper understanding of the text in its "direct meaning". For removing these doubts one interprets the linguistic expression using certain means.'

12 This variant includes a wide range of approaches, including the creative use of strong discretion (Hart, 1961, pp.138–44), radical analogical reasoning within Common Law approaches (Allan 1993; and MacCormick, 1990, p.556): 'rational reconstruction means the production of clear systematic statements of legal doctrine, accounting for statute law and case law in terms of organizing principles, relating to actual or hypothetical decisions both to their factual bases and to governing norms elaborated out of the authoritative materials'. Also Dworkin (1986, p.52): 'constructive interpretation is a matter of imposing purpose on an object or practice in order to make it the best possible example of the form or genre to which it is taken to belong'.

13 For a sophisticated version of this caricature, see Davidson (1984, p.141): 'we interpret a bit of linguistic behaviour when we say what a speaker's words mean on an occasion of use'; and, perhaps, Schauer (1991, p.206): 'every application of the use of a term is an interpretation'.

14 Dummett (1986, p. 484): 'when the hearer does not have to search for the speaker's meaning, but takes for granted that he is using words in just the way with which he is familiar, there is ... no process of interpretation going on'; also Schauer (1991, p.207): 'Rules are normally unobtrusive and doing much of their work without inducing conscious interpretative doubt in the addressees'; Barnes (1988, pp.8–10), where she argues that if something is obvious to the reader she is not interpeting it; Wittgenstein (1968, 212e): 'it is easy to recognize cases in which we are interpreting. When we *interpret* we form hypotheses, which may prove false'. As Barnes notes, obviousness is not merely relative, for it is clear that we sometimes know that we know something, and this applies to some cases of language use. Marmor (1992, Chapter 2) takes it to be analytic to say that interpretation is a matter of seeking a speaker's communication intentions in situations where the meaning of a sentence is not determined by semantic rules. This is helpful but overly restrictive.

15 Thus Wroblweski (1992, p.122): 'Rule R has meaning M can be true or false in a determined language of legal discourse if it is relativised to the directives of interpretation and to evaluations, and if this relativism fulfils certain conditions.' These criteria are 'evaluative' but not necessarily direct moral judgments. This interpretative process is sometimes said to be 'real' judging: Perelman (1980, pp.143–4): 'there is no need for a judge where the rules lead everyone, provided no errors are committed, to the same solution and where correct rules of reasoning from indisputable premises exist. We need judges when these rules are equivocal, when reasoning does not end in a conclusion, but justifies a decision.'

16 See Raz (1975, Chapter 2).

17 Fish (1982, 1983).
18 See Hunt (1992, pp.33–9).
19 In the interests of presenting law as a system, Kelsen (1967) takes law to be a system of directives to law enforcers.
20 Thus *Regina* v. *Barnet* LBC ex p. Shah [1983] 2 AC 309, per Lord Scarman at 345:

> By giving the words their natural and ordinary meaning one helps to prevent the growth of a multiplication of refined and subtle distinctions in the law's use of common English words. Nothing is more confusing and more likely to bring statute law into disrepute than a proliferation by judicial intepretation of special meanings, when Parliament has not expressly enacted any.

21 See Cross (1987, p.14) and Pearce and Geddes (1988, p.16).
22 The idea of literal meaning is often made to look unduly simplistic or unattractive. Thus Summers (1992, 147): 'An interpretation is highly formal if it merely focuses on literal meanings of words or on the narrow confines of normative conduct or other phenomena to be interpreted ... it is less formal if it goes behind the words (or conduct etc.) into any relevant underlying substance reasoning to determinate meaning.' In particular, plain meaning is often castigated as ridiculous on the grounds that it assumes that there are 'objective' meanings which are 'out there' and independent of cultural context. No such assumptions are necessary. 'Plain', when applied to language, can only be relative to the meaning rules employed by the audience.
23 Thus, to cite just one example of the importance of context, in *Rex* v. *Liggetts-Findlay Drug Stores* [1919] 3 Western Weekly Reports 1025, where there is a simple ambiguity of 'close' as between 'close and stay closed' or 'close and open again'. The latter was rejected as 'absurd' but in fact it is a possible plain meaning. Yet, according to Stuart J.: 'no-one but a lawyer – I mean a person trained in legal technicalities such as a Judge or a lawyer – would ever think of imputing such a meaning to a by-law'. In fact, the 'absurdity' depends on an appreciation of the context of requiring shops to close at a certain hour late in the day. The purpose of the legislation of this sort is not difficult to determine and this is sufficient to resolve the ambiguity.
24 From *Sussex Peerage* (1844) 11 Cl & Fin 85 at 143.
25 The so-called 'Golden Rule' of statutory interpretation is that 'ordinary signification' is to be preferred 'unless when so applied they [the words construed all together] produce an inconsistency, or an absurdity or inconvenience so great as to convince the Court that the intention could not have been to use them in their ordinary signification, and to justify the Court in putting on them some other signification, which, though less proper, is one the Court thinks the words will bear'. See *River Wear Commissioners* v. *Adamson* (1877) 2 App.Cas.743 per Lord Blackburn at 764. Mere anomalies are not enough unless 'they produce an absurdity which Parliament could not have intended, or destroy the remedy established by Parliament to deal with the mischief which the Act is designed to combat' *Stock* v. *Frank Jones (Tipton) Ltd* [1978] 1 WLR 231, per Lord Scarman at 238). On the equally familiar 'Literal Rule' such absurdities are to be corrected by Parliament. Both are clearly prescriptive stances within judicial ethics. The reason given for the literal rule by Lord Bramwell in *Hill* v *East and West India Dock Co* (1984) 9 App Cas 448, 464 is that 'what seems absurd to one man does not seem absurd to another'.
26 There is an ambiguity in talk about 'hard' cases between the difficulty of understanding the language and the difficult of accepting unpalatable conseqences of the plain meaning. See Schauer (1988) and Marmor (1992).
27 See Murphy J. in *FCT* v. *Westraders Pty Ltd* (1980) 30 ALR 353 at 371. Thus Deane J. in *Westraders*:

> The result may seem both contrary to the general policy of the Act (if it be possible to discern any general policy other than that people pay income tax)

and unfair to the ordinary taxpayer who willingly or reluctantly contributes without resort to tax avoidance, the share of his net income which the parliament had determined is required by the nation for the common good. If there be, in truth, such contrariety or unfairness, the fault lies with the form of the legislation at the relevant time and not with the courts whose duty is to apply the words which the parliament has enacted. For a court to arrogate to itself, without legislative warrant, the function of overriding the plain words of the Act in any case where it considers that overall considerations of fairness or some general policy of the Act would be best served by a decision against the taxpayer would be to substitute arbitrary taxation for taxation under the rule of law and, indeed, to subvert the rule of law itself.'

28 This need not reduce to a narrow empiricist view according to which truth conditions must involve the decisiveness of sense observation but pragmatically it can serve as a recommendation that laws should be expressed if at all feasible in such 'observation sentences' (Quine, 1960). The weaker idea of 'assertability conditions' in which it is sufficient to indicate what kind of evidence is indicative of the truth of a sentence (Dummett, 1978) provides a more embracing theory of actual language but is not very helpful in the search for modes of expression which minimise semantic disagreement (Kripke, 1982).

29 Wilson (1992, p.8).

30 I take this to be the position adopted in Wittgenstein (1968). See Lewis (1969).

31 Wroblewski (1992, p.319): 'interpretation is not axiologically neutral, and the degree to which the interpreter follows the letter of the law depends on the directives of interpretation he uses'.

32 See Gabel (1980).

33 See Kennedy (1976).

34 This is what is meant by open-texture, at least by the originator of this overused catch-phrase: Waismann (1945). On the distinction between vagueness as a matter of fuzzy conceptual boundaries and vagueness as excessive generality, see Sorensen (1989).

35 Schauer (1992, p.213): 'Unless we embrace an implausibly particularist theory of meaning, under which the notion of meaning collapses into what a decision-maker in a particular environment should do on a particular occasion, it appears that Hart was correct. There are core meanings of rules (clear cases under the rule), even though they may not always be congruent with the core meaning of the ordinary language of the canonical formulation.'

36 Thus Fuller (1958, pp.662–3).

37 See *Potter* v. *Minahan* (1908) 7 CLR 277 at 121. Also *American Dairy Queen (Qld) Pty Ltd* v. *Blue Rio Pty Ltd* (1981) 37 ALR 613. *Hocking* v. *Western Australian Bank* (1909) 9 CLR 738 per Griffith C.J. at 746: 'It is a sound rule to be applied in the construction of all Acts altering the common law, that they are to be taken to alter it only so far as is necessary to give effect to the express provisions of the Act.' For a discussion of these and other cases, see Pearce and Geddes (1988, pp.104–6). See also Sunstein (1989, p.503): this 'would convert some hard cases into easy ones, by providing principles with which to determine cases that might otherwise be in equipoise'.

38 For broad definitions of purpose which provide no effective guidance for interpretation, consider the discussion of Emerson (1963, p.878) on the purpose of the First Amendment of the US Constitution as being 'to guarantee the maintenance of an effective system of free expression'.

39 For speaker's intent as what people mean by what they say, see Grice (1957). This is readily distinguishable from what the words mean to the audience. Even Grice does not say that meaning *is* intention. See also Dworkin (1986 p.50) on 'conversational interpretation', MacCallum (1970, p.239), and Schauer (1992, p. 215).

40 For an example, consider the ambiguity of 'cost' in *Pepper* v. *Hart* [1993] 1 All ER 42, HL(E). 351, a recent case in which the rule against judicial use of *Hansard* in the UK was overruled. Here it was unclear whether it was the average cost or marginal cost of providing a free service that was relevant for the tax objectives in question. See Walker (1993).

41 Stress on speaker's meaning fits best with personalised forms of Positivism which focus on the model of the commands of the powerful: Posner (1986). Evidently, there are some areas of law, such as succession, where there are special reasons to establish speaker's meaning. Identifying these areas is a matter of substantive jurisprudence: Schauer (1992, p. 221).

42 Thus Atiyah (1986, pp.24ff) considers the judgment of Lord Simon of Glaisdale in the House of Lords in *Black-Clawson International* v. *Papierwerke Waldhof-Aschaffenburg A.G. [1975] AC591,* which concerns the interpretation of a statute giving effect to the report of a committee. Simon seems to allow for interpretations which conflict with what Parliament clearly intended in the sense of legislators' intent, for he says it is the words not the intention that count; arguing from costs, expectations of citizens and good drafting, he contends that it is the words which give the intention. Atiyah agrees for the most part, on the grounds that statutes are not passed lightly and are the formal expression of Parliament's will. This is what he means by formalism. Atiyah treats precedent as being different in so far as there is the assumed possibility of distinguishing apparently similar fact situations, but with higher courts the outcome is much the same when finality is important, as with a declaration of legitimacy: *Russell* v. *Russell* [1924] AC687. Interestingly, Atiyah (pp.43f), noting the trend to go beyond formal reasons to substantive ones in relation to the substantive fairness of a contract, considers that this arises from the realisation that the fairness of the price is not in general properly considered elsewhere in the process, as it would have been with good legislative practice.

43 For an uncontentious example of how a straightforward knowledge of context can help clear up an ambiguity, consider legislation limiting the hours of work being used against a person found ironing his own shirt during the proscribed hours: *Ingham* v. *Hie Lee* (1912) 15 CLR 267. See Pearce and Geddes (1988, pp.25f).'Literalism' is sometimes identified with the idea of trying to read rules outside of their evident context of application. Consider examples noted in Wilson (1992) of absurd literal meanings, as when picking up a Chinese take-away meal is argued to be 'loading' a vehicle (*Boulton* v. *Pilkinton* [1981] RTR 87) or that an intentional car crash is not an 'accident' (*Chief Constable of Staffordshire* v. *Lees* [1981] RTR 506).

44 MacCallum (1970, p.239) makes the legislative purpose the sixth possible meaning of 'legislative intent' to cover 'what he intended the statute to achieve'. On p.241, he notes the 'major source of confusion has been the belief that we must always guide our understanding of statutory words by an understanding of legislative purposes, as though we could not understand the words without prior knowledge of the purposes'.

45 Ibid., p.242.

46 Thus there is a tendency to confuse MacCallum's sense 7 – 'his interest in enacting the statute' – with sense 5 – 'how he intended the words to be understood'. MacCallum (1986, pp.239–40).

47 MacCallum (1970, p.270): 'Once it has been stated it provides part of the institutionalized background against which legislators recognize themselves to be acting when proposing, investigating, discussing and voting for bills.' For what this may involve, see Walker (1993) which discusses the position adopted in *Pepper* whereby there may now, in the United Kingdom, be judicial use of *Hansard* and clear statements by a minister or promoter of a bill if there is ambiguity, obscurity or absurdity involved. Of course, it has long been acceptable to look to the 'mis-

chief' leading to an alteration in the legal status quo (from *Heydon's* case) and legislative history has been extensively used in the United States since 1940. See *United States* v. *American Trading Association*, 30 US 534 (1940). There is currently some back-pedalling on this matter, particularly when the natural meaning is not in doubt. Thus Justices Scalia and Blackman: 'when we find the terms of the statute unambiguous, judicial enquiry should be complete except in rare and exceptional circumstances' (*Freytag* v. *Commissioner*, 111 S.Ct 2631 (1991) 1636).

48 MacCormick and Summers (1992, p. 520). Compare Henry Hart and D. Sacks, *The Legal Process: Basic Problems in the Making and Application of Law* (text ed. 1958), the central document in the so-called 'legal process school', which argues for an examination of what legislators intended to achieve through looking at reports and other documentation. There is clearly a danger in this of reconstructing a view ascribed to 'rational' legislators with 'good' purposes, yet, if we can see what they were publicly expounding, and even appreciate the political deal involved in the legislation, if it is honest (as is required for the Economic Analysis of Law and Public Choice Theory), then we are on the track of the actual intentions in a legitimate form.

49 [1942] AC206.

50 Ibid., p.256.

51 Of course, an interpretative principle may license the use of specified statements or conventions of basic or human rights.

52 Bell (1986, p.47): 'Even a fairly elementary understanding of the purpose of tort law would reveal that there is no tenable distinction between the rules of liability governing floor-layers and those governing electricians.'

53 Schauer (1992, p.222).

54 See *The King* v. *Barger* (1908) 6 CLR 41, 67. Recent House of Lords reasoning shows a tendency to ignore the words of the Act and the traditional principles of construction and resort to general principle in an open-ended way. Thus *W T Ramsay Ltd.* v. *IRC* [1982] AC 300 and *Furniss* v. *Dawson* [1984] AC 474. See Wilson (1992, pp.7–8).

55 Thus the Land Tax (Revision) Act 1991 (Victoria) has as its purpose clause 'the purpose of this Act is to make certain amendments to, and revision of, the Land Tax Act 1988'.

56 I am indebted to Mr Jonathan Woodger for this point and related materials.

57 See Fuller (1957–58, pp.662–3).

58 This rather crude summary of the end-point reached in Dworkin (1986) is endorsed by a number of the essays in Hunt (1992). Dworkin presents a legal theory in competition with LEP in so far as it is openly a systematic value commitment, in his case to a form of justice based on fundamental moral rights. In principle, the Herculean method of legal reasoning recommended by Dworkin could meet the Positivists' need for a line of judicial action when confronted with bad or no law since it does offer a prospect of a right answer which is in theory knowable to all legal participants. However, this prospect is not fulfilled because of the element of moral reasoning involved in his method of 'law as interpretation' whereby the adjudicator is required to consider which construction of the law not only coheres or fits with existing law but, within these constraints, gives the best moral reading, in that it is capable of the most acceptable moral justification in the context of law as a whole, given what we take to be its best purpose. In fact such innovative 'interpretation' (in his terminology 'constructive interpretation') is an interesting and valuable enterprise in art and literature but has little to do with the communication as distinct from the adoption of regulative political choices. In the end the ultimate dominance of the 'best that it can be' criterion in the theory is enough to remove Dworkin's approach from the LEP camp. See Campbell (1988b, Chapter 2); also Westmorland (1991, p.174): 'Law as integrity, Ronald Dworkin's theory of

jurisprudence, often requires judges to make highly controversial decisions that have no roots either in popular morality or in the understanding of the authors of the black-letter law which judges are pledged to interpret'; and Sheldon Leader, 'Impartiality, Bias and the Judiciary', in Hunt (1992, p.249).

59 There are special features involved in constitutional interpretation which are only touched on in this chapter, but the political uses of literalism are as common as they are with respect to purposive approaches. See Craven (1992), Galligan (1987) and Zines (1992, pp.371–5).

60 See Llewellyn (1934, 1233–41).

61 Hence the need to present descriptive Positivism in a weakened form in which almost anything can be part of a rule of recognition: see Waluchow (1994).

62 See pp.69–72.

63 See pp.17–18.

64 For a collection of central theoretical essays on this topic, see Tushnet (1993).

65 Thus Ackerman (1984).

66 See Sunstein (1993a).

67 Thus Cardozo (1921, p.113) says that judges 'fill the open spaces in the law'. See also Raz (1979, pp.70–77).

68 Thus Kelsen (1992, p.84): 'Genuine gaps ... do not exist' for a decision can always be made not to allow a claim. According to Schauer (1992, p.222) the problem of gaps is not a problem of interpretation but what to do with gaps. He argues that gaps are the product of the conjunction of two distinct conditions in the system: the purport to be comprehensive and the absence of a closure rule.

69 Barak (1987, p.7): 'discretion is the power given to persons with authority to choose between two or more alternatives, when each of the alternatives is lawful'. On Dworkin's view this is 'strong discretion', which is never required or authorised since every legal issue has a correct answer. The only discretion that judges have is to decide what that right answer might be.

70 Posner (1985, pp.280–89): 'Imagine as best he can how the legislators who enacted the statute would have wanted it applied to situations they did not foresee.'

71 This is the Austinian line. See Collins in MacCormick and Birks (1986). Thus the appeal to 'contemporary standards' in *Gregg* v. *Georgia* 428 US 153 (1976). For the view that this is unrealistic, see Bell (1983).

72 In Campbell (1988a), my initial essay on Ethical Positivism, I gave this thesis more emphasis and endorsement than I do here.

73 The failure of impartiality to deliver a complete methodology for making moral choices is a recurrent theme of moral philosophy. For examples of failed attempts see Smith (1976), Kant (1948), Hare (1963) and Rawls (1972).

74 For an impressive and sustained effort to work out some such line, see MacCormick (1978). See also Bernstein (1978).

7 Humane Rights and Freedom of Expression

Introduction

The discussion of interpretation in the previous chapter shows that interpretation in the strict sense, that is the selection of meanings from a fairly narrow range of possible alternatives, requires that the rules to be interpreted are specific enough to be related to actual situations and relatively clear in terms of the normal contexts of their use.[1] Where this is not so, because, for instance, they are no more than broad abstractions or contain ambiguities which relate to relevant points of dispute, then the creativity required by 'intepretation', in some looser sense, a creativity which is essential if the rules are to be applied to concrete cases, can be seen as the exercise of political (or perhaps simply arbitrary) judgment by adjudicators who, thereby, become de facto legislators. The conclusion that a certain limited degree of legislative power is inevitable, and often desirable as an interim solution to immediate legal problems, contains the proviso that such delegated legislation or bounded discretion be subject to review by elected legislatures. It follows that a legal system which approximates to the model of Ethical Positivism can have no place for highly general statements of rights which can be used by judiciaries to overrule otherwise valid legislation.

As a political philosophy, LEP contains many affirmations of basic rights. These feature, for instance, in the legitimation of the state and the justification of rule governance to empower and delimit government activities.[2] What LEP rejects is that the articulation or 'creative interpretation' of these rights is a task for judicial authority. Where this occurs massive political power is given to a small number of non-accountable persons in circumstances which tend to produce substantive rights which are often protective of vested interests threatened by government regulation and frequently restrictive of positive efforts by government to deal with the inequalities and inhumanities which flourish in modern societies. Humane and effective basic rights require a greater degree of democratic responsiveness and initiative than courts can be expected to provide.[3]

LEP has no problem with the idea of overriding rights based on fundamental human interests shared by all persons. Indeed, one of the virtues of LEP is that it requires that we make clear the hierarchy of rules in cases of conflict and identify the obligations whose performance gives effect to rights. Moreover, it makes no assumption that basic rights must be stated in such broad and loose terms that their meaningfulness and hence their usefulness is always at risk. Thus a relatively precise right, such as the right not to be killed, except in precisely delineated circumstances, can override lesser rights of other people, like the right to enter into contracts. Often such overriding is simply a matter of giving a precise exception to less specific rights, as when the right of one person to communicate is limited by right of another to preserve her good name. However, human rights are characteristically not only overriding (by definition) but also very general, such as the right to own property and the right to freedom of religion, as befits a rhetoric originating in revolutionary politics. In these cases the process of concretising a right to give it sufficient specificity to have an impact on an actual situation is essentially to create rules that have some evident connection with particular fact situations. Where such general overriding rules are used to strike down relatively specific legislation then we have judicial legislation which, on the Positivist model, is an abuse of judicial power and a standing danger to the concretised rights on which reliance can be based.[4]

The undoubted attractions of court-centred Bills of Rights have their chief ideological base in hostility to government, a hostility which, as the paradox of politics makes clear, has substantial basis. The 'downside' of institutionalising basic rights under the control of judiciaries is that this places responsibility for the specification of these rights in the wrong place. The ethical perspective from which human rights are articulated is too narrow, and too detached, to be an expression of the will of the ultimate political sovereignty which resides in populace as a whole. Of course, this may be a selling point for those who distrust majority opinion and have a strong belief in the moral superiority of persons with a professional legal education. It also accords with the idea that a major point of having human rights is to protect minorities against majorities. However, it is simplisitic to view courts as inherently better able to protect minority interests, particularly where these are threatened by private power based on social and economic advantage.[5] LEP does accept that courts have an important role in protecting minorities by requiring rule governance, but, beyond this, the positivist view is that a humane and equal society is best achieved by institutionalising the basic right to government, including the right to render specific the overriding rights of citizens, through the primary democratic process as an essential part of community self-determination. While 'Bills of Rights' may seem to offer an easy way out of the paradox of politics, if these are entrenched against effective democratic review by legislatures, then they undermine the most basic of the rights they are created to protect.

The problem is compounded when the rights in question have no clear purpose and hence it is difficult to use the purposive reasoning which we have conceded may be helpful for the attainment of positivist ends in those cases where a clear legislative purpose can be found. While some human rights, such as the right to life, approach this ideal, since they are clearly intended to prevent the evil identified in the rule, others, such as freedom of expression, have a more instrumentalist role in political discourse, but no agreed purpose lies behind them. And even in the case of the right to life, a court-centred system will tend to concentrate on the right not to be killed at the expense of government measures to save and prolong life by positive measures and protect the individual against the life-threatening impact of private power and public neglect. For such reasons, whatever the initial attractions of constitutionally protected overriding rights administered by courts, they are clearly suspect from the positivist standpoint. Judge-controlled Bills of Rights threaten the values of freedom and efficiency with which we began this analysis.[6]

Of course, very general rights can be rendered more specific by developing case law with the Common Law methods, producing a bank of precedents to render more specificity to rights at the moment of application to specific circumstances. It is also possible to draw on the vast international jurisprudence on human rights which has been built up around the United Nations, the European Convention of Human Rights and the constitution of the United States. But these constitute no cohesive body of law. Much of their content is so unspecific as to be unjusticiable by positivist standards. And where there are fixed points, as in the case law surrounding the US Supreme Court, or the European Court of Human Rights, they are as contentious and parochial as any other pieces of legislation.

It follows that, accepting the notion of human rights as having an important role in political and legal debate, we must be wary of any system which depends to any great extent on the interpretion of abstract or very general constitutional rights. This chapter develops this thesis, first in the round, and then more pointedly in relation to recent development in Australian constitutional law with respect to freedom of expression.

Rights and Human Rights

The idea of human rights is at this time so well accepted and internationally utilised that it is difficult to acknowledge just how flimsy are its philosophical foundations.[7] While it can hardly be politically correct to express grave doubts about such a venerated aspect of western political tradition, we cannot evade confronting the practical fallout of this philosophical weakness. In particular, the absence of any reputable methodology for determining the content and scope of human rights means that it is rash to subject ourselves to the largely unchallengeable authority of courts by giving them the power to decide on our behalf some of the most important moral and political issues affecting modern life.

There is, however, an approach to rights which takes on board this epistemological weakness without abandoning the central contention of the rights' view. This, the prescriptive positivist approach, acknowledges that there are certain important values, both ethical and humane, which ought to be ascribed political priority and deserve particular protection, often in the form of secure, specific, overriding and precisely administered rules.[8]

The standard view is that rights are *moral* entitlements and human rights are those moral entitlements which are the possession of *all persons everywhere*.[9] Traditionally it is argued that, either through a careful examination of what it means to be human or by attending to allegedly self-evident moral truths about what it is to be a moral agent, it is feasible to come up with a specification of such rights, rights which are seen as indefeasible moral claims against all other persons and more especially against governments.[10] These claims are held to be so strong that there is scarcely any reason for failing to respect them absolutely, and to give rise to duties so basic that their neglect denies any government, even a formally democratic one, its legitimacy.

This idea of human rights as indefeasible moral rights, the valued moral entitlements of all persons, expresses the vision of individual pre-political rights which dates from the beginnings of the modern state and serves as its legitimating and limiting basis. In this tradition, the state is formed to protect human (or natural) rights and is restricted by this remit with respect both to its objectives and its methods.[11] The notion of knowable basic moral entitlements for all persons is immensely attractive even if its attempted instantiations have proved distressingly vacuous on both historical and geographical parameters. Inconveniently, what has seemed evident at least to some people at particular times and places does not appear that way to others, particularly if they are spatially or temporally disparate. Moreover, these 'self-evident' moral rights have been recruited in the service of repression and reaction as well as of reform. Thomas Hobbes was only the first to start with hopeful-looking premisses about individual inalienable rights, only to end up with almost total subservience to political authority. Even his residual natural right of self-defence is one which is now frequently used to legitimate acts of war under international law.[12]

And so, although some agreement can be reached on highly indeterminate affirmations of rights to such matters as life, liberty and happiness, even these allegedly timeless and placeless moral truths have not withstood philosophical criticism of their epistemological base. Nothing within the functionalities of reason or sense has been identified as a reliable mode of moral apprehension of even these simple affirmations. This becomes evident as soon as we try to be specific as to what such basic rights actually involve. Little by way of detailed agreement has arisen to make the hypothesis of available moral truths plausible. Only part of what is natural to humankind has a clear claim to be good and right, and we disagree radically as to what part this is. Moral intuition has proved an elusive facility with no identifiable reality beyond the personal subjective certainties that lead us to posit such mysterious paths to knowledge in the first place. Assertions of clear and comprehensive universal entitlements have not stood up well against the vast diversity and range of human belief systems and social practices. Long before we were caught up in the ironic detachments of postmodernism, universal moral rights seemed intellectually vacuous in their epistemological foundations and possibly morally suspect in their anti-pluralistic imperialism.

Whether or not human rights are intellectually defensible or culturally tolerant, we do have need of them, at least at the edges of civilisation and in the tangle of international politics. They now have an undeniably important role as the basis for international criticism of evil regimes and are a constant source of inspiration for the protection of individual liberty rights and increasingly for challenges to the inadequate responses of governments to soluble deprivations. The single most important impetus to our contemporary system of human rights was the Nuremberg war crimes trials, from which emerged the United Nations framework that is now being brought to bear on the atrocities in Bosnia–Herzegovina. And increasingly it is to human rights that we look to provide a transnational basis for world order, a basis that cannot be had without a certain commitment to recognising the internationally agreed systems of human rights within all national boundaries.[13]

These developments are, however, doomed to disappointment if they proceed on the basis of a flawed model of rights which underplays the difficulty of arriving at defensible agreement as to the content of human rights and legitimates giving the power of defining their content and force to persons whose skills are legal rather than political and whose authority is professional rather than democratic. What is required is an alternative philosophical basis according to which rights in general and human rights in particular can be seen as empty and malleable forms which we can shape, and into which we can pour such content as we choose, in the light of such agreement as we can attain with respect to our basic values and the specific ways in which we can instantiate them within the particular social and political environment we inhabit.[14]

The prescriptive positivist approach to rights starts out from a more sociological, less rationalistic, stance and asks what social practices give substance to the discourse of rights. It prompts us to ask: what is the political benefit in being the acknowledged bearer of a right? And it leads us on to consider how to institutionalise the communal embodiment of humane and autonomy values within this framework. From this perspective a right is seen as a normatively protected interest, it being an open matter which interests receive such protection and precisely what that protection involves.[15] By 'interest' is meant anything that a conscious being is capable of being interested in ('first order interests') or anything which is causally related to the protection of such conscious subjective interests ('second order interests'), there being no prior assumption that all first order interests are equally or even minimally deserving of protection. This is what provides the strong individualistic associations of rights discourse.

By 'normatively protected' is meant recognised in those rules or standards or principles which are effective within a community, either in relation to informal expectations ('societal or community rights') or in the official regulator system of a group or society ('legal rights'). 'Protected' here refers to some sort of systematic social or legal response which legitimates and promotes the exercise of the interest in question as well as systematic criticism and correction of (in)actions which interfere with or fail to promote that interest. Standardly, this involves the recognition and enforcement of a rule-defined duty which is laid on others with respect to that interest. This protection involves, at the very least, a prima facie case to permit those activities which involve the pursuit of the protected interest ('liberty rights') and against actions which are in some way contrary to its realisation ('claim rights'). At the most developed it may involve unconditional correlative duties to ensure that the objective of the interest in question is realised ('positive' as distinct from 'negative' claim rights).[16]

This essential element in the concept of a right is grounded in the same analysis as was applied to rules. Indeed, rights simply are rule-protected interests.[17] Rules have the function in decision making of removing certain factors which would otherwise be relevant from consideration, and identifying those matters which alone are to be treated as relevant. This analysis applies to action-guiding rules in general; the sub-class of rights rules are those where the rules in question are construed or justified as defending or furthering the interests of those persons who are the bearers of the rights in question and the beneficiaries of any correlative duties involved.

For there to be any sort of right, the rule protecting the interest must exclude at least some countervailing considerations which might, if it were not for the right, possibly override it. In this dimension rights may vary from having very weak overriding thresholds to near absolute ones. While there can be no sharp distinction between rights and human rights in this respect, human rights are at the absolute end of this continuum and are therefore relatively invulnerable to being overridden by other considerations, including other rights.

The idea of human rights, on this analysis, presupposes that there are certain interests common to everyone everywhere which ought to be given (at least near) overriding significance when they conflict with anything else, including interests of lesser significance. Of course, strict universality and great significance do not necessarily go hand in hand, but the idea of human rights requires that at least some highly valued interests are universal ones, and vice versa. So much so that these universal interests are often taken to be constitutive of what it is to be a human being. This scheme is neutral as between other important variables, such as (a) the scope of the right in terms of the precise delineation of the interest in question; (b) the existence of a correlative duty, if any; (c) whether this duty is a negative duty to refrain from damaging the interests in question, or a positive duty to further its fulfilment; (d) the power, if any, of the right holder to waive or claim that right; and (e) the mechanisms involved in so doing.

All this has a strong positivist flavour since the idea of rights is related to interests which are recognised and furthered by positive rules or other actually operable normative standards. It may therefore be thought to be inimical to moral rights and hence to human rights as a sub-class of moral rights. By excluding the rights which people in some mysterious way already have solely by virtue of an objective morality which is independent of its human recognition – social or legal – we would appear to be precluded from developing a theory of human rights as those rights which are the moral possession of all persons.

In fact, the positivist analysis does not prevent us claiming that there are some rights which *ought* to be the actual possessions of all people. There may be absolute positive rights that morally ought to be guaranteed to everyone. Indeed, it is only the positivist analysis that enables us to give substance and political point to such prescriptive contentions. It is possible to formulate this position by saying that everyone *does* have such (moral) rights, rather than that they *ought* to have such (positive) rights. However, the point of making such assertions is to argue that these 'moral rights' ought to be accepted into particular societies or social groups (ordinary rights) or ought to be recognised in the case of all human beings (human rights), and the argument that people ought to have certain rights is not in general assisted by the assertion that they already have them. Moreover, the possession of moral rights is of no value unless they are positivised and nothing significant is lost by translating statements about the existence of such moral rights into statements about the social or legal rights that ought to be recognised and enforced. It is therefore both clarificatory and pragmatic to interpret statements about moral rights as statements about the positive rights that ought to exist.

This Benthamite reductive analysis of rights has the advantage that it brings out the fact that the significance of rights derives from an operative system of norms to which appeal can be made to instantiate a claim or resist the conduct of others in real social and political situations. The value of rights is that, if we have them, this prevents others from thwarting our interests or failing to facilitate them in specified ways, a mechanism which does not work unless the rule is generally recognised as binding and routinely followed or enforced as such. Rights are important because they enable us to reduce our vulnerability to the conduct-justifying arguments of others in particular instances and makes available reliable cooperative support by asserting the recognised claim which renders such argument irrelevant.

The positivist account is not in itself morally superior to a natural law conception, but it does give defensible sense to a distinctive role for the language of rights, namely to argue from the existence of a social norm to the validity of a claim to the protection or furtherance of interests, an important mode of social practice. Unless so-called 'moral rights' are encapsulated in societally recognised norms, the language of rights loses its distinctive role in societal organisation and becomes simply another way of referring to a value-based reason indicating why we ought to be treated in one way rather than another. Such rights do not trump other moral considerations, they simply compete with them.

All this may be thought to ignore the moral depths of rights language by failing to bring out that the rights approach to morality involves a specific form of morality which provides distinctive reasons why there should be positive rights and perhaps much else besides. Indeed, the positivist account of human rights may seem appallingly poverty-stricken from the moral point of view. Of itself it provides no basis for the criticism of positive rights, be they legal or social. It provides no way of distinguishing those rights which are human from the common or garden rights of everyday legal existence. And it leaves no room for using the language of moral rights to recommend policies which do not involve the instantiation of positive rights.[18]

It may be argued that a significant conception of human rights must identify something of what it is that prompts us to institute the appropriate positive rights or adopt preferred policy objectives. Thus, if we are discussing the right to park my car in the street, for instance, we may argue that I ought to be so entitled for a variety of reasons, such as that it will give me pleasure and harm no one else, or that I own the street, or that this right will further my personal development. That is, rights-justifying arguments may appeal (a) to utility (the increase in pleasure they bring), (b) to positive law (such as ownership), or (c) to personal moral values (such as self-development). It is often argued that only the third type of reason is really a rights reason. Mere positive rights may be justified by other positive rights or by utilitarian arguments, but 'real' rights are based on specific types of values, values perhaps of humanity, but more likely of moral choice, or self-development, or autonomy, since these are the values that are regarded as being unique to humans. This narrower, specific type of moral reason is required, it is said, to explain the distinctive role of rights discourse: the protection of the individual against the predations of despotic power, majoritarian or otherwise, the delineation of an area within which we can be human beings. With respect to freedom of speech, it may be argued that this is a human right because speech is a necessary part of an autonomous human existence and any diminution of speech takes away from an activity which is of the essence of human nature. With similar arguments all human rights may be traced to aspects of human flourishing with respect to those properties which make us distinctively human, particularly the capacities of reason and moral choice.

There is every reason to articulate the values which might prompt us to instantiate or maintain priority positive rights, but there are more powerful reasons for refusing to identify these values as themselves human rights. In the first place, this encourages the mistaken idea that such meta-rights have the specificity which we aspire to in the formulation of good positive rights, that is rights which are of use to us. But since we cannot read off from values such as moral agency any particular duties sufficiently detailed to make them candidates for acceptable positive law, that is a law whose meaning is sufficiently clear for us to determine without dependence on the moral valuations of others, it is not clear what protection and support is available from the normative order of our society.

A positivist account of rights is a formal one and requires to be substantiated by value-directed political choices which render operationally precise the sort of conduct which we believe will embody that interpretation of our values that we wish to adopt. However, the particular account of rights (as protected interests) that I have outlined can be used to give individual interests a central place within political philosophy and, in so far as this is the case, the account is rights-based simply because it regards individual interests as an ultimate locus of value. But this does not mean that there is some sort of super-right from which we deduce the value centrality of individual interests.[19]

What the positivist approach to rights can and should involve is a commitment to discussion and decision in which it is an accepted premiss that individual interests are what count and that the choice between these should be on morally relevant grounds which respect the equal worth of everyone. Spelling out what this involves is not, however, principally a matter of drawing up a Bill or Charter of Rights, although these may be a useful first step in articulating the value-protecting goals. Rather, the definition and selection of what rights are to be human rights is a process which should inform every political activity. Nothing specific follows uncontroversially from the idea of equal worth itself, an assumption which needs to be brought into conjunction with the selection of precious human interests and priority modes of human relationships. That this is not a matter of purely utilitarian investigation and calculation may serve to dignify it with the label of a rights-based approach, but it does not support the contention that there are existing fundamental moral rights from which we can deduce the proper content of positive rights.[20] Further, identifying rights with values which may lie behind positive human rights can, not accidentally, lead to a very restricted conception of the values which are relevant to the choice of human rights. More particularly, it focusses on the values of autonomy rather than the disvalues of suffering, the deontologies of liberty rather than the disutilities of inhumanity. The emphasis of moral rights rhetoric is on moral agency rather than human distress and the autonomy values serve to displace the more humane and mundane ones.

The tendency to overemphasise moral agency over humanity arises in part because it is easier to identify non-consequentialist values as absolute because their significance is not so dependent on any calculations of consequence which might turn up some countervailing factors. Thus, if free speech is based on the inherent dignity of speech, or the value of self-expression for its own sake, then there is no need to enquire into whether it has good or bad consequences. Its absolute status seems all the more secure thereby. And yet, in the sphere of freedom of communication, it is clear that the most powerful arguments for institutionalised protection of speech are highly consequentialist appeals to the social utility of truth and the adequate functioning of representative democracy.[21]

Making a choice of fundamental rights, therefore, requires recourse to a variety of value bases and a multiplicity of consequentialist considerations. This takes us far indeed from a world in which we can intuit the content of human rights into a much messier situation in which we need to consider, not the abstract idea of the freedom of speech, but the proper content of defamation law, the details of the regulation of political advertising, the better protection of whistleblowers, the consequences of pornography, the value of parliamentary privilege, and so on. It is possible to see the human rights movement as an attempt to identify these basic values and implement them in an egalitarian way in operable rules, in principle for all actual societies but primarily for our own and cognate ones. This approach to rights is not only compatible with Positivism, it actually requires such a theoretical basis. It requires that we pursue an ideal of rules that are specific enough to guard us against empty rhetoric and hopelessly fuzzy conceptual edges, and are defined in ways which make them as protected as possible from the moralising or self-interested interpretations of their administrators.

This positivist ideal can incorporate human rights as rights which have priority in that, in cases of conflict or doubt, they prevail over lesser rights. For this to be effective, human rights must be expressed in terms of a hierarchy of rules in the articulation of which Positivism excels. Further, Legal Positivism more than accommodates the idea that there are rights which belong to all, for there is nothing inherently vague in such an idea, provided that we specify their application at the debatable margins, such as when human life begins and ends.

Positivism also has the virtue of opening up for discussion the choice between the different possible ways of securing political and legal priority for certain selected interests. In the democratic form of Positivism with which we are dealing, what matters is that the processes of arriving at the specification and implementation of human rights be a dialogue which results in difficult choices being made in a democratically legitimate manner, rather than being imposed as the end-point of a specialist professional discourse aimed at eliciting the correct meaning of some simple formulations, or an appeal to the abstractions of 'justice' or intuited moral rights, or some extrapolation from a highly general concept such as 'responsible government' or 'contract'.

The method for reaching politically acceptable determinations of what a society is adopting and adapting from its social practices as human rights and precisely what that entails is not derived from any positivist dogma as to the legitimate expression of the will which emanates in law. However, in its democratic versions, at any rate, it can be closely associated with the ideal of political dialogue, whether in terms of the rather abstract Rawlsian method of reflective equilibrium[22] or of an imaginary constitutional dialogue as conceived by Ackerman,[23] or, less speculatively, of the Habermasian strategy of uncoerced dialogue in conditions of free and equal debate.[24] Whatever precise methodology is adopted, what is crucial is that they be part of the mainstream political process rather than a part of democratically peripheral legal argument centred on a limited and limiting document.

The Articulation of Human Rights

The arguments concerning the proper locus of decision making with regard to the articulation of basic rights come under four adjectival headings: (a) epistemological, (b) democratic, (c) ideological, and (d) positivistic. These represent four types of argument against implied or explicit court-articulated fundamental rights. The example I take by way of illustration is *Australian Capital Television Pty Ltd* v. *The Commonwealth* (1992),[25] in which the plaintiff challenged Part IIID of the *Broadcasting Act* 1942 (Cth) introduced into the Act by the Political Broadcasts and Political Disclosures Act 1991. Part IIID prohibits political advertising on radio or television during an election period but allows for politically oriented radio programmes and the allocation of free television time for political parties. It was held by the High Court that 'Pt IIID was invalid in its entirety because of its severe impairment of the freedoms previously enjoyed by citizens to discuss public and political affairs and to criticise federal institutions – freedoms embodied by constitutional implication in an implied guarantee of freedom of communication as to public and political discussion'.[26]

We are dealing here with alleged implications within a federal constitution rather than the interpretation of an overt Bill of Rights, but the structural features of the case are essentially similar with respect to the analysis of what is going on in the dynamics of such a decision. In both cases authoritative constitutional words are being interpreted in the context of the alleged invalidity of an exercise of legislative power. Maybe it is more controversial to find a Bill of Rights within a constitution from which the drafters consciously excluded a Bill of Rights, but we may let that pass for the moment.

Many of the arguments apply with even greater force to the more extreme argument, recently propounded by one member of the High Court, to the effect that implied human rights may be derived from the Common Law 'freedoms' which were assumed to have normative supremacy at the time the Constitution was approved.[27]

The Epistemological Argument

The confidence with which human rights enthusiasts approve the adoption of court-centred fundamental rights is based on unsupportable assumptions about the distinctive epistemology of human rights. Only the assumed uncontroversial nature of content of human rights enables us to hold that courts are able to identify, in a non-partisan way, certain fundamental rights which may then be superimposed on normal political decision making so as to keep the latter within its proper bounds. The justification for the courts being involved in this way is that they have the requisite skills for fact finding and are used to applying given rules in a manner which is impartial enough to command our respect. All this rests on unsupportable ideas about the nature and justification of rights, namely that human rights may be captured in relatively pellucid and simple rules. The prime task in securing human rights is thus viewed, not as knowing what these rights are, but in seeing that they are observed and remedies for their contravention implemented. Thus it is assumed that we all know what torture is, and we all agree that torture is never justified; the remaining – and demanding – task is to find out when torture happens and provide mechanisms for its prevention.

This model of human rights as an intuited or agreed set of absolute prohibitions – which we may call the torture model – has important uses in the exposure of human rights abuses by such agencies as Amnesty International, and is of considerable importance in the realm of international relations, but it has little relevance to the pursuit of human rights in countries such as Australia. Once we move on from prohibitions on the grosser barbarities to the articulation of policies within a basically humane system we soon discover that the content and form of even the least controversial rights is a matter of some difficulty and no agreed methodology. Does the right to life exclude capital punishment? Does it require the best available emergency medical care at no cost to the indigent? Does it give a right of action against a department of state that fails to prevent deadly child abuse? Indeed, as soon as we try to lift our standards from crude extremes, even the definition of 'torture' becomes problematic in relation to aggressive methods of interrogation and disgusting prison conditions.

Further, there is no simple way in which such rights as are agreed have the form of absolute prohibitions on certain types of wrongful conduct. With highly indeterminate formulations, exceptions are always allowed, especially in situations of conflicts with other rights. Absolutist formulations are fine in political rhetoric but they are always qualified in any formulations accepted by governments. In either case, in practice there will be many exceptions. So the vaunted absoluteness of human rights is no special protection until the specifics have been spelt out and difficult choices made. Nor, unless we endorse an extreme libertarian ideology, are the correlative duties confined to negative ones of non-interference and inaction, so there is no agreement on the form of rights either.[28] In fact, our consensus on human rights goes little further than a common cherishing of certain very important human interests which we value highly, and a commitment to some form of human equality and a highly unspecific notion of what is fair. These broad ideals are almost meaningless until they are worked out in detail in relation to different areas of activity and the endless competing priorities are brought into some form of working relationship. These values are inevitably socially acquired and articulated and we can only choose within the options our cultural context enables us to express. It follows that participation in the process of articulation and choice should be one of the most prized ideals of the human rights tradition, not simply the spectator sport that it becomes when these crucial choices are left to litigants, lawyers and courts.

Ostensibly, *Capital Television* does not appear to be in the business of making political judgments based on the moral intuitions of the judges. Rather, what appears to be going on is the working out of the presuppositions of the idea of 'representative government' the explicit datum of the Constitution from which the relevant implied fundamental right is to be deduced. The determination of these presuppositions may be regarded as a factual matter within the normal provenance of judicial activity. Is the questionable legislation destructive of something that is causally necessary for representative government? The court approaches these issues in two stages, first arguing that there is an implied right of freedom of political communication, and then going on to the view that Part IIID violates that right in an unacceptable manner. In the first leg of the argument Mason C.J. contends:

> The point is that the representatives who are members of Parliament and Ministers of State are not only chosen by the people but exercise their legislative and executive powers as representatives of the people. And in the exercise of those powers the representatives of necessity are accountable to the people for what they do and have a responsibility to take account of the views of the people on whose behalf they act. Indispensable to that accountability and that responsibility is

freedom of communication, at least in relation to public affairs and political discussion.[29]

In other words, freedom of communication is indispensable to representative government.

This argument is unexceptionable if it is simply an assertion that some communication is a prerequisite of political representation but it does not establish some specific set of rights (dubbed 'freedom of communication') that is indispensable in this regard. Indeed, it may be plausible to say that the more communication there is the more representative the system will be, so that in a fully representative system there will be maximal communication. Mason C.J. says something like this: 'Absent such freedom of communication, representative government would fail to achieve its purpose of government of the people through their elected representatives; government would cease to be responsive to the need and wishes of the people and, in that sense, to be *truly* representative.'[30] However, what he refers to is not actual or maximal communication but 'freedom' of communication, that is, some notion of normative order bearing on the governance of communication.

It is at this point that the assumption is made that the court simply 'knows' what this normative freedom of communication amounts to. The fundamental right is in this sense 'intuited' or, more accurately, taken as uncontroversially clear and beyond question. The 'intuited' moral judgment comes when the court simply discounts the corrupting influence of money in the election process, a corruption which does affect the equal competition of ideas which could be regarded as what freedom of communication is meant to be all about. The majority of the court 'knows' that what is involved in Part IIID is a limitation of freedom of communication rather than an enhancement of it. The issue is dogmatically assumed to be freedom of communication versus competing public interests, such as political corruption.[31] The same confidence in the ability of the court to know what freedom of speech involves is demonstrated by its quick dismissal of the possibility that giving representatives special and cost-free access to the media enhances rather than reduces 'freedom of communication'.

Given that the court has this intuitive confidence in its judgment of what is involved in the fundamental right of freedom of communication, namely something like the existing rules relating to communication, the second stage of the argument for the invalidity of Part IIID is relatively easy. If a law in any way further restricting communication is a violation of the right to freedom of political communication then it follows that outlawing political advertising even for a restricted period is a violation of freedom of communication. The only question then is whether there are any sufficiently good reasons for permitting such a violation. The majority opinions then centre on whether corruption of the political process or undue influence are sufficient grounds for going along with what is taken to be a clear incursion on the right to political communication.

The argument looks very different if we construe it as a debate about what constitutes freedom of communication. The majority on the court avoid the debate about whether freedom of communication might be enhanced by the legislation. Yet corruption may be a matter which is internal to the processes of communication. If it is communication that is corrupted, by being available only to those with large sums of money, then it is not a matter of freedom of communication versus corruption, but of articulating an acceptable set of free communication rights. However, even after allowing that the legislation may have a bearing on access to the media and so to the problems of democratic politics in an age of expensive and restricted media outlets, Mason C.J. simply states that the common practice of regulating political advertising in nearly all other comparable democracies 'does not refute the proposition that Pt IIID impairs the freedom of discussion of political and public affairs and freedom to criticise federal institutions in the respect previously mentioned'.[32] This displays an unwarranted confidence that the court 'knows' what freedom of communication involves and that, in particular, it is not a matter of providing access to the media. If the argument is made that Part IIID would reduce the dependence of political parties on large contributors, this may be seen as tantamount to saying that it will *increase* freedom of communication in that what is available to electors will be less controlled by wealth. The fact that wealth and property dominate modern communications may be seen as a corruption of the political process precisely because it diminishes the sort of freedom of communication that 'truly' representative government requires.

Nor do the other majority opinions show much awareness that the argument that television advertising trivialises political debate[33] is an argument about the proper content of freedom of communication rights, something which needs to be determined after an examination of the rationales for freedom of communication in the political context, rationales to which they are happy to appeal when arguing for the existence of an implied right of communication but then ignore when passing over what constitutes that right.[34] So the pivotal role of the court's assumption that it knows what freedom of communication is may be appreciated by noting the way in which this enables it to avoid addressing the question of whether or not the provisions of Part IIID enhance or diminish the democratic system. The point here is, not that the answer is obvious, but that it is not. If the question had been directly addressed then the speculative and political nature of the issues would have been so evident as to disqualify the court from having an authoritative opinion on the matter. As it is, the Chief Justice is able to accept the political and evaluative arguments of the Senate Standing Committee which considered the matter, but dismiss them as irrelevant. Had the court undertaken such a study itself, it would have been clearly involved in a political process more suited to the legislative branch of state. It would certainly have been evident that no answer could be read off from any uncontroversial formulation of a right to freedom of communication. The issue comes down to a matter of whether the legislation will make the Australian system more or less representative. This must be a highly speculative matter of political science and political philosophy which is very dependent on what particular conception of representative government is involved and what are the economic realities of effective communication. While the dissenting judgments do not themselves directly address the conception of freedom of communication, they do show much more awareness of the political nature of the issues raised by the challenge to the legislation.[35]

The Democratic Argument

Perhaps the most powerful argument for having court-based fundamental rights is that democracy itself is neither self-justifying nor self-correcting. Democracy as a system of government cannot itself be justified by democratic means without circularity. It follows that democracies are not entitled to choose to abandon democratic institutions. Further, even if democratic process is accepted as the sole basis for political legitimacy, this legitimacy depends on the system actually being democratic. The majorities that count are the majorities within properly constituted democratic regimes. It is evident, therefore, that there is reason to look for some institutional procedure to provide external oversight for electoral rules and procedures and to limit the capacity for even properly constituted democracies to resile from democratic norms.[36] Moreover, actual democracies, in seeking to give institutional form to the justificatory idea of equal political power, have to operate according to some less than unanimous decision procedures which inevitably place the interests of minorities at risk. It can therefore be argued that it is actually democratic (in that it furthers the objective of equal power) to limit what majorities may do in relation to the interests of those individuals who are not of their number. Hence the idea of fundamental rights as a device to protect those interests, interests which not even majorities may thwart. Again, as part of democratic aspiration, it seems natural to look to courts to prevent majorities violating such rights. However, while these powerful considerations do point up important roles for the *idea* of fundamental rights as moral limits on unprincipled majorities, it is by no means clear that they legitimate a role for courts in actually developing the content rather than merely applying such right-centred rules as are deemed appropriate to protect the vulnerable interests in question.

Indeed, it is apparent that the solution of giving such power to a small number of unelected and unrepresentative persons, drawn from the membership of a not always admired profession, may turn out to be much more inimical to these rights than the undoubted problem with which we started. Given selfish or foolish majorities, neither courts nor parliaments seem attractive mechanisms. If we are sure that we all know that rights are to be enforced, it is evidently proper to give courts the task of determining when such rights have been violated. But there are strong arguments for giving neither courts nor parliaments the power to determine the content of these rights. The former are not democratically accountable at all and the latter only imperfectly. Giving either branch of state the power to determine the content of rights which trump majority decisions raises the eternal political dilemma: who is to control the controllers? In these circumstances the determination of fundamental rights by referendum has some advantages, although this in itself does not solve the problem of who establishes the electoral ground rules for referenda, nor does it overcome the problem of minority rights. Moreover, such referenda generally involve a decision for or against brief and unspecific rights which effectively places a great deal of unaccountable power in the hands of the interpreters who have the task of applying these indeterminate rights to specific circumstances.[37] It is more appropriate, therefore, to give the task of rendering fundamental rights more specific to the elected representatives of the people who retain thereby at least some control over the all-important task of positivising priority rights. This removes from the courts the power to reject any legislation which can be viewed as an attempt to instantiate fundamental rights and retains the power to determine the content of fundamental rights as part of those political rights which are inseparable from democratic citizenship. Any viable justificatory theory of democracy centres on the idea of equality in the exercise of political power. Scarcely any aspect of political power is more important than the determination of what is to count as those priority interests which are to overrule and out-prioritise all other considerations. To hand this role over to a non-representative body is to hand over such a major aspect of political authority as to undermine the initial basis which is used to justify that move. To despair of the capacity of majorities to recognise rights for minorities is to despair of democracy itself. Indeed, if the populace does not retain an idea of and commitment to fundamental rights, courts are in no position to sustain the vitality and force of this essential element of democracy. Democracy was not achieved by judicial activism and is unlikely to be sustained by it. If the people and their representatives do not a have a lively sense of human rights, and a strong sense of responsibility towards the values they represent, fundamental constitutional rights, implied or otherwise, will be ineffective. And so, while it is true that democratic decision making presupposes democratic process and majority sensitivity to the rights of minorities, it is mistaken to look to the maintenance of democratic culture and process outside of majoritarian electoral process.

In *Capital Television* the unelected judges decided what is an appropriate ordering of communication during election periods. They did so through an application of their conception of freedom of communication and its particular significance for representative government. In so doing they took on the role of protecting democracy against a violation enacted by elected representatives. In the judgment, judicial suspicion of politicians is clear: Mason C.J., 'The Court should be astute not to accept at face value claims by the legislature and the Executive that freedom of communication, unless curtailed will bring about corruption and distortion of the political process.'[38] More particularly, the system of distributing free television time on the basis of previous elections was seen to favour the political status quo and hence the politicians who had enacted the legislation. All this fits the 'representation reinforcing' thesis of John Hart Ely which interprets the Bill of Rights as giving the US Supreme Court the task of sustaining the preconditions of fair elections.[39] Certainly, the High Court takes this as the paradigmatic area for the inquisition of legislative acts: 'The Court must scrutinise with scrupulous care restrictions affecting free communication in the conduct of elections for political office for it is in this area that the guarantee fulfils its primary purpose.'[40]

Now, of course, the High Court's suspicions may be justified in that the proposed reform would have benefited incumbent representatives (but not therefore always a particular political party). But, given that television time is a very scarce commodity and given the relevance of representative authority to the allocation of such a scarce resource, to say nothing of the highly restricted de facto access which holds at present, it is not clear what alternative system of allocation is appropriate. As Dawson J. (dissenting) points out, 'free access to the airwaves by all who wish to put a point of view during an election period is an impracticality, and, if there is to be free time, then there must be some method by which it is granted'.[41] Indeed, only by discounting the disproportionate influence of wealth is it possible to consider that the enacted reforms did not provide an appropriate move towards a 'more even playing field'. If this is so, it demonstrates that the court is taking a very particular and controversial line on a matter of how freedom of communication is to be spelt out. Further, there is no reason to believe that in so doing they were following the electors' view of fair political process against that of their representatives.

In any case, it is part of my argument that it is corrupting to the political process that such matters are taken out of the political arena and settled by judges. Dawson J. (dissenting) points out that the constitution makers explicitly rejected the American model (a point also emphasised by Mason C.J.) and that this 'choice was deliberate and based on a faith in the democratic process to protect Australian citizens against unwarranted incursions upon the freedoms they enjoy'.[42] Dawson J. does not deny that freedom of expression is as fundamental to a free society in Australia as it is in the United States, but rests his position on the constitution's commitment to an alternative way of protecting rights: 'The fact, however, remains that in this country the guarantee of fundamental freedoms does not lie in any constitutional mandate but in the capacity of a democratic society to preserve for itself its own shared values.'[43] This not only seems an accurate account of what the constitution implies but represents a political direction which is more thoroughly democratic than the alternatives. Dawson J. again: 'To say as much is not for one moment to express disagreement with the view expressed by Murphy J. that freedom of movement and freedom of communication are indispensable to any free society. It is merely to differ as to the institutions in which the founding fathers placed their faith for the protection of those freedoms.'[44] As it was Parliament rather than the High Court which enacted universal adult suffrage so it is to Parliament that we should look for dealing with the immense dangers facing democracy from the commercially dominated media which now have an extraordinary power over public opinion. It is a matter for considerable regret that an initial (and no doubt imperfect attempt) to deal with this matter has met with such negative response under the guise of the protection of democratic rights.

The Ideological Argument

Capital Television demonstrates one way in which courts can claim to be impartial in relation to fundamental rights. Judges do not benefit or lose from changes in electoral process in a way that politicians may do so. More generally, courts may also be seen as detached from political conflict in a way which renders them able to take at least a relatively unbiassed view of conflicts between majorities and minorities.[45] However, while such impartiality is a reason for entrusting courts with the application of specific rules to particular factual circumstances, it is not a sufficient basis for entrusting them with what is in effect legislative power, particularly when such judicial legislation is immune from review by legislatures.

The familiar arguments on this matter derive from the fact that any individual or group of individuals has their own value viewpoints, which means that they cannot be politically neutral when handed a specifically political task, such as legislation. It is no accusation of improper bias to say that courts, along with any other institutional collection of individuals, cannot be impartial in relation to the choice rather than the application of rules. It is not necessary to invoke any extreme Realist argument as to the impossibility of any neutrality even in the interpretation and application of the clearest and most specific rules, in order to question unelected legislative power. While this argument against implied constitutional rights does not depend on establishing that there are any specific value preferences involved in the exercise of judicial legislative power, it is arguable that the class, gender and age characteristics of court members are helpful in predicting and understanding their judgments on such matters. Certainly there are reasons for believing that court-based articulations of fundamental rights will tend to be both conservative and biassed towards a negative idea of human rights, while a political process is more open to a more progressive and positive approach.[46]

In *Capital Television* the conservative tendency is illustrated in that the assumption is made that *existing* laws and practices represent a bundle of free speech rights which are the measure of what is justified in this sphere. It is the fact that the Act *alters* the existing rights of Australian citizens that makes it suspect and a prima facie violation of the right to freedom of communication. This is simply a status quo argument: 'Pt IIID was invalid in its entirety because of its severe impairment of the freedoms *previously* enjoyed by citizens to discuss public and political affairs and to criticise federal institutions.'[47] Further, this has the ring of truth only if freedom of communication is equated with the absence of legal prohibitions on any form of communication, the right of communication correlating with a duty on government not to prohibit any form of speech. But fundamental rights are capable of being viewed as positive rights in the sense of correlating with the duty of government (or other) to take positive steps to further communication by, for instance, the provision of free time on television. Such positive rights are not those which courts routinely reflect but a creative community-oriented ideology which is not dominant within the legal profession. Indeed, although the plaintiff's submission that the provision of free time is a violation of their property rights is not explicitly addressed by the court, it is possible that the court's composition made it receptive to such views, as it is in general to US free speech jurisprudence which is similarly affected by the rights of media owners to control their own property.

Certainly the court exhibits no awareness of ideological bias in detaching the definition of freedom of communication from the consequences of existing rules on the quantity, quality and distribution of the capacity to communicate within the community. The centrality of the absence of prohibitions is evident in the court's disinterest in consequential arguments: 'the prohibition is no less antagonistic to and inconsistent with the freedom of political communication which is implicit in the Constitution's doctrine of representative government simply because the parliament or those in government genuinely apprehend that some person or groups may make more or the more effective use of the freedom than others involved in the political process'.[48] In other words it is formal, negative freedom that counts when fundamental rights are at stake.

The Argument from Positivist Values

We have been viewing Legal Positivism as more of a prescriptive than a descriptive theory. The legal theory of Ethical Positivism has been characterised as the view that we are better governed through a system of explicit, precise and comprehensive rules which can be applied without recourse to the moral and political views of the adjudicators. The familiar benefits which are said to flow from this version of the rule of law are a serendipitous bundle: freedom for individuals and groups who can plan their conduct in the light of known legal consequences; formal equity in that differential treatment is according to some rule rather than official whim, with the prospect that if the rule is a good one then there will be substantive equity as well; and governmental effectiveness in that, with clear and specific binding rules there is an increased prospect of altering conduct in an intended direction.

Less frequently noted are the democratic benefits of approximating to the positivist ideal. In its democratic form, Positivism holds that the people or their elected representatives are the sole or at least the superior source of law. The positivist ideal of specific, impartially applicable rules enhances democracy by giving a focus to decisions which are sufficiently detailed to have some practical effect. In other words, choosing rules gives real and effective choices to the people or their representatives. Electing officials who are given wide discretionary power over individual matters involves a measure of accountability in so far as re-election is a matter of consequence to those officials, but far greater democratic control is obtained by requiring such officials to govern in accordance with rules which are subject to the outcome of democratic process. This control is, of course, even more important in the case of unelected officials, such as government bureaucrats and judges, who are not constrained by electoral discipline. This last point is crucial in *Capital Television*, if only in relation to the conduct of non-judicial officials, in that the absence of clear criteria for the allocation of 10 per cent of free television time is given as a reason for rejecting the legislation. The court notes disapprovingly that the allocation of 10 per cent of the free time depended on 'the exercise of discretion by the Tribunal'.[49] This means that it is not possible to anticipate how this discretion will be exercised. However, essentially similar criticism may be made over allowing an interpretative discretion to courts that enables them by a process of very loose and inevitably political reasoning to make decisions which strike down legislation which is clear and precise. On the positivist model the High Court is on strong grounds when it objects to what in the United States is called 'unconstitutional vagueness', but the very same considerations count against court-centred Bill of Rights of court-engendered implied constitutional rights.[50]

The values which lie behind the desire for human rights can be captured within specific and neutrally applicable rules selected from existing social practices. Human rights can be positivised. Indeed, given that the crucial decisions are decisions about just what these values import, they must be positivised if they are to be effective, and if they are not to violate these values themselves, particularly those of freedom, equality and effective response to fundamental human needs. If we are given to such rhetorical talk, we might say that it is a human right to be governed by democratically chosen rules which approximate to the positivist ideals of clarity, specificity and consistency. There are fundamental human values and some of these need protection in laws of specific content. But this does not mean enacting Bills of Rights whose specific formulations become the object of legal interpretation, as if this could take the place of political debate. It does mean identifying certain key valued interests which should be protected and furthered by duty-imposing rules which are adapted to particular social and economic circumstances. Thus the Political Broadcasting and Political Disclosures Act 1991 can be seen as an effort to instantiate a human right by democratising the election process so as to render more attainable political equality in a specific type of social circumstance. The assumption by the High Court of an arguable discretionary power to disallow such legislation is an affront to positivist ideals and a move away from the rule of law.

Of course, courts are able, albeit unsystematically, to positivise abstract rights through the standard processes of case law development, as happens routinely in those jurisdictions with entrenched rights. However, the more this happens the more the courts take on the role of legislators and, as the scope of these rights becomes interpreted in an expansive manner, there is scarcely a political decision that may not have to be reargued in an ostensibly legal framework. Further, by drawing the courts into a more overtly political role we will in the long run reduce their capacity to fulfil their prime role of administering rules chosen for them in an impartial and non-political manner.

Conclusion

This chapter concentrates on important aspects of disquiet concerning the near universal trend towards Bills of Rights and implied constitutional rights as a focus for political choice. However, it needs to be stressed that this is not to denigrate the importance of the idea of human rights and the significant value commitments they represent. Indeed, one of the more convincing reasons for being in favour of court-centred fundamental rights is that this may be a way of affirming the importance of these values. There is no doubt that the veneration for fundamental rights is tied in, to an extent, with the fact that they are seen as removed from the banalities and trade-offs of routine politics. It can be argued, therefore, that encouraging the Australian High Court to develop an implied Bill of Rights may have immense symbolic significance and help to generate a sense of the nature and significance of human rights in Australian society.[51]

On the other hand, the message that such an institutional arrangement gives is an essentially undemocratic one, not because majority decision making is beyond reproach, but because it despairs of majorities being capable of thinking and voting in human rights terms, recognising the equal worth of all citizens, appreciating the need for attending to the basic needs of everyone and appreciating the importance of protecting the happiness as well as the autonomy of individuals. The symbolic impact of removing the articulation of human rights from the elected representatives of the people may be even more damaging than the symbolic advantages of setting up a countervailing political institution to oversee human rights.

Further, if we despair of politics then courts will not save us. A danger of entrenched Bills of Rights is that ordinary politics is given over to hard-nosed majoritarianism and unadulterated utilitarianism. It must remain part of any acceptable political culture that the democratic process in all its aspects is receptive of arguments that certain interests require the sort of protection which leads us to enshrine them in positive rights, that is interests which are protected by specific mandatory duties on others to protect and further the interests in question without rendering these interests vulnerable to the calculation of utility (or any other calculation for that matter) in particular circumstances. The idea that only judges can be trusted to formulate and uphold rights is a facile and dangerous contention.[52]

The upshot of this discussion is the importance of finding an institutional way of emphasising and facilitating the democratic expression of human rights which does not involve major judicial input, an institutionalisation which preserves the idea of fundamental rights but reclaims it for democracy. There are a number of options and these cannot be explored here. Unentrenched Bills of Rights can help in focussing attention on human rights, in that legislatures may be called upon to reconsider their enactments if they seem to the courts to be in conflict with the current bill or charter.[53] This approach, however, still gives the judiciary the unfortunate task of reading what they can into highly unspecific rights. If, to avoid this, Bills of Rights are made very detailed, then they become generally indistinguishable from ordinary legislation. A less dramatic alternative is to use the approved statement of rights in the context of a parliamentary committee which reviews all legislation in the light of the human rights perspective, something which goes neatly together with a review of draft legislation in relation to international treaty obligations emanating from the many human rights conventions to which countries are signatories.[54] To this can be added further functions for such a statement of rights, in particular their use as a guide to statutory interpretation and Common Law development, provided that this is subject to legislative review.

Without canvassing the pros and cons of these possibilities, we may note that it is possible to find ways of institutionalising human rights considerations without making the courts the prime locus of their substantive articulation. A regard for humane values, and even a commitment to the ideal of autonomy which underlies much of the human rights conception, point definitively to the need for keeping the power of defining the content of fundamental rights with the mainstream of democratic politics. It is important that this be done, if only because it may serve to inhibit moves into what may be seen as a human rights vacuum within states that lack Bills of Rights on the American model, a vacuum which is more a matter of international comparison than actual neglect of human rights. Indeed, a main worry relating to the current Australian development is that genuinely democratically led human rights developments may be struck down by the High Court on the basis of its own unlegitimated ideology. This can only bring the ideal of human rights into disrepute, to the ultimate detriment of the humane values and human interests that they ought to serve.

Notes

1 A version of this chapter, 'Democracy, Human Rights and Positive Law', is published in *Sydney Law Review*, **16**, (1994), 195. My thanks are due to John Tasioulas for his expert comments on the original paper.
2 See Chapter 2.
3 For a fuller analysis of 'humane', see Campbell (1974a).
4 For the notion of 'concretisation', see Campbell *et al.* (1986, Chapter 1).
5 This is particularly the case in the American constitutional tradition. But see Sunstein (1993a).
6 Thus Dworkin (1990, p.23). In the UK context, Dworkin argues that incorporating the European Convention on Human Rights into the law of the United Kingdom will mean that 'Law and lawyers might then begin to play a different, more valuable role in society than they may now even aim to have ... might think in terms of principle and less in terms of narrow precedent' and so be 'the conscience, not just the servant, of government and industry'.
7 For a more extended discussion, see Campbell (1983).
8 The classic statement of the essence of this approach is to be found in Mill (1910).
9 'Human Rights are the rights which all persons equally have simply insofar as they are human' (Gewirth, 1978, p.1).
10 Thus Gewirth (1978) grounds human rights in the capacity for action.
11 For the Social Contract tradition, see particularly Locke (1960).
12 The right of self-defence is used to legitimate pre-emptive actions which would otherwise be classified as acts of aggression.
13 The ideological base of the United Nations is inseparable from its Universal Declaration of Human Rights (1946). Increasingly, it is permissible for individuals to raise domestic violations of human rights with international courts and commissions.
14 For a more functional and detached, but equally demythologised view of human rights, see Gaete (1993).
15 A view particularly associated with Bentham. See Hart (1982).
16 This scheme is derived from Hohfeld (1919).
17 Thus Hart (1973, pp.171–201).
18 Thus Frey (1980, Chapter 1) and Nelson (1975, pp. 145–55).
19 See Campbell (1983, pp.192–103).
20 As Dworkin (1977) in effect suggests.
21 See Campbell and Sadurski (1994).
22 Rawls (1974).
23 Ackerman (1977).
24 Habermas (1984).
25 *Australian Capital Television Pty Ltd* v. *the Commonwealth* (1992) 66 ALJR 695, at 695: 'PtIIID was invalid in its entirety because of the freedom *previously* [my italics] enjoyed by citizens'. Perhaps more extreme is *Leeth* v. *the Commonwealth* (1992) 174 CLR 455, particularly Gaudron J., who argued that an implied doctrine of equality entails that 'in constitutional context discrimination is constituted by different treatment of persons or things that are not relevantly different'. This may be a very acceptable moral principle but as a constitutional rule it enables courts to decide that any piece of legislation which they believe to be morally misconceived is invalid.
26 Ibid.
27 Toohey J., above, n.9.
28 Consider Menlowe and McCall Smith (1993).

29 *Australian Capital Television Pty Ltd* v. *the Commonwealth*, above, n.25, at 703.
30 *Australian Capital Television Pty Ltd* v. *the Commonwealth*, above, n.25, at 703; emphasis added.
31 *Australian Capital Television Pty Ltd* v. *the Commonwealth*, above, n.25, at 705. The contrary view was put to the Senate Select Committee on Political Broadcasts and Political Disclosures November 1991 (1993) at 4.6.5 by Dr Ian Ward and Dr Ian Cook, both political scientists from the University of Queensland.
32 *Australian Capital Television Pty Ltd* v. *the Commonwealth*, above, n.25, at 700.
33 Ibid., at 703.
34 Ibid., at 696.
35 Brennan J., ibid., at 724, and Dawson J., ibid., at 703.
36 These definitional limits of 'democracy' are explored in Chapman and Wertheimer (1990). See Dworkin (1990, p. 13). 'Democracy is not the same thing as majority rule.'
37 On referenda, see Walker (1987).
38 Ibid., at 696.
39 Ely (1980).
40 Ibid., at 705.
41 Ibid., at 725.
42 Ibid., at 722.
43 Ibid.
44 Ibid., at 723–4.
45 Thus Dworkin (1990, p.13).
46 Griffith, *The Politics of the Judiciary*, 4th edn (1991).
47 Ibid., at p.719; emphasis added.
48 Ibid., at p.695.
49 Ibid., at p.707.
50 For the morality involved in interpreting vague rights, see Perry (1982).
51 The symbolic point is made in Dworkin (1990, pp.56f).
52 Chambers (1993, p.247): 'People who doubt that inclusive rationalized debate is the means of strengthening our rights tradition must either doubt the capacities of human rationality or doubt that there are good reasons for justifying rights.'
53 As in the New Zealand Bill of Rights Act 1990.
54 For one suggestion, see Kinley (1993); see also Lester (1968).

8 The Political Choices Within Freedom of Speech

Introduction

The moral and political articulation of the form and content of fundamental rights is a matter for the democratic political process. The principal ground for this contention is that the concretisation of abstract rights is an integral part of the political right to self-determination. We have also noted that democratic dialogue places more emphasis on humane values and less on the acontextual individualism which characterises court-based legislation. In the last chapter these claims were explored in relation to an example in the area of the regulation of political broadcasting. Here we take up a more general discussion of freedom of speech in order to illustrate the complex moral and political issues which are at stake in the determination of the rules that are to apply to the processes of communication. This discussion seeks to bring out that the variety and nature of the considerations which have bearing on these issues are such that they are unsuited for judicial determination. More specifically, it is argued that the diverse and incommensurate values and purposes involved in developing rights and duties governing freedom of expression make it difficult to view the articulation of 'the' right to freedom of expression by way of an interpretation of a brief and abstract affirmation of basic rights or an extrapolation from a constitutionally enshrined concept such as 'representative government'. The choices which require to be made are substantial, controversial and political and, therefore, in accordance with LEP, require to be expressed in the form of rules which are capable of being applied without recourse to controversial moral and political views. This chapter concentrates on these political choices.[1] In the next chapter we consider whether it is feasible to formulate acceptable free speech rules which satisfy positivist criteria.

Freedom of expression is a major test case for LEP. The claim that governments must articulate a basic democratic right of free speech comes up against the immediate objection that governments are the prime offenders against such freedoms. Indeed, it is traditionally assumed that freedom of speech is a right which is directed entirely against government. In the dilemmas which arise from the paradox of politics, freedom of speech is usually portrayed as a bulwark against the ever-powerful forces which prompt the political Leviathan to curb individual political freedoms. To leave democratic rights in general in the hands of governments appears to resolve the paradox of politics by abandoning the effort to restrain the abuse of government power. The problem must be acknowledged. Indeed, consciousness of the endemic abuse which is inherent in the operations of all political authority is an essential ingredient in any mature political culture. But the response must be that the involvement of government is essential to the attainment of many aspects of freedom of expression and that the furtherance of rights in this as in other areas requires working within the accountable democratic process rather than seeking to impose constraints from the outside.

In the jurisprudence of the First Amendment to the Constitution of the United States, which requires that 'Congress make no law abridging the freedom of speech or of the press', the standard theme is that the underlying objective of the First Amendment is to promote a free market in ideas, the assumption being that this is the path to truth.[2] However, if we look to a wider range of sources, we find that, in addition to the market argument for truth, freedom of speech (or expression or communication) is also commended in terms of self-determination,[3] democratic process,[4] promoting tolerance,[5] sustaining pluralism,[6] the efficient allocation of resources[7] and the intrinsic worth of the communicative experience.[8] Interestingly, many of these justifications are instrumental ones, in that they relate to the posited outcomes of a free speech, such as truth, tolerance, pluralism and efficiency. It follows that there may be reason to restrict communication when its outcomes run counter to these same outcomes, or other valued ends. Moreover, even the more deontological justifications, such as self-determination, or communication for its own sake, are in competition with other basic values, such as protection from physical and psychic harm, countering error and falsehood, protecting reputation and privacy, reducing social animosities, discouraging offensiveness, undermining hierarchy and the protection of property. With so much at stake, no society accepts an unlimited right to freedom of expression in the sense that everyone can communicate what they like when and how they choose. It is always assumed that there will be some laws concerning such matters as defamation, obscenity, breach of confidence, broadcasting, copyright and, normally, blasphemy, pornography and vilification as well.

On the other hand, it is widely believed that basic right to freedom of expression has a special status which renders it invulnerable to circumstantial qualification. Certainly, the right to free speech must be presumed to hold generally, in that it is not to be dependent on establishing that any of its justifying rationales have force in each particular circumstance. Moreoever, the right to free expression can hardly be overridden by just any negative factor, otherwise it is not even a common-or-garden right. Every right must trump some counter-considerations or exclude the relevance of some otherwise significant factors, and none more so than freedom of speech. There is, it is generally assumed in liberal societies, something special about speech that puts it at the absolutist end of the inviolability spectrum, so much so that free speech standardly takes precedence over otherwise advantageous activities, such as public order and privacy. Some account must be given of this very powerful normative status, even if only to note that freedom of speech is peculiarly vulnerable to political suppression and therefore in need of special protection.[9]

At this point absolutists sometimes go down a number of more or less unfruitful tracks. The first is to fuss over what counts as real 'speech'. It is *speech*, not pornography, not vilification, perhaps not even commercial advertising that is to be unconditionally protected.[10] At an extreme, this line may lead us to a defence of something like an absolute right to freedom of political speech in a democratic context to the exclusion of such communications as the 'speech' element in scientific reports and works of art.[11] Or the 'real speech' track may lead us to stress the cognitive aspect of communications to the exclusion of words or representations with primarily emotional impact. Even to a committed legal positivist such formalistic conceptualism may seem a desperate ploy, particularly if it is taken as a move within political philosophy, however useful or necessary it may be for interpreting constitutional rights to freedom of speech so as to accord with our preferred political philosophy. In practice, little independent force is given to the philosophical analysis of ordinary meanings of 'speech'. The analyses offered are in effect nutshell theories as to what is significant about speech, or why certain types of speech are significant. The hunch – and in the United States it is a hunch backed by the almost sacred dignity of the First Amendment – is that there is something that sets speech (and the press) apart. In trying to identify what this (these) unique feature(s) is (are) we find ourselves back where we started, in the realm of freedom of expression rationales.

The second, slightly more fruitful track, is to be relaxed as to what counts as speech, and to search for a few bases, or preferably a single base, for all 'exceptions' to freedom of expression, such as the 'clear and present danger' test, which gained its prominence in the area of sedition but has been applied in other areas where harm is alleged to occur, such as obscenity. Or it may be argued that whatever speech restrictions are imposed, these must be neutral in relation to the content of the speech in question. We may be offered a combination of a definition of real or protected speech with one or two allowable exceptions, as, for instance, that there is an absolute right only to political speech and even then only in situations where there is no clear and present danger.[12] While it is not inconceivable that a simple set of rules could be devised and constituted as a fundamental right, in practice the outcome of judicial development in this area is a complex web of dubiously consistent rules and exceptions which cannot be captured in the sort of simple formulations required for a Bill of Rights. Further, at every stage in the development of such case law, crucial political choices are being made which are as dependent on political philosophy and historical circumstance as any piece of legislation. However necessary such rules may be to concretise abstract constitutional rights, their articulation and justification require us to know what the positive value of speech might be and, if there is to be a single overriding clause, this must be more specific about what dangers we have in mind when we speak, for instance, of clear and present danger.

Certainly, the absolutist search for a core right of freedom of speech is understandable and attractive. If there is somewhere we can take a stand and exclude all infringements, then we have a right indeed, legal power with which to trump all-comers. Moreover, once we allow exceptions to a right of free speech this will be used by powerful or cautious people to curtail an unacceptably wide range of discourse. Only absolute rights, it may be said, can be immune from the misuse of exceptions.

Perhaps this core right may be secured by emphasising the centrality of a particular free speech justification, which helps to explain the distinctive significance of free speech and gives us reason to accord it special status. A single powerful rationale seems to go neatly with giving freedom of speech particularly high priority. It is understandable, therefore, that much ingenuity is exercised in the search for one underlying ground for all legitimate free expression rights.[13] Yet the scope of such a core right is going to be far too restricted to instantiate the area we will want to defend in the light of the full range of available free communication justifications. Maybe we can say anything we like about politicians, but how does that help with the pursuit of non-political truth or the attainment of artistic self-determination? In any case, if free speech is special, it may be so for a combination of reasons rather than the unique application of one overriding rationale.

And so we are back in the messy world of multiple rationales and an open-ended set of potential limiting factors. We therefore have no alternative to sorting out what these theories are about: what values they involve, what forms of speech, communication or expression are important for the furtherance of such values, and what factors threaten their embodiment in social realities. Then, for purposes of assessment and institutional instantiation, we must identify what the various theories presuppose, (a) philosophically, that is by way of epistemology, theories of meaning and so on; (b) sociologically, in relation to the type of human relationships and social structures that are assumed to pertain; and (c) politically, in terms of the institutionalisation of power in the polity in question. Thus J.S. Mill's familiar argument from truth assumes an empiricist philosophy, a relatively egalitarian and educated population, and a political system which guarantees a rough balance of competing interests groups between which an educated and enlightened elite can hold a benign balance.[14]

Other rationales, however, come up with a very different set of assumptions presenting other difficulties in justification and instantiation. Thus the argument from democracy may be founded on a radical subjectivism which justifies freedom of communication by reference to the epistemological impossibility of rejecting any opinion as 'false', perhaps in combination with a belief in the total harmlessness of all expression when compared with the oppressive tendencies of governments. Such analyses are very important from a number of points of view. They enable us to see which legislative or constitutional proposals may be philosophically defensible, which may be realistic ideals in different types of society, and what sort of political institutions may be required to implement them. They may also reveal embarrassing divergences which require us to pick and choose between free speech justifications. Thus some of our favoured justifications assume objective theories of knowledge, others presuppose radical subjectivism. Naively, we may be cheered by the thought that, on either (or any) epistemological premisse, we may defend freedom of speech. Either free speech matters because it leads to the truth, or speech cannot be legitimately curtailed because no one statement can be known to be better established than any other. In fact, of course, one supposition serves to undermine the other: on objectivist premisses we may pick and choose between manifestly false and possibly true beliefs and exclude the former if they are deemed harmful; on subjectivist premisses, there can be no basis for saying that open debate leads to the adoption of the best grounded beliefs for any purpose, including establishing what is harmful. In such cases we must choose between, rather than accumulate, such rationales.

Another such running sore in amalgams of free expression rationales is that some insist that speech is of vital importance for society because it has profound effects on us all, so that is must not be in any way curtailed, while others stress that speech itself can do no real harm, so that it is wrong to restrict speech on the basis of its effects, for these are minimal. Again, we have to choose, or qualify. Is speech power or puff? Evidently, also, it emerges in the study of various freedom of communication rationales that there are very many different versions of what counts as a limitation on such freedoms. Spectacularly, in present-day contexts, there is a gulf between the defence of a liberty right and a negative claim right of free speech, on the one hand, and freedom of speech as a positive or affirmative claim right, on the other hand.[15] A liberty right to free speech is defined in terms of the absence of legal prohibitions on speech, with no implications that anyone has a duty to allow the right holder to speak. Such rights may be important in excluding censorship or warding off defamation actions, or in giving significance to silence as an indication of tacit consent.[16] Liberty rights of free speech are usually closely associated with a number of negative claim rights in terms of which one person's freedom of speech correlates with other people's duties to refrain from interfering with that speech in specified ways, as in preventing communication between persons. Article 19 of the International Covenant of Civil and Political Rights, which proclaims the right to hold opinions and to receive them from others, may be interpreted as supporting negative claim rights. In contrast with both liberty and negative claim rights, affirmative or positive claim rights involve correlative duty holders who are obliged to empower the right holders to participate (and/or have others participate) in successful communicative activities. It cannot be assumed that such affirmative claim rights are simply supplementary to the liberty and negative claim rights, for the attainment of the former, for instance, enabling us all to have a voice on the media, may require curtailing the latter, for instance, the media owners' right to exclude what they dislike.

Moreover, there is a constant ambiguity between freedom of expression in two further dimensions: as an individual or a social right, and as an intrinsic or an instrumental right. These distinctions relate more directly to the justifications which may be offered for having specific liberty or claim rights of free speech. Thus the right to communicate is an individual right if it is construed as being for the benefit of the right holder. However, it may be of benefit either because the individual has an interest in freedom of communication as such and for its own sake, in which case it is an intrinsic individual right, or else because the right holder wants the right in order to protect or pursue further interests, such as commercial profit, in which case it is an instrumental individual right. On the other hand, freedom of communication is a social right if one person's right is justified by the benefits which accrue to other people, such as the autonomy which derives from having the information received through the exercise of this right by the right holder. Again this social right may be intrinsic, as when the beneficiaries of the right desire autonomy or information as such and for their own sakes, or, as is more likely, it may be an instrumental social right, as when the recipients desire the communication for ulterior purposes, such as protecting their political interests. In cases where the benefits of freedom of communication as a social right cannot be restricted to identifiable persons or expressed in an aggregative way, then we may think of the right to freedom of communication as a public good, as when it is said to promote a progressive economic culture, or tolerant political pluralism.

Clearly, these distinctions are of vital importance when it comes to assessing the proper scope and force of freedom of communication rights and the adoption of some such scheme will help to clarify any free speech debate. In particular, these distinctions may help us to evaluate arguments for a unique and singular free speech rationale, which tend to rest on the significance of individual negative claim rights, such as freedom of intrinsic individual expression for its own sake. Such arguments are standardly preferred to more socially based instrumental rights, such as political communication for the welfare of a polity, which are more readily interpreted as affirmative claim rights. As against the tendency to assume that intrinsic individual rights have greater moral and political force, it is worth noting that the classic argument for truth most often takes the form of a social right, in that its justification normally derives from the maximisation of true belief within the relevant community.

Passing now to the closer analysis of particular justificatory considerations, we can consider the arguments for freedom of communication by way of both clarification and critique. The objective is to work through to a framework of rationales which assist with ordering and clarifying our thinking about the worth and implication of freedom of communication justifications in specific contexts and at the same time reveal the complex competing considerations which are at work in the choice of free speech rights. There is no one rationale and no one conception of freedom of communication. Speech is an element in almost every worthwhile human activity, and is central to many of the forms of conduct which have most bearing on human wellbeing. Once we depart from unhelpful generalities we must expect to find multiple reasons for its nurture.

Starting with the classical trio of free speech values: truth, self-determination and democracy, we explore ideal type versions of these free speech rationales with a view to focussing on their more convincing versions and raising into view some of their crucial distinguishing presuppositions. It may be assumed that we are looking for freedom of communication rationales which are capable of generating reasons for defending freedom of speech even where there are significant counter-considerations, reasons which not only generate an assumption of freedom but have a resilience against countervailing factors which is sufficient to vindicate rules of strong exclusionary force.

The Argument for Truth

The argument for truth seems the most dated of the standard justifications for freedom of expression. The view that the operation of unrestricted speech is the only basis for justified truth claims bespeaks an enlightenment rationalism according to which speech expresses beliefs and most citizens are capable of testing arguments both in terms of consistency and by reference to self-evident truths or empirical evidence, a world in which truth is an evident value and an undoubted force for good in the fight against superstition and authoritarianism.[17]

Nowadays we are more aware that much of actual speech has little if any potential truth value, in that it is either not directed at the expression or vindication of justified belief or is not the sort of expression which is capable of having a truth value. From this post-enlightenment perspective we might restrict any right to freedom of speech to 'truth-oriented' speech, that is speech which expresses a putative truth or evidence bearing on some such truth. A great deal would thereby be excluded, including, importantly, expressions of opinion about matters which are not capable of truth or falsity. This could include all pure value judgments (that is, value judgments which do not contain or imply factual suppositions) and even highly speculative factual claims which are in principle beyond the reach of testable evidence. Nevertheless, enough may be left within the sphere of decidable facticity to provide a powerful rationale for freedom of speech, even if it is confined to the truth-oriented aspects of speech.

It is an argument, however, whose validity ultimately rests on an objectivist theory of knowledge, according to which epistemological relevance and evidence is not simply a matter of personal opinion or existing community standards.[18] Moreover, its force and scope depend on some view as to what sort of discourse and evidence is relevant to the determination of truth and falsehood. The development and implications of the argument for truth depend, therefore, on establishing an acceptable range of working epistemologies. Thus, in those areas which are left within the scope of truth-oriented discourse, it seems strange to think of the weight of evidence for any factual claim depending on the availability of the largest possible number of individual expressions of truth-oriented speech. Accumulation of communications is in itself of no significance except in special circumstances where these communications are part of an indicative enumeration, as when we are making assertions about the content of positive morality, or existing patterns of consumption. Even a 'democratic' approach to truth as the agreed outcome of a discussion in which all have an equal say can have little epistemological weight, however important such an approach may be when questions of value and consent are at issue. The way in which freedom of expression may contribute to justified belief therefore needs careful exploration and may lead us to give special weight to some forms and sources of communication.

This exploration is not helped by the unfortunate 'market place of ideas', so popular with the US Supreme Court.[19] The market model suggests that justified belief is the result of a preference selection between the widest possible range of different assertions on the basis of the tastes and purposes of the 'purchaser'. The more opinions available, the more likely that the seeker after truth will find what she is looking for. By being able to make comparisons the truth hunter will get the best bargain relative to her needs. There are echoes here of J.S. Mill's idea that any assertion might be true in that we cannot know in advance of examining it whether or not it is correct, but it does nothing to illuminate the bases of distinguishing truth from falsehood. In the market, the fact that someone buys an item is taken as demonstrating that she wants it more than the available price-comparable alternatives. This is a primitive datum of the market. However, the fact that someone 'selects' an opinion is not in itself evidence of its truth. Nor is 'market success', namely the fact that an opinion is selected by large numbers of people, convincing evidence of its accuracy.

The market model is better suited to the idea of a market in information which is not directly concerned with the discovery of truth but with its distribution. Assuming that some information has a market value, in that people and organisations are often prepared to purchase that information, we can construct an argument for unrestricted entry to that market in the interests of its efficient functioning, so that information gets into the hands of those ready and willing to pay most for it. However, such a model presupposes the ownership of ideas and the right to control their circulation, concepts which are intrinsically inimical to freedom of speech. It can be argued that a market on these lines is an incentive to the development of new ideas, a systemic view which has affinities with the argument for truth but, in this case, the argument favours the regulation of speech by market mechanisms and the protection of proprietary interests in information. However, in so far as it can be used to condemn legal restrictions on entering the information market, this 'efficiency argument' does provide reasons for having rights to communicate the commercial information without which market choices will not be properly informed. It is hard to see, for instance, how financial markets can operate efficiently without uncensored financial journalism. The general inappropriateness of the market metaphor is further evidenced by looking for some analogy to 'price' in the market-place of ideas. Ease of understanding and ready availability seem the best candidates for representing the price of ideas, since the least effortful purchase might be regarded as the cheapest. As a criterion of truth this seems even less promising than democratic consensus.

Pragmatic theories of truth fit best with the market analogy according to which consumer preferences are confirmed by past purchases which fulfil the purchasers' high expectations and are changed when purchases prove disappointing. This may be thought to parallel maintaining those beliefs that sustain successful action and discarding those which do not work in practice. However, while this model may be appropriate to the truth of some claims which depend on summations of the experiences of large numbers of people, this does not hold for truth in general. In most spheres it is expertise, not numbers, that count. Most truth-oriented speech has to be taken as conveying information or suggesting conclusions which might be drawn from the data conveyed. This means that evidence from those who have been witnesses to events or phenomena which relate to the truth value of assertions is clearly significant. Evidence from those who have deployed, with proven skill, recognised techniques for the discovery of truth, such as scientific experiments, historical research of primary sources or social surveys, also has a preferential claim on the attention of the truth seeker. Comments which relate to the logical consistency and argumentative general coherence of truth-oriented arguments also qualify. Further, only when the recipient of such speech is able to make a proper assessment of the evidential value of the reports and comments of others is there a feasible claim to knowledge.

Very loosely, then, if the function of some speech is to assist the individual, in discussion with others, to make a sound judgment as to what to believe, freedom of communication is generally desirable in so far as it results in new information or new ways of looking at the available information. Other things being equal, the more speech a person is exposed to the less likely it is that she will miss something important for the evaluation of competing views. However, it remains unlikely that anything other than suppression of particularly important pieces of information, or systematic suppression of a particular view of available information, will seriously affect the legitimacy of existing claims to justified belief. On the other hand, the mere existence of freedom of expression, even given that it is widely utilised, is in no way a guarantee that truth will emerge. The market-place analogue gives the unfortunate impression that the argument for truth depends on the unlikely claim that free discussion is a sufficient condition of progress in relation to general community knowledge. In fact, all that the argument can possibly do is to establish that freedom of communication is a necessary part of the successful pursuit of truth, or at least increases the likelihood of knowledge development.[20]

This means that critics are able to dismiss the argument for truth on the grounds that people are not rational consumers of information and that actual belief depends on factors other than the force of the available evidence. Truth is not readily recognisable. But, granted all that, it may still be the case that, in so far as rationality is attainable, it involves scrutinising different opinions. In this case it is evident that freedom of speech is not a sufficient condition for the emergence of truth. The argument for truth can only support the weaker claim that diversity of expression and openness to deviant views is a necessary condition of intellectual progress. Or, indeed, it may come down to little more than the assertion that, other things being equal, communication helps the advance of knowledge.

The apparently restricted scope of the argument for truth, when presented on the objectivist assumptions that I have been defending, may prompt us to look more closely at variations which make no such claims and therefore do not have such limitations. A non-objectivist alternative version of the argument from truth may be derived from the 'fallibility' argument used by J.S. Mill in Chapter 4 of *On Liberty*. Mill argues that we cannot use such certainty as we have to suppress an allegedly false belief because, without hearing all opinions, we cannot claim to know that it is false. The acceptance that we may be wrong is an inextricable part of the mental attitude which justified our claims to justified belief. It is only because our belief is based on considering and testing all opinions that we have grounds for confidence in it.[21] This powerful argument suggests that the argument for truth commits us to at least allowing all truth-claiming assertions to be heard – at least once – by all those concerned. However, the application of the fallibility argument to limitations on belief to the exclusions of limitations on action depends in part on the assumption that speech causes no harm (see below). Indeed, if we take the assumption of fallibility seriously, we are not going to be in a position to interfere in the conduct of any harm-causing person because we may be wrong about the allegation that the conduct causes harm. While this possibility may make us hesitant to enforce conduct it does not exclude such intervention where the evidence of potential harm is strong. Only if speech cannot cause harm does the same logic not apply to restricting speech as applies to restricting conduct.

This is not to say that speech and action are on precisely the same footing in relation to the legitimation of belief. Speech has a role in testing putative truths which is not in general shared by action. Speech may therefore require greater protection than action. Equally, the fallibility argument should give us pause when we argue for restrictions on action which are based on claims as to the harmfulness of that conduct. Further, an admission of fallibilism is much too weak for those who see radical scepticism as the only feasible epistemology in a postmodernist setting. Mill's fallibilism, of course, was part of an objectivist empiricist epistemology, but more radical versions make the claim that there is ultimately no basis for selecting one factual claim over another. According to this subjective fallibilism, truth is a matter, perhaps, of coherence with the propositions already accepted by the subject, none of which rests on any foundation external to the perceiving and believing person; or, perhaps, truth is a function of the degree of subjective certainty, again something which is not amenable to external critique; or, perhaps, truth is a merely pragmatic concept of 'what works for me'; or, perhaps, truth is a matter of intersubjective agreement incorporating some of these aforementioned criteria.

Positions like these certainly undercut the limitation of the argument for truth to truth-oriented communications as defined by some objectivist epistemology. But they also undercut limitations on communications that are based on assessments of harm caused, the truth of which is not, on the theory, open to determination. Without an objectivist theory of truth, no-one can have the right to interference on the basis of superior knowledge, certainly where basic premisses are involved and probably in every particular circumstance. It would seem then that non-objectivist approaches to truth (such as subjective fallibilism) do not provide alternative versions to the classical argument for truth, although they may incorporate elements which give the argument for truth a limited foothold, as when they incorporate the need to eliminate logical inconsistencies. We are left, therefore, with a powerful but limited defence of freedom of communication in relation to authenticated ways of promoting the discovery of truth, perhaps in accordance with some minimally defensible range of epistemologies. This certainly does not take us as far as the strong thesis that complete freedom of expression is a sufficient condition for truth and maybe not even as far as the weaker thesis that unrestricted communication is a necessary condition of truth. We can, however, espouse the weakest version of the argument for truth, that unfettered discussion can make an important and distinctive contribution to knowledge.

These relatively weak forms of the argument for truth can be strengthened in practice so as to protect strongly, or even absolutely, all truth-oriented assertions. If we take into account sociological factors relating to the tendency of those who are regarded as authorities with respect to truth to suppress factual beliefs which conflict with their own cherished convictions, and the tendencies of political authorities to censor any factual expressions which they believe might undermine their hold on power or the achievement of their political objectives, then it may be that only unconditional support for freedom of communication can protect the valuable truth-oriented elements within the variety of human communications. These are, however, contentious and difficult philosophical and moral opinions which are not determinable by legal argument or amenable to resolutions without reference to the prioritising of truth as a value over competing considerations.

The Tendency to Abuse and the Harm of Speech

The 'tendency to abuse' speech restriction is a major and convincing factor in almost all free speech rationales, and one which is central to the implications of the paradox of politics. Bad faith censorship generally drives out good censorship. While this phenomenon is relevant to the establishment of any rules and procedures for protecting and furthering speech, whatever its rationale, its general significance can be examined effectively in the context of the argument for truth.

At its strongest, the tendency of those in power to abuse legitimate restrictions enables us to argue that no restriction on expression can be allowed, even if there is a good prima facie case for it, because it will nearly always be malappropriated by vested powers. This extreme form of the tendency to abuse theme assumes (a) the impossibility of 'institutional objectivity' in speech-limitation regimes, in that no institutional devices can be put in place to reduce abuse to acceptable levels, and/or (b) the 'no-real-harm' argument, to the effect that any harm done by permitting evidently false and harmful statements is pretty minimal.[22] Institutional objectivity is a major topic and one which requires us to explore both the possibility of formulating limitation rules which are applicable without recourse to personal opinions and the prospect of institutionalising application of rules by persons who do not have a vested interest in speech limitation. Thus the distinction between matters of fact and matters of opinion, which is required to give a plausible scope to the argument for truth, must be legally operationalisable if special protection is to be given to those expressions which can convincingly be included under the truth-seeking (factual) heading, while excluding those matters of opinion, such as value judgments, which are not candidates for truth.

At the extreme, it is argued that no precision is possible here, so that no clear distinctions between types of speech can be used to formulate objectively applicable limitation rules. This claim is not, however, very convincing unless it is tied in with a distrust of those who are applying the rules. All that can be said briefly is that these are matters of degree. It follows that the argument from abuse has force only to the extent that appropriate rules cannot be formulated precisely and the adjudicative process is not free from bias towards existing political and intellectual authorities.

The tandem argument for making free speech rights unconditional, even if the rationales do not themselves warrant such an extreme position, is based on the thesis that speech does no real harm. This contention may be questioned on several grounds.

1 In relation to the argument from truth, given that speech is, ex hypothesi, a means for the attainment of truth, this seems to assume that speech does affect belief and it is impossible to accept that action-guiding beliefs do not have a major impact on the outcome of actions. The modifying contention that only true statements affect belief is not itself part of the argument for truth and in any case lacks plausibility. Moreover, the harm caused by assertions may not relate to any truth value which they may or may not have but to their evaluative or expressive or imperitival import.
2 However 'truth' is defined, it must include or imply at least the claim that action based on true factual beliefs is more likely to be successful than action which is based on false assumptions about the instrumentalist involved. Hence false beliefs, which may result from unlimited speech, can lead to the loss of intended benefits and the production of unintended harms.
3 It is dogmatic to exclude psychic harm which is a major consideration when considering the effects of speech as distinct from action. Speech can offend, insult and shock, even if it is considered by others that such responses are inappropriate.

To counter all these points, we may adopt the free speech analysis of Baker,[23] who argues that, although harm may result from speech, these results are standardly produced non-coercively, in that its eventuality depends on others adopting 'certain perceptions or attitudes', so that the speaker is not responsible for the harm unless she has been coercive, which comes down to a failure to respect the rights of the others, in which case she has applied 'improper pressure', as when 'the person manifestly disrespects and attempts to undermine the other person's will and the integrity of the other person's mental process'.[24] This relates to Baker's major contention that freedom of speech is fundamentally a matter of the liberty of the individual, the idea of free speech being a matter of respecting the integrity and autonomy of the individual, and therefore excluding speech which is used for such purposes as fraud, perjury, blackmail, espionage and treason. Baker's argument shifts the focus of debate from the prevention of harm to the responsibility for its production. Harm caused by speech is mediated by the reactive attitudes of others who suffer or directly cause the harms in question.

However, even if we adopt this perspective, it is not clear that non-coercive speech which is a foreseeable ingredient of a process which results in harm is not accountable simply because the process involves the uncoerced actions of others. Such intervening events do not normally negate criminal responsibility, as when one person asks another to kill a third party, and it is not clear that the shared culpability in such cases is such that the person who takes out a murder contract is less culpable than the person who carries out the homicidal actions. Similarly, from the point of view of prevention, if the suppression of speech is effective in preventing a harm, then it makes perfect sense to say that speech in some sense causes harm, since in some situations it is a sine qua non of the harmful event, and it is no objection to preventing the harm by preventing the speech that it takes away the choice of the person who would have received and possibly acted on the message suppressed. Moreover, speech is itself a form of action which can in some cases be regarded as harmful in itself, something which is not confined to overtly 'performative' utterances but applies in all cases where communication establishes or alters the relationships of those involved.[25]

The Value of Truth

Assuming, then, that institutional objectivity in speech limitation is approachable and that actual and ostensibly truth-oriented assertions may be harmful, where does this leave the argument for truth as a candidate for guiding politically neutral applications of the right to freedom of expression? A great deal depends here on the sort of value we ascribe to truth. Knowledge may be valued for its own sake, as an intrinsically worthwhile possession or state of mind. Thus it may be valued simply as the object of a desire: for example, curiosity or, more grandly, the thirst for knowledge for its own sake. Value of this type must vary with the sort of knowledge in question. Are we after deep scientific understanding or finding out what it is that the neighbours are up to in their garage? Only in relation to significant truths can knowledge for its own sake claim to have overriding importance. Otherwise, the evaluation of truth for its own sake is simply the expression of one desire amongst others. Then there is the instrumental value of truth, which is high in relation to such matters as applied science, organisational efficiency and legal justice, although in itself morally neutral as being a matter of means not ends.

Endorsement of the argument for truth as an instrument has to make the supposition that those in a position to utilise truth are enlightened with respect to both their objectives and their skills. This may often be an overoptimistic assessment of the social and political situations into which truth is to be released. The argument for truth as an instrument is, therefore, only as strong as the social and political arrangements for the use of knowledge.

From these ingredients we can construct an argument for a strong presupposition in favour of a right to freedom of truth-oriented expressions where the truths at issue are of intellectual significance or have potential beneficial uses. However, this presumption may be overridden by the probability of instrumental harms arising from the dissemination of the assertions or associated harmful side-effects, particularly when truth is being valued simply as an object of desire. In general, taking on board the potential benefits of knowledge and the pervasive effect of the tendency to abuse otherwise justifiable restrictions, it would seem right to take the presumption in favour of freedom of truth-oriented discourse as holding generally, without argument in relation to individual expressions, whereas restrictions require to be justified more particularly, in relation to specific types of assertion or specific circumstances. In other words, the truth benefits of freedom of expression are to be viewed either as intrinsic to each and every case of knowledge, or in more general utilitarian terms, it not being possible to demonstrate the truth utility of each specific utterance or type of utterance, while exceptions to freedom of such discourse call for probabilistic justification in relation to the specific harms claimed.

Not only are these complex considerations which call for closely debated political determination, the point at which the presumption of freedom is overridden will depend on the value which we attribute to knowledge for its own sake, the scale of values used to measure harm and the available capacity to control the uses of new knowledge and the benefits it might bring, none of which are the province of distinctively judicial wisdom and only some of which are closely related to the control of political power.

The argument for truth is multifaceted with respect to our preliminary analysis of the types of free speech right. Freedom of expression clearly has an individual dimension with both instrumentalist and intrinsic forms, since it may be vindicated as enhancing the speaker's grasp of the truth for its own sake, and as a means whereby the individual may acquire useful information which enables her to protect her own interests. However, individuals gain knowledge through listening to others, knowledge which may be as important to them as it was to the speaker, and in the same diverse ways. The argument for truth is therefore as much a social as an individual right; in fact its chief application is probably in relation to the public good of the general enhancement and distribution of reasonable belief within a community.

Similarly, it is clear that the argument for truth portends far more than any mere liberty right to freedom of expression. In the interests of truth, special weight could be given to the communications of those who are in a position to contribute significantly to the search for truth, as eye witnesses, as knowledge experts or as skilled analysts. Perhaps this dimension has import only where there is need to distinguish between potential speakers, either in relation to the possible harms which may result from their contribution or because priorities have to be allocated in giving access to the means of communication, but it is an affirmative claim right, albeit of a less than universal application. One such priority is access to audiences, but of prior importance is the matter of access to research resources. Even if discussion is an element in the discovery of truth, it is certainly rarely sufficient to this end. The resources for scientific, historical, journalistic and other research procedures are scarce and can rationally be distributed in accordance with the capacities and training of those available to do such work. Such matters may be thought to go beyond the sphere of freedom of expression. However, if freedom of speech rests on the value of truth and if truth requires supports beyond negative claim rights to free speech then these other matters have ostensible equal weight in the determination of social and political priorities. If intellectually significant truths are what we value, then governments which limit the allocation of resources to scientific and other research are mistaken for the same reason as those which limit freedom of the appropriate speech, with the reservation that it is proper to take into account the forgone benefits of alternative uses of such resources. Only if the protection of negative free speech is thought to be economically costless can such freedom of speech be regarded as a right in a different category from the affirmative freedom to research, even in this respect.

Of course, we standardly distinguish between freedom of speech as a negative claim right to the absence of government or other prohibitions, and freedom of research as a positive or affirmative right to receive the resources to carry out research. However, the clarity and relevance of this distinction is undermined by the truth benefits of a positive right to freedom of research publication and dissemination of acquired knowledge, which may be as significant as the absence of prohibitions on research for which the research has available funds. In other words, if freedom of speech is valued for its role in the attainment of truth – a type of instrumental social right – then modern conditions require that the liberty and negative claim rights be supplemented by less universal but equally significant rights to the means for acquiring knowledge. The argument from truth is not just an argument for negative freedom of expression.[26] However, such affirmative arrangements can lend credence to the charge that free speech is a legitimating myth which furthers the interests of intellectuals, a charge that has some force if we accept that intellectuals are not more trustworthy than anyone else when it comes to exploiting the instrumental value of knowledge.[27]

The Argument for Self-determination

Self-expression/self-development/self-determination/autonomy arguments for freedom of expression are perilous in their potentiality for tautology and thus their inappropriateness for judicial articulation.[28] We may simply be going round in the circle of saying that freedom of expression is an absolute right because expression is fundamental to human nature, part of the very essence of humanhood, a contention which is itself based on convictions about human beings have free expression rights. Moreover, at first sight the idea of self-determination offers little guidance as to the scope and weight to be ascribed to such a right, which may be as little as the provision of an outlet or as much as the necessary condition of a morally good life.

Nevertheless, if such a claim can be given intelligible and plausible content, it provides an argument which is important because it is relatively immune to empirical critique. If we add to this the sceptical argument (if they can be rendered compatible) against curtailing the expression of others on the grounds of superior knowledge, we have a strong deontological argument which does not depend on the proof of any consequential advantages and disadvantages arising from freedom of expression. This is given experiential content by the affront felt by one human being who is silenced by another on the grounds that this is an unwarranted assumption of superiority.

The argument for self-determination tends to be sidelined in political contexts because the significance of this individual right does not seem to be derived from the role of speech in the political process. However, while the argument for self-determination as an *intrinsic* individual right is certainly a contrast to political rights in free speech which are, as we shall see, grounded more in the idea of *instrumental* individual rights, there is an instrumental form of the argument for self-determination which sees speech as a means to further the wellbeing of the speaker. Self-determination or autonomy is, therefore, a concept which bridges the private and the political spheres.

The ambiguous associations of self-determination may be clarified by making a sharp distinction within the right to self-determination between, on the one hand, the intrinsic individual right which derives from the inherent value of individuals expressing themselves and, on the other hand, the instrumental individual right which involves individuals using the opportunity to express themselves in order to protect their interest or further their projects beyond mere self-expression. The former may be called *the self-expression argument*, the second *the self-projection argument*. I use this latter phrase to incorporate those aspects of self-realisation which involve the further objective of developing individual capacities and the broader range of ways in which individuals use speech to promote their own enterprises and defend their own projects. Certainly, there are many instrumental aspects of expression which may need to be separated from whatever constitutes its intrinsic worth. Thus speech may matter to an individual person because it may help her to get what she wants, to influence others, or to protect herself, all of which have an importance which is quite independent of the intrinsic value of exercising her human capacities for self-expression. Even the activities of making up one's own mind and making one's own choices may be valued both as an exercise of autonomy which is significant in its own right and as a means of furthering and protecting one's own interests.

Whatever the precise interpretation we give to the idea of self-expression, there are strong reasons for accepting a self-expression argument as a distinct ground for justifying certain speech freedoms. The intrinsic values of authentic self-expression and frank communication are sufficiently distinctive to represent a particular argument for freedom of expression, one which is not subsumed under either the argument for truth or some version of the argument for future self-realisation. Indeed, some apprehension of the intrinsic worth of self-expression may lie at the base of some of our most profound intuitions about the significance of freedom of expression and the tendency to regard it as a distinct and inviolable right irrespective of its political context and cognitive content. Further, the self-expression rationale has the advantage of empirical impregnability (at least if we ignore its possible harmful side-effects), a privileged position which cannot be extended to other important rationales which are based on the alleged consequential benefits of freedom of communication.

However, while the intrinsic value argument may not be endangered by evidence of failed instrumentality, it may still be overridden by harmful or otherwise unacceptable side-effects of expression and communication.There are other intrinsic goods, some of which are found at the end of instrumentalist chains. This is particularly so when the chosen sphere of self-expression has a general communicative objective, such as art, music and literature, rather than expressions which flourish in more private contexts. It is a mistake, therefore, to reduce the whole justification for freedom of communication to such a basis. The fact that pure self-expression may constitute a core intrinsic individual right which is immune to consequentialist evaluation does not drive out other more empirically vulnerable rationales. Self-expression has to take its place along with different and often competing justifications of freedom of communication. For instance, self-expression may get in the way of self-projection: individuals may not do their projects any good by overexercising a right to speak out.

Moreover, the attempt to utilise the concept of self-expression to cover all free speech rationales involves serious distortions in the meaning of much communication. Thus there is clearly something wrong with Baker's thesis that, from the point of view of freedom of speech, political protest is to be seen as a process of self-affirmation. This does not capture the point of view of participants who, routinely, are not interested in self-expression as such, but in changing the world for some ulterior purpose, such as spreading a message they believe in, changing government policy or protecting their own interests.[29]

The argument for self-expression is a speaker-oriented approach which may be extended to take in the communicative function of speech by drawing attention to the human significance of making honest communication with other people. Since this is a two-way process, expression is then seen to have intrinsic importance both for the recipient and for the speaker. To bring this fully into the picture we have to talk of freedom of communication rather than simply freedom of expression. Indeed, we may move towards the line once taken by Scanlon to the effect that freedom of speech is important because of the autonomy it affords to the *recipients* of the speech.[30] A strength of the pure intrinsic worth of expression and communication is that it is not defeasible with respect to the content of the expressions and communications in question; it is content-neutral. This strength is shared in part by the wider version that incorporates the use of speech and communication to form considered beliefs and make personal choices: the autonomy function of expression when detached from its instrumental aspects. However, the self-projection justification is defeasible both in the face of evidence that particular exercises of that freedom are not protective of that person's interests and in the light of the quality of the objectives adopted by the communicating persons. The freedom of speech of a person who wishes to protect his activities as a fraudster may have some intrinsic content-independent significance, but it is vulnerable to curtailment in the light of the uses to which that freedom is put in a way which would not apply in the case of a person who chooses to pursue morally approved goals.

Similar points may be made by relating expression and communication to the notion of self-development, that is the nurturing of selected talents and abilities in ways chosen and endorsed by the individual. There is both a content-independent aspect of self-development and a defeasible approval which depends on whether or not the talent in question is acceptable or approved. Sociologically such valuations would seem to represent the outlook of certain types of society in which individualism, creativity and Protestant-style faith and vocationalism dominate, but, particularly in its communicative aspects, it may also cohere with communitarian values such as empathy and cooperative activity in so far as the reciprocal aspects of communication are emphasised.

The instrumental value of speech and communication is, analytically, equally at the service of a multiplicity of values and compatible with endless variations of institutionalised settings, but, as a rough generalisation, the self-projection utility of communication will be of far greater importance in societies which minimise organised social concern and depend on individual responsibility. In the latter type of society, freedom of expression cannot be expected to fulfil its defensive and projective function in an equitable way if there are major inequalities of capacity, education and access to communicative means. Since this is the normal situation in individualistic societies, instrumental arguments for freedom of speech seem to be particularly relevant to the defence of the interests of the articulate and powerful sections of society. However, starting with this framework, it is possible to think of ameliorative measures, at least with respect to the access to communicative means. The right to freedom of instrumental expression need not be regarded as a purely negative right.

Beyond this, it needs to be noted again that instrumental arguments vary enormously in their strength in accordance with the ends to which expression is regarded as a means. Further, the importance of freedom of expression will vary not only, as we have noted, with the communicative capacities and resources of the right holders, but also with the form of life and employment that they adopt: writers and journalists have more at stake in relation to instrumental freedom of expression than plumbers and farmers, although the contrast needs to be refined by acknowledging the significance of audience interests.

The Argument for Democracy

The argument for freedom of communication as a precondition of democracy is perhaps the most popular basis for the assertion of an absolute right at least to freedom of political expression,[31] and the one which is most closely connected with the reasons for placing the interpretation of that right beyond the control of elected politicians. This may be because freedom of expression can be seen as partly constituent of democracy itself, and democracy is accepted as a universally shared value within the relevant constituencies. However, this then shifts the argument to the nature of acceptable democratic processes: that it is the majority election of rulers, that it is the equal distribution of political power, that it is the pursuit of consensus, that it is the recognition of diversity, that it is a process of deliberation, and so on. All of these will have a role for speech and rationales for its freedom, but perhaps the most important thing about the argument for democracy is that the particular freedom of communication rights that are intrinsic to democracy will vary with the model of democratic process that is adopted.

Talk of absolute freedom of communication is strong in the political sphere because it is here that the danger of abuse of any legitimate restrictions of freedom of speech is thought to be greatest (although this may be to underestimate the significance of economic power). Moreover, the argument from abuse has a more positive form: namely that freedom of speech about the activities of government is a necessary means of control.[32] This may be taken as an application of an instrumentalist version of the argument for truth, namely that it is public knowledge of what politicians are up to that keeps them on the straight and narrow. But clearly, more than discussion is required for effective accountability even in countries where public opinion is powerful through elections and simple publicity. In this context the right to freedom to communicate as an instrumental social right takes us into an argument for access to information as well as the opportunity to disseminate it. Here the rationales for freedom of communication and freedom of information come together.

Further, because the abuse is most likely on the part of elected politicians or their sponsors, it is easy to see why it may be thought that such a right may be best protected by putting it beyond legislative power in the form of an entrenched Bill of Rights. This does not mean that the democratic rationale for freedom of communication is necessarily stronger than other rationales, but simply that the vested interests of political power in suppressing political speech make it appropriate to institutionalise its protection in a way which is relatively independent of first order political processes.

There is also a less combative form of the argument which fastens on the idea of discussion with a view to reaching agreement as basic to the democratic process. On this view discussion is inherently democratic since the opinion of each person is given equal weight, thus maximising autonomy within the political arena. This position is often combined with the more instrumental view that discussion has an important role in promoting social stability. That said, the content of the right is varied and to an extent dependent on the nature of the democracy in question. Particularly in relation to positive versions of free communication rights, the dialogic form of democratic theory points to the need for actual opportunity to engage in dialogue, not just to receive information and impart it.

Those democratic theories which take democracy to be a process of discussion aimed at continual consensus on governmental objectives will be more inclined to require freedom in relation to ongoing discussion rather than simply for the process of choosing rulers. Within such theory, expression is likely to be regarded not only as the exchange of relevant information but also as access to the means for persuading others to adopt the values and viewpoint of the speaker. This latter point is of fundamental importance since it requires freedom of speech and communication for all those who wish to persuade and not just for those who have some new information to impart. Or again, while all versions of democracy which give a role to citizen choice must value freedom of communication as a way of making such choices better informed, a democracy which rests on mere majority power may not be concerned with the freedom of minority opinions, whereas one which emphasises some ideal of equal political power will see majority decision making as second-best to consensus and place special emphasis on the role of the minority views. Hence also, perhaps, the common emphasis on diversity as an objective of state regulation of the media.

Also, a democratic theory which sees electoral procedures as a way for individuals to protect their self-interests by giving them leverage over the actions of elected politicians will require the maximal flow of information about the details of governmental activity and its effects, whereas a theory which sees politicians as being elected for their personal capacities and representative qualities as persons to be entrusted with the complexities of government will be more focussed on the passage of information about candidates than about the minutiae of government. The choices presented by alternative models of democracy are profound and profoundly political. Whichever is chosen, it is clear that no answer can be read off from any abstract conception of 'representative government' or 'popular sovereignty'.

The argument for democracy overlaps both with the argument from truth, in that what is required for genuine choice or control is informed consent, and with the argument from self-determination, particularly in its instrumental form, as political expression has utility in making others aware of one's views or demands. Democracy can, of course, be defended as a way of valuing aggregate individual choices as ends in themselves, quite independently of the worth of the choices made, a sort of mass intrinsic self-expression. If unfettered discussion is a prerequisite of choice then this is because self-expression is the value embodied in free political speech. But if all that matters is choice, good or bad, it is not clear why open discussion is necessary. Any justification for free speech on these grounds must be agent-oriented, in that the right is to express opinions, not to receive them. Following this line, the significance of political speech has to be that it is the most important area of self-expression.

However, it is hard to hold to this view unless politics is also taken to have instrumental functions in relation to self-interest or the general good. In this case we are not dealing with pure self-expression but with the instrumental value of self-projection. If the instrumentality is protecting the interest of the individual, this is best done if the individual is well-informed. If the instrumentality is more in terms of the public good that all have in attaining the best government, then it can be argued that this is also best served by free discussion. In either case we are then back with something like the argument for truth, albeit an instrumental form in which truth is itself valued instrumentally in terms of the political objectives prioritised in the theory of democracy. In so far as the argument from democracy centres on political application of the argument for truth, it has some cogency. Openness of discourse gives everyone the opportunity to bring to the attention of others relevant facts about candidates, governmental activities and other material relevant to the evaluation of the causal aspects of policies. If it is argued that voters cannot assess such data then this must be seen as an argument against democracy as a means for obtaining governments which best serve the interests of their citizens. The persuasiveness of the argument is that, if it fails, it brings down democracy with it. On the other hand, democracy, however defined, is a matter of degree, so that the free speech which is partly constitutive or causally required for it may also be a matter of degree.

Further, it is clear that there are many individual citizens who have information which is highly relevant to the choices which fall to be made by electors. Equally, there are many reasons why those holding and seeking power should seek to suppress such information. It follows that an absolute right to impart factual data of any possible relevance to the political process has a clear function within a democracy. However, truth is not a concept which applies to political discourse generally, in that much of political communication consists in, perfectly proper, expressions of values, self-interest, persuasive rhetoric and personal commitments. These disparate forms of expression may be put together under the inadequate label 'opinion' to distinguish them from assertions which are in principle capable of refutation. Opinions have the advantage over factual assertions that, if viewed as opinions, they do not have the same potential for damaging a candidate or a cause as statements of fact which undermine electoral credibility. There is, therefore, a basis for saying that opinion should be unrestricted whereas factual claims must be evidenced in some acceptable way. On the other hand, if opinion is not susceptible of proof, or perhaps any strong form of critical assessment, it would not seem to come under the argument from truth. In that case, there must be some criterion other than truth which leads us to say that open debate of opinions leads to the selection of the 'best' candidates and policies.

We might adopt the – highly democratic – view that the best policy is that which gains a consensus, the one that is favoured by most people. Here acceptance is not a test of truth but the very quality that makes the policy the one which ought to be adopted: consensual government is to be preferred as such. If this is incorporated in the view that such consensus only legitimates government if it is the outcome of informed and equal discussion then we have arrived at the discourse theory of democracy according to which discussion or discourse is a means which enables a group to approximate, if not to truth, at least to fair and reasonable agreement. All such theories use the idea of neutrality or impartiality as a basis for saying that, if we can eliminate or reduce the factors which render us different and therefore generate disagreement, we may have the basis for reaching morally defensible agreement.

Foremost about what separates us is our distinct personal beings and interests. What benefits one person does not thereby benefit another. If this can be overcome, either by a veil of ignorance or an infusion of benevolence, or by an act of imagination, then agreement becomes more possible. We can go down a Rawlsian path of removing from our knowledge particular facts about ourselves which might bias our choices, like our beauty or our gender,[33] thus putting us in something like Rousseau's ideal democracy in which all citizens participate in a legislative assembly which passes only general laws that have an equal impact on all because everyone is in roughly the same economic and social position.[34] This model of democracy has only a limited role for actual debate since, given that one individual has all the relevant information, she is in a position to choose on behalf of all. A more discursive alternative fastens on the role of open and fair debate as a means of mutual persuasion approximating to a situation of reasonable communal decision making. Thus the Habermasian model of ideal communication can be seen as a modified version of the argument for truth, or as a hypothetical model posited on the significance of consensus (the position to which Rawls would seem to have retreated).[35] If it works as an epistemological cum political theory then it fits well with the communitarian model of democracy as a process of attaining harmony of opinion and lifestyle and civic organisation. Such a model is very attractive to the free speech absolutist, as it places discussion at the centre of the political stage.

However, the call of the Habermasian for 'unfettered discussion' includes a call for the removal of inequality and oppression in the process of debate. It could therefore involve silencing the powerful and empowering the weak, indeed any other action which is conducive to uncoerced dialogue. Habermasian freedom of communication must seek in some way, even if it is not by coercive intervention in debate, (a) to control biassed speech, (b) to promote equal rights of access to media, (c) to afford minority protection by disproportioned assistance and maybe even (d) to encourage cultural homogeneity, (e) to educate for self-expression, and (f) to ensure the dominance of civic over commercial rights, for example in advertising. If this cluster of affirmative free speech rights and duties all seems just too much, we may backtrack from subsuming the argument for democracy under an argument for truth or rationality, and resort to some more instrumentalist view of the rationale, either in the traditional terms of providing better informed voters who are therefore more able to protect their own interests, or in terms of more subtle sociological claims, such as the view that freedom of communication, even freedom of divisive and hateful speech, leads to the highly valued virtue of tolerance.[36] Or we may argue that restricting speech serves to exclude diverse groups from membership in society.[37] Or, if we adopt the view that democracy is to be valued because people are in some sense ruling themselves, however badly they do it, we may proffer a parallel rationale for freedom of speech, including freedom of political speech, as simply one element of self-expression and hence an intrinsic good for each individual which does not need any further justification.

Conclusion

More than enough has been explored to establish the point that the justifying grounds of freedom of speech are so complex, intertwined and in the end incommensurable that they are no arena for simple slogans and evident legal applications of pre-established clear and simple rules. It is clear that there are several plausible, but often quite limited, distinct rationales for freedom of communication. It may be reasonable to stick with the centrality of the traditional trio of rationales, truth, self-determination and democracy, though with some provisos, but it cannot simply be assumed that there are not also other important considerations. Perhaps the argument for truth should be limited to truth-oriented speech. Perhaps the argument for self-determination needs to be divided into a self-expression variant and a self-projection variant. The argument for democracy incorporates several distinct instrumental arguments posited on a wide range of mechanisms and values, only some of which relate to informed choice of rulers.

Moreover, none of the rationales can justify an absolute right to freedom of expression, even of a specified category of speech, although this does not mean that we may not be persuaded by pragmatic arguments for an absolute legal right to participate in certain types of speech which cause little direct harm, contribute significantly to important values and are at risk from the abuse of power. Although these rationales are cumulative in some combinations, particularly with respect to the argument for truth and versions of the argument for democracy, they compete in other ways, particularly in the case of the disparity between those rationales which focus on individual benefit and those which highlight social consequences. Further, all justifications for freedom of expression would appear to have implications far beyond the mere removal of legal restrictions on communicative acts which suggest complex rights of communication that correlate with the duties of government to promote and even ensure the means for the development of knowledge, access to technology for effective communication and the disclosure of politically relevant information.

Finally, only the argument for pure self-expression as an intrinsic individual right is not internally limited by its own premisses. Even that argument is vulnerable to evidence that the side-effects of such an intrinsic right may be unacceptable in terms of other values. To sum up: just because there is no one overarching rationale for freedom of communication, there cannot be any simple and straightforward politically uncontroversial formulations of acceptable freedom of communication rights.

Notes

1 This chapter is a modified version of Chapter 2 in Campbell and Sadurski (1994).

2 For the background to the First Amendment to the Constitution of the United States, see Tribe (1989).

3 Baker (1989).

4 Ely (1980).

5 Bollinger (1986).
6 Shiffrin (1990).
7 Posner (1986).
8 Richards (1986).
9 Note the concern in Schauer (1982) with the tendency of governments to be intolerant: pp.12, 68, 83, 106 and so on; also Schauer (1983). On this 'negative' theory, see Cass (1987).
10 Thus Schauer's exclusion of pornography from the domain of speech on the grounds that it is equivalent to a sex aid (Schauer, 1982); see *Miller* v.*California*, 413 US 15,34 (1973).
11 Meiklejohn (1962).
12 For this principle, see *Schenk* v. *U.S.*, 249 US 47,52 (1919): speech is not protected if there is 'clear and present danger that it will bring about the substantive evils that Congress has a right to prevent'.
13 Thus Baker (1989) fastens on self-realisation. Greenawalt (1989, pp.3–4) asks, 'what is the speech that is to be protected?' and answers, 'The constitutional guarantee of free speech reflects the important political principle that government should not suppress the communication of ideas.'
14 See Campbell (1971).
15 See p.279.
16 Pettit, Chapter 3 in Campbell and Sadurski (1994).
17 Mill (1910).
18 Baker (1989, pp.12–13).
19 *Whitney* v. *California*, 274 US 357,375 (1927); *Furman* v. *Georgia*, 408 US, 238, 467 (1972); *Red Lion Broadcasting Co.* v. *FCC*, 398 US 367, 392 (1969); *New York Times* v. *Sullivan*, 376 US, 254,a72,279 (1964); *Poe* v. *Ullman*, 367 US 497, 514–5 (1961). See *Abrams* v. *United States*, 250 US 616,630 (1919): 'The ultimate good desired is better reached by free trade in ideas … the best test of truth is the power of thought to get itself accepted in the competition of the market.'
20 Bollinger (1986, pp.43–75).
21 Duval (1972).
22 Thus Emerson (1963, p.881): 'expression is normally seen as doing less injury to other social goals than action. It generally has less immediate consequences, is less irredeemable in its impact.'
23 Baker (1989, pp.57f).
24 Ibid., p.59.
25 See the discussion by Rae Langton in Campbell and Sadurski (1994, Chapter 6).
26 Greenawalt (1989, pp.22–3); Baker (1989, pp.37–46).
27 Coase (1977).
28 This rationale is central in Baker (1989, p.5). See also Richards (1986, *passim*); Scanlon (1972).
29 Baker (1989, p.53).
30 Scanlon (1972, p.204).
31 Ely (1980); Meiklejohn (1960); also Bork (1971).
32 Blasi (1977).
33 Rawls (1972).
34 Rousseau (1963, pp.143–229).
35 Habermas (1984, 1987, 1989).
36 Bollinger (1986); contra Schlag (1986, pp.281–2).
37 Raz (1991).

9 Positivist Defamation Law

Introduction

We have considered the positivist and democratic disadvantages of empowering courts to override legislatures through the application of abstract and overriding principles, such as freedom of speech. These disadvantages arise from the fact that in determining the specific content, scope and force of these principles the courts are involved in highly controverisal political questions. This amounts, it is argued, to an ascription of massive, unaccountable and politically arbitrary power. This critique presupposes that there is a feasible alternative, namely the legislative establishment of rules which embody and convey precise political choices in the form of specific rules establishing positive rights and duties which can be impartially applied and subject to meaningful political debate in a framework of electoral accountability. It is to this question that we now turn in an examination of the prospects for attaining rule governance in the sphere of defamation law, a particularly vexing and contested area of law which bears on freedom of expression.

LEP does not itself indicate a preferred approach to the substance of defamation law beyond its general commitment to significant freedoms, effective democratic government and formal justice as a necessary condition of substantive justice. However, the previous chapters make it clear that good positivist law requires the preselection of specific legislative objectives which identify public purposes that enable us to formulate rules, at the appropriate level of specificity, and provide a background for the understanding of the regulations which require or permit particular actions. In the case of defamation this is superficially easy. Defamation law, it might be assumed, is designed to protect the good name and reputation of individuals against unwarranted and damaging assertions and innuendoes. To damage or destroy a person's reputation is to inflict serious injury which it is an injustice to ignore, thereby justifying the regulation of criticism of the conduct and character of other people.

Immediately, however, uncertainties and ambiguities emerge. Does 'unwarranted' refer to the falsity of the assertions, or their subject matter? That is, are we dealing about damaging falsehoods or invasions of privacy?[1] Further, is the object of legal intervention to deter or punish such injurious assertions, to provide redress in the form of compensation, or to do something to salvage and restore the good name of the defamed person?[2] Further analysis brings out that warrantability may refer, not to the intrinsic merits of the assertions, but to the assumed countervailing advantages of permitting unfettered communication, whatever its reputational or other consequences.[3] For instance, the purposes of defamation law may be thought to include the negative objective of not restricting or inhibiting freedom of expression. Indeed, as we shall see, it is possible to view the furtherance of free speech values as a positive objective of some aspects of defamation regimes.

Identification of the purpose or set of purposes of any area of law does not in itself ensure that the rules are clear and objectively applicable. Purposes have to be translated into rules establishing identifiable patterns of conduct and relevant moral distinctions have to be formulated in rules that can be followed, and be seen to be followed, by those who do not accept the moral significance of the distinctions so drawn. Defamation law is a particularly challenging area for the application of LEP in this respect. Defamation deals directly with the slippery phenomenon of language and is for this reason alone hard to capture adequately within specific rules.[4] Defamation occupies a battleground between the competing interests of the rival elites of journalists and politicians, both of which are adept at the use and misuse of language. The phenomenon of defamation is itself somewhat intangible, dealing as it does with variable subjective reactions to verbal symbols and the distress which can arise from what people believe others to be thinking or saying about them as well as the more tangible consequences for the careers and incomes of those who have been defamed.

Actual defamation systems are replete with confusing and often conflicting rules and procedures which have less to do with the intangible nature of the subject matter than with the considerable confusion about the role of defamation law. Defamation is standardly and not incorrectly presented as a principal area of conflict between freedom of communication and the desire to impose communicative restrictions for the protection of private and public interests. If people are allowed to say whatever they like about others then some of this, whether true or false, is likely to cause a great deal of loss and hurt, certainly to individuals and perhaps to beneficial systems of political and community life.[5] Even true defamations may cause harm, with no adequate compensating benefits. On the other hand, the interests of significant truth, self-expression and democracy are often well served by the circulation of information and opinion, some of which bears negatively on the reputation and/or deals with the private concerns of individuals. In the normal course of events, much of this material will be false or unprovable but its publication may be directly or indirectly valuable nonetheless.

As is made clear in the previous chapter, no simple reconciliation between these competing values is theoretically possible and difficult prioritising choices have to be made. Unsurprisingly, therefore, defamation law, as a product of the Common Law, is a mesh of confliciting principles and procedures which leave these underlying tensions unresolved. Always the questions remain: what are the proper objectives of defamation law, what price is worth paying for the free speech benefits of weak defamation law, and what sort of defamation regime might benefit free communication goals? For LEP, a central question is whether it is possible to make political determinations of the priorities and balances in this area of social dispute which can then be captured in precise rules that may be effectively and fairly administered in the context of such prejudices and biases as currently threaten these outcomes. Certainly, there are few areas of defamation law that are characterised by clarity of purpose or content. In practice a great deal tends to be left to the intuitions of juries and the balancing acts of judges, both of which are suspect to the Positivist. Defamation law reform is, therefore, an enormous challenge to the aspirations of LEP.

Given the problems of drafting good defamation law, the prospect that this is an unsuitable sphere for legal regulation has to be considered very seriously. Yet, unless we adopt a very strong form of the argument from truth, it seems impossible to allow without exception the deliberate dissemination of damaging falsehoods about individuals without in effect sacrificing the interest of defamed persons in the cause of some abstract ideal of truth. And it seems unlikely that the democratic advantages to be derived from unfettered debate can be used to justify the complete absence of sanctions designed to limit unfounded personal criticism, even if this is confined to the political sphere. We seem doomed, therefore, to having some rule-defined limits to utterances bearing on the reputational interests of others. This goes with a political obligation to see that those who are actually harmed by unjustified defamatory statements have access to effective and affordable remedies. State regulation is always unwarranted if it does not attain the objectives which confer legitimacy on its operations. On the other hand, there is nothing intrinsically superior in the absence of regulation in any aspect of life where substantial injuries are being inflicted and significant benefits forgone.[6]

If those who criticise the conduct and character of others have to substantiate their allegations in court this presents immense disincentives to making such criticism. Uncontroversially, what courts determine proven or unproven is not necessarily true or false. Further, the imprecision of legal rules in this area and the unpredictability of legal outcomes, particularly in relation to the amount of damages that may be awarded by juries,[7] leads to self-censorship, even of matters that are believed on good grounds to be both true and socially or politically important.[8] Depending on the regime in operation, the allocation of legal costs can be such as to deter the publication of critical material which might lead to the initiation of a lawsuit irrespective of its merits and the eventual outcome. All these factors serve to undermine open discussion about those with wealth and power.

The great champions of freedom of expression, at least in the form of negative rights, are media owners and professional journalists. The motivation of the media advocates of freedom of communication varies from serving the public interest in obtaining full and correct information, to the pursuit of personal advancement, political power and material gain. On the other side, politicians depend enormously on what is said in the media about them and their policies and have an intense private interest in protecting themselves from the disclosure of damaging information about their conduct and political activities, while not being averse to the availability of such data relating to their opponents. 'Gagging writs', a familiar phenomenon in many jurisdictions, greatly inhibit honest investigative journalism and straightforward news reporting.[9] Notoriously, particularly where juries are involved, there are large sums of money to be had from successful libel suits even in cases where little real harm is done to the defamed person and where the material concerned may be correct, but cannot be substantiated in accordance with current rules of evidence and resources available or without violating the confidentiality under which information was imparted to journalists.

Although there is an evident public interest in obtaining information about any individual whose activities affect the welfare of others, it cannot be claimed that everything that the public is interested in has such legitimacy. The satisfaction of curiosity is harmless in itself and good business for the media, but these benefits are not the sort which readily outweigh the protection of individual privacy. Moreover, it is not simply the interests of defamed individuals that is at stake. The integrity of the democratic process itself requires that political choices are not manipulated by the dissemination of false 'information' about those involved, particularly when the purveyors of this material are mass circulation newspapers or television stations which allow no effective opportunity for reply. The fact that the motives of plaintiffs may often be tainted and their injuries exaggerated does not mean that the system does not have overall desirable results.[10]

Difficult problems also arise in relation to the application of any defamation rules, even those which may be thought acceptable in themselves. In some jurisdictions, judicial protectiveness towards public figures and lack of respect for unconventional and dissenting views, to say nothing of oversensitivity to specifically judicial reputations,[11] often makes the judiciary a problematic tribunal in defamation cases. Involvement of juries may help with assessment of how allegedly defamatory material is understood by the reader or listener, but juries may not be representative of the relevant social group, can be unreasonably hostile to some media outlets and, understandably, have difficulty in assessing the economic 'worth' of a reputation, to say nothing of following the enormous complexities of defamation law as it stands.[12]

The cumbersome ineffectiveness of external controls of media practitioners and the ways in which these can be evaded and abused to silence communications which are in fact in the public interest raises the question of whether self-regulation may not be a better means of minimising unwarranted defamation than litigation, despite the lack of effective sanctions to back up journalistic self-discipline. The record here is not good and the explanations for the poor performance of self-regulation are easily traced to the commercial pressures involved and the absence of effective sanctions for conformity to agreed codes of practice.[13]

The relevance of Ethical Positivism to these debates is clear. In the first place, LEP draws our attention to the importance of having precise and objectively justiciable rules which are effective in relation to their politically determined purposes.[14] Unless there are specific and operable rules within which media persons, authors and political activists can operate, the effect of defamation law inhibits investigative journalism, whistleblowing and the general free flow of information relevant to democratic process, historical truth and self-expression. The 'chilling' effect on speech of defamation actions relates directly to the uncertainty of the law which makes it prudent for lawyers to advise clients not to publish or, when their published comments are challenged, to settle out of court. This pursuit of 'good' defamation law goes along with a commitment to determining the best form of tribunal and procedure for the administration of defamation rules in the light of the likelihood of bias through the impact of majoritarianism, economic power and improper political influence. Both matters cannot be approached until we have some idea of our preferred political objectives.

Our particular interest here is how the values of communication bear on the issue of what constitutes good defamation law. While those familiar with the operation of defamation regimes often perceive them to be unduly restrictive of freedom of communication, it is a common public perception that the suppression of false allegations against individual citizens does not represent any real threat to the purpose which freedom of communication is meant to serve. Thus, for a long time, the US Supreme Court treated defamation as outside the scope of the First Amendment.[15] At least since *New York* v. *Sullivan*,[16] this is no longer the case, since defamation actions by public officials (and later 'public figures') are now curtailed on First Amendment grounds, the view being that the object of that amendment is to promote robust and open public debate and encourage 'the free flow of ideas and opinions on matters of public interest and concern'.[17]

Not only is it necessary to take on board the major adverse impact of defamation law on freedom of communication, it is possible to envisage that certain elements within it which foster the discovery of truth may serve free speech values, so that defamation law may in some respects actually be supportive of freedom of communication. With this in mind, this chapter examines the relationship of defamation law to the standard rationales for freedom of communication with a view to demonstrating how the clarification of policy objectives can contribute to the development of good law. But first it is important to explore how far we can, and how far we cannot, go towards the positivisation of defamation rules even before adopting any specific policy objectives.

Defamation Criteria: Fact or Value?

An initial positivist objection to defamation law is the concept of defamation itself, the legal deployment of which appears to invite the sort of direct evaluative judgment that is excluded from the positivist paradigm of rule application. When a judge or jury is asked to decide if certain material is 'defamatory', LEP requires the deployment of appropriately precise standards which can be applied without recourse to subjective value judgments. Thus it is not appropriate to ask if the jury or jury believes that the plaintiff is justified in feeling aggrieved or offended by the assertions in question. Yet it appears that the traditional Common Law criterion for defamation, which requires an assessment of how 'right-thinking' people would react to allegedly defamatory material, requires just such moral determinations.

In the basic common law tradition, exemplified in England and Wales, and with some variations in Scotland and the various Australian jurisdictions, a statement is defamatory if it undermines respect for an individual and damages his or her reputation as a human being or with respect to his or her work or place in society. Defamation is 'lowering the plaintiff in the estimation of right-thinking people generally' or 'injuring the plaintiff's reputation by exposing him to hatred, contempt or ridicule' or 'tending to make the plaintiff shunned and avoided'.[18] It is for the judge to decide if the material is 'capable' of having a defamatory meaning. Whether or not it is actually defamatory is treated as a matter on which the plaintiff must convince the jury (or sometimes a judge) on the balance of probabilities. The plaintiff must also establish that the defendant was responsible for publishing the defamatory material and that it would be taken as referring to the plaintiff. The defendant may then seek to justify what was written (or, in the case of slander, said) as true, or, if it is a matter of opinion, that it is an opinion based on alleged facts that he can prove to be true.[19]

There are certainly many examples of these legal definitions of defamation being used by a court to impose its values via such vague and value-inviting criteria.[20] However this is not the only possible approach to the 'right-thinking' formulation, and it is not one which serves what may uncontroversially be taken as a purpose of defamation law, namely to protect the reputation of the person at large (rather than within the courtroom). One alternative approach is to take the criteria as referring to the way people in general actually react to such words in such a context, thus replacing a partly evaluative criterion by an empirical test. Ideally, if what is at stake is a matter of fact as to actual public reactions, appropriate evidence should be introduced and tested. But it is possible to view a jury as a representative sample whose reactions can be used as a way of deciding how the allegedly defamatory words would be understood by, and affect the attitudes of, those to whom they are communicated. A jury may be asked how they would react to such material, not to give or justify their own values, but in their role as a representative group.

However, it may be that defamation is not concerned with the responses of just any citizen, but is intended to exclude the responses of irrational, immoral and deviant members of society. If we assume that this is indeed to legislative intent, it is still possible to regard juries as representative of majority or dominant social opinion, provided that irrationality, immorality and deviance are assumed to be minority attributes which are unlikely to have any significant representation on a jury. Provided juries are asked, and accurately respond, how they react to the alleged defamation rather than how they believe that they ought to react, then the empirical test remains as a way of getting at the moral distinctions favoured by the legislature. In this respect there is a positivist preference here for the Scottish test of how words are *in fact* understood, rather than the English test of how a *reasonable* person would understand them.[21]

Juries as representative groups are problematic in a pluralist society, and there may be a role for expert evidence here, particularly with respect to distinctive audiences. The empirical approach to 'defamation' is even less plausible where no jury is involved and seems inapplicable to the prior procedure whereby the Common Law judge is required to determine whether the words in question are capable of having a defamatory meaning. Unless this is viewed as simply a threshold matter to do with whether the plaintiff's case has sufficient prima facie plausibility to justify the cost of proceeding with a trial, it would appear to place unwarranted trust in the judge as representative of the community reactions. Alternatively, if the judge addresses the question of the meanings certain words and sentences can bear as essentially a matter of a basic knowledge of the language in question as recorded in authoritative dictionaries, this detaches defamation from the way communications are actually understood by particular audiences.[22]

While some progress can be made in thinking through what positivist defamation criteria would look like, it is not feasible to be precise about the empirical tests that are to be applied without coming to a decision about the specific purposes of defamation law. In particular, for instance, we need to know more precisely what injuries we are seeking to prevent or compensate. Adequate precision in the formulation of defamation criteria can only be obtained by specifying whose opinion counts from the point of view of defamatory understandings. This is not evident in the Common Law tradition because, unusually in tort law, there is no requirement to prove that any actual injury has in fact resulted. Specification of the nature of the injury would, however, bring more precision to bear on the question of whose reaction counts. Is it the bad opinion of neighbours, of fellow employees, of superiors or customers that leads to the loss or harm at issue? That can be answered only by reference to the injury that is claimed to have arisen from the defamatory publication. Once this is established then it is possible to answer the question of defamatory meaning in a manner which is in principle objective, since it relates to factual questions about the understandings of an identified group of persons. Although this judgment concerns the subjective reactions of these persons and their likely subsequent conduct prompted by these reactions, which may be difficult to determine with precision, it is plainly a matter of fact and capable of a degree of objective determination. Framing the issue in this manner removes some of the dangers of value bias which might otherwise operate and provides a way of settling the issue of whether a publication is 'defamatory'. Moreover, it also provides a manageably precise question for publishers to ask when they are considering whether or not the material they wish to publish will be considered defamatory or not. They will have to consider the understanding of those persons whose bad opinion may adversely affect the recognised interests of the person(s) whose conduct or character is being mentioned.

This is an example of the level of 'appropriate precision', which relates to the purpose of the determination rather than a contextless dictionary-style definition or judicial opinion concerning linguistic usage. In summary, Ethical Positivists may go along with defamation tests which in effect raise answerable questions of sociological fact relating to public or specific group opinions, provided that these can be established with some precision and subjected to relevant counter-evidence. In a pluralist and complex society, this is unlikely to be clearly understood or properly dealt with in judge or jury reaction alone without reference to relevant expert evidence.

The Elusive Distinction between Fact and Opinion

A second area of obscurity which is the despair of positivist commentators on defamation law is the elusive distinction between fact and opinion. This distinction is vital in a number of ways. Thus statements of opinion are highly protected (sometimes totally) but statements of fact are not, including the facts on which opinions may be based. Thus *Gertz* v. *Robert Welch* (1974) established the absolute constitutional protection in defamation of actions for the publication of opinions in the United States.[23] Just one problem with this distinction is that what appears to be a statement of fact may not be taken as such by the audience.[24]

The distinction is often assumed to be self-explanatory, but closer examination reveals that fact and opinion are 'vague familiar terms into which one can put whatever meaning is desired in order to reach a particular conclusion'.[25] Where these difficulties are recognised, little assistance is provided by courts for their solution. Thus courts are enjoined to 'consider all the words used' and 'all the circumstances surrounding the statement, including the medium by which the statement is disseminated and the audience to which it is published'.[26] But this does not tell us what we are looking for when we examine the material contextually. Certainly, we must distinguish normal from rhetorical meanings,[27] and, in terms of our earlier discussion, the issue will then be whether the relevant audience would have understood the expression literally or as rhetorical hyperbole. However, this does not settle the fact/opinion question, for both the real and the rhetorical meanings may be either factual or opinionative. For instance, the term 'blackmail' may rhetorically apply to unfair emotional pressure, but this amounts to a moral judgment ('unfair') on a matter of fact ('the use of emotional pressure'). We may agree that expressions of dislike alone are not factual (unless these are viewed as merely reporting subjective feelings), but most criticisms do imply that there is a factual basis to the opinion and these implications may be false. On the other hand, just because it is contextually clear that a statement is fictional, this does not mean that it is an opinion. Fictional statements may themselves be divided into those which are fictional facts and fictional opinions.[28]

Further, we talk of having 'opinions' about factual matters when, for instance, we are not certain of their truth or falsity. Courts sometimes use the idea of verifiability to distinguish fact and opinion.[29] 'Opinions' are what cannot be proved true or false. But lots of unverifiable statements, such as particular historical matters, are clearly factual. And it is unclear why unverifiable assertions should be less vulnerable to liability on the grounds of defamation as they may cause equal harm.[30] Post suggests we adopt a distinction between those matters on which we can expect convergence of view, as in science, and those, on which we cannot, as in ethics, but he gives no real explanation of the significance of the distinction, apart from claiming that the former is not group-dependent and relates to standards that transcend particular communities. Yet this means that in theory factual truth is not so dependent on open debate, and this is the converse of the argument that there be no enforcement of opinion.[31]

This highly complex matter must be settled in this context by a determination of what is at stake rather than through abstract philosophising. In fact there are two crucial dimensions to be considered. The first is the distinction between fact and value, and the second is that between knowledge and belief. The crucial first distinction is in principle lucid, in that we can readily grasp the difference between saying that something is the case and saying that this is a good or bad thing. Much of our of language (for example, 'liar') conjoins these two dimensions but they are analytically distinguishable. Clearly, to protect publishers, and hence open debate, it is necessary to concentrate on the idea of fact as having to do solely with assertions which are understood as saying that something is or is not the case. This excludes evidently fictional accounts as well as value judgments. On this basis we can make a strong positivist criticism of those cases where value judgments are treated as statements of fact because they are not overtly based on associated factual claims. In such cases courts may require defendants to establish a value judgment as 'true', which leads to an adjudication of the matter on the basis of the moral views of those involved, which is precisely the sort of situation that Positivism seeks to avoid. Moral 'truth' should not be at stake in the process of law application.[32]

This does not go far enough, for factual assertions may be 'opinions' in the sense that they are based on belief, not knowledge, in that the person making the assertion is not justified in claiming that the belief is correct. This does not mean that the 'opinion' is a value judgment. Neither does it mean that the assertion is unjustified, since it may be a factual matter on which there is insufficient evidence to make it possible to have knowledge of it and yet one on which we need to have a view for pragmatic reasons. This distinction enables us to raise the question as to whether or not it is legitimate to make factual assertions which cannot be known to be true, as the relevant evidence is not accessible, when these assertions have a defamatory implication. This is a policy matter requiring a decision on the extent to which belief-based factual assertions are permissible. If the answer is that belief-based assertions should not be acceptable where there is evidence available that would render them open to a judgment of truth or falsity but, in matters of practical and immediate importance, they should be permitted where such lesser evidence as is available has been taken into account, then these matters can be dealt with by deciding which party has the burden of proof in such cases, and articulating a burden of proof which is relative to the determinability of the matter in question. This would enable a clear distinction to be drawn between 'opinion' as value judgment and 'opinion' as belief about matters of fact. The former can then be fully protected, while the latter will be subject to tests of 'reasonableness' in relation to appropriate evidence and standards of proof.

To introduce 'reasonableness' at this stage is to appear to jump from the frying pan into the fire, but a reductionist empirical approach can be applied to the 'reasonable person' in law similar to that which we used to save the concept of defamation from evaluative subjectivity. What is involved, on this view, is an appeal to accepted community standards. However, it has to be accepted that there is no agreed community standard on such matters as whether an issue of fact bearing on reputation may be raised without having sufficient evidence to convince a jury on the balance of probabilities. In the absence of such common standards, progress towards the positivist ideal can be made by specifying the standards of care that are required in relation to the dissemination of opinions by going into whatever detail is required to specify the steps which must be taken to verify the empirical grounds of defamatory factual opinions.[33] It is on such matters that the crucial political choices have to be made about the extent of evidence that is required to justify bringing a factual issue into the public domain.

Ultimately, therefore, it is not feasible to arrive at good positivist defamation rules in relation either to the legal criteria of defamation or to the fundamental distinction between fact and opinion without bringing to the fore a coherent specification of the policy objectives which the rules are intended to serve.

Defamation and Freedom of Expression

As a contribution to the clarification of the policy choices that fall to be made in formulating positivistically adequate defamation rules, we take up the line of thought outlined in the introduction to this chapter, to the effect that defamation law and freedom of speech can have important overlapping objectives, beginning with a brief consideration of the conflicting and reinforcing rationales relating to freedom of speech in general, to assess their impact in relation to defamation. This will illustrate how the clarification of objectives can enhance the prospect of formulating positivistically good defamation rules.

Abstracted from its subsidiary role in the argument from democracy, the argument for truth is strongest in relation to the consideration of ideas as general truths about the world. Establishing general truths may involve the inductive use of alleged facts about individuals, but these particulars are not significant for their own sake but only as part of the evidence from which conclusions are drawn inductively. For this reason defamation law, which is normally restricted to libel or slander against individuals, may not be considered a threat to the discovery of the truths which are at stake in the market-place of ideas. Thus in US Supreme Court jurisprudence it is often held that the First Amendment is only for the protection of 'any exposition of ideas'.[34] Nevertheless, limitations on defamation law may be grounded in the argument from truth. Thus Sullivan, which permits uninhibited comment on public figures unless it is made with 'knowledge that it was false or with reckless disregard of whether it was false or not', is based on the view that the object of the First Amendment is to 'assure unfettered interchange of ideas' and presupposes confidence in 'the power of reason as applied through public debate'.[35]

Putting aside the case of political speech for the moment, there is something in the view that defamation rules which protect the reputation of individuals do not directly impinge on freedom of expression in so far as they are justified solely by the argument for truth. Criticism of individuals is not the sort of truth-oriented speech that the argument is all about. In the terminology of Chapter 2, defamation law does not curtail significant freedoms, or at least not morally significant freedoms. The same could be said of those forms of the argument for truth which apply to matters of evaluative opinion rather than empirical fact, since what is principally at stake, for the argument, is the desirability and undesirability of certain types of conduct and certain sorts of policy, rather than a judgment on specific individuals. Yet, where information about individuals can be shown to have significance as contributing to useful general knowledge, perhaps for scientific or political purposes, the argument for truth has force in relation to those aspects of potentially defamatory statements which are truth-oriented. Thus, in order to establish generalisations about political elites or business conduct it may be necessary to offer as evidence assertions about identifiable individuals.

Moreover, truth or falsity in relation to particular persons and events has its own significance. The truths we desire to have include historical truths in the sense of knowledge about unique particulars, whether or not these fit into any general patterns. Leaving aside for the moment the political significance of such individual truths, it can certainly be argued that, where the conduct of individual persons is material in relation to the causation of important historical events, deprivation of the opportunity to establish such particular truths is a significant infringement of liberty. It is not so clear that knowledge of the individual conduct of persons whose conduct is not historically important has the sort of weight which goes with the argument for truth. Unless individuals have good reason (that is, something beyond mere curiosity) to have information about other people, it is not an evident violation of their morally significant liberty to be deprived of giving and receiving such communications.

In some circumstances, however, there is a social interest in having ways of communicating this sort of particular evidence and finding ways of resolving the truth or falsity of allegations bearing on individual conduct and character. Indeed, a defamation action could (not always very plausibly) be presented as providing a forum in which expression is encouraged and required for purposes of establishing socially significant truth. Reputation matters to people in relation to their private relationships as well as their public lives. And the practice of assessing and criticising the conduct of fellow members of a social group may have its own moral legitimacy and purposes. It is therefore a prime matter of policy consideration whether defamation actions promote or inhibit open debate and fair resolution of disputes about truth-oriented and opinion-oriented speech in both private and public spheres. Indeed, law reforms may be instituted with these objectives in mind. Thus if the duty to publish a correction rather than an award of damages were made the relevant liability, this could be said to make the objective of factual accuracy central to the action.

Even without resort to such devices as enforced corrections, it can be argued, with respect to the objective of truth, that the sanctions of defamation law correct inequalities in the so-called 'market-place of ideas' in so far as they inhibit careless journalistic practices by the media outlets that dominate the productive side of that market. The idea of defamation law as a corrective to market failure resulting from inequalities of communicative power is far from fanciful. In short, the argument for truth is in itself not always a strong basis for objecting to the tort of defamation in general. It has to be established that the truth in question requires debate about the individuals concerned, and that there is some countervailing access to the communicative market by those allegedly defamed.

The second principal argument for freedom of expression is based on self-realisation. Commenting on the lives and conduct of others does not seem closely related to the development of the individual speaker, except in the case of those, such as journalists, who adopt this form of self-expression as a channel for their autonomy. Nor does receipt of defamatory information appear to have any bearing on the general run of audience self-realisation. Further, publication of defamatory information about individuals may harm their autonomy by undermining their position in society and their general self-confidence. No doubt, in some cases, the activity of defending one's reputation may provide an avenue for self-realisation, but this can only rarely be the case.

Some speaker self-realisation interests are to an extent bound up with the opportunity to let off steam by expressing strong opinions about significant others, which argues that there should be some considerable latitude allowed to such emotion-releasing mechanisms, but this can hardly be viewed as a central aspect of self-realisation. Yet it is important for individuals to develop the self-confidence and sense of responsibility which manifests itself in the open criticism of those whose conduct falls short of what they have a right to expect or a social duty to demand. Provided that there is reciprocity and social equality, criticism of others is, in many situations, an activity to be admired and encouraged and therefore an appropriate avenue for self-realisation. Not all negative evaluations are based on malevolence and self-interest. Self-realisation through criticism of others applies particularly if self-fulfilment is regarded, not as a private matter, but something which is achieved in the context of a community. The interactions and achievements of communal life often require a setting in which the honest criticism of others plays an important role. Equally, the harmony of community life requires some way of resolving disagreements which arise over the dissemination of information which is critical of others. In any genuine community there can be no general bar on personal criticism of others, but there must also be ways in which these criticisms can be considered and community relationships restored.

Particularly in communal settings, which could be taken to include neighbourhood, work and associational contexts, freedom of communication in relation to discussing the conduct and character of others may call for protection on the grounds of the self-realisation rationale. Interest in and a critical attitude towards the conduct and character of others, and the attempt to formulate and express opinions about others, have an important role in the development of the capacities of social beings. We learn to be critical about ourselves through observing and assessing the conduct of others and taking into account the criticisms that others make of us. Mutual assessment is a socially significant activity. The argument for self-realisation can, therefore, be used not simply to resist defamation laws which restrict those aspects of self-realisation which involve expressing views on the conduct and character of others, but to urge the development of defamation regimes which encourage the acceptable forms of such self-realisation, namely those in which the truth of the matters at issue are not lost sight of.

The third principal argument for freedom of expression is the democratic one. Both ideas and information are vital to democracy, particulary information about those personally involved in the democratic process. Electoral judgment and the continuing process of democratic debate presuppose a legitimate interest in such ideas and information as bear on the assessment of the policy, conduct and trustworthiness of those who are or aspire to be active participants in the process of democratic government. The argument from democracy seems, therefore, to imply that there should be no law of defamation in relation to the political process, widely conceived.

Some personal matters about politicians and others involved in matters of genuine political concern may be irrelevant to sound political debate, but relevance is a matter which itself has to be determined by open discussion. While a politician may believe that his sexual conduct is irrelevant to the evaluation of his political worth, this may not be a view shared by members of the electorate. It is not for a majority to prejudge the issue of public relevance or private data. Additionally, there are grounds for saying that it should be possible for any citizen or commentator to raise suspicions about matters which cannot be readily established but which are of political importance, just so that these may be overtly debated.

It can, of course, be argued that deliberate or careless falsehoods actually damage the democratic process, particularly when they cannot be countered within an electorally significant period. The well-timed falsehood can have an unwarranted determinative impact on electoral outcomes. There may therefore be democratic reasons to regulate expression from outlets that are open to the manipulation of those who control effective means of communication so as to avoid the immediate impact of defamatory assertions. Equally, however, any defamation law which is aimed at such evils can readily be abused by those wealthy and powerful people who tend to dominate the political process in such a way as to exclude the public from information which is highly relevant to the political choices that they are called upon to make. Moreover, those who offer themselves as participants in the political process may be regarded as voluntarily assuming the burden of being the target of criticism and comment.

It would appear, then, that the argument for democracy gives weight to the view that defamation law should have a very limited role within the political process, but there may also be substance to the view that there can be defamation regimes which actually assist the sort of democratic dialogue that serves the goal of informed debate in a manner which assists the discovery of politically relevant truth.

The brief analysis of defamation law objectives in the context of free speech rationales has revealed that we are not dealing here with a simple opposition of the protection of reputation to the values of freedom of expression. It may be that the selection of a priority goal, such as furthering effective debate relating to the determination of disputes bearing on reputation, can expedite the articulation of positivistically good defamation rules. The principal justifications of freedom of expression can be deployed in favour as well as to counter elements of defamation law. This approach to the analysis and reform of defamation law is by no means an account of actual defamation law. In fact, defamation rules and procedures in different jurisdictions are highly variable, a point which is itself worth noting in the light of the tenacity with which some cling to the status quo with which they are familiar. Indeed, striking contrasts may be drawn between defamation law in the United Kingdom, the United States and continental Europe.

The Common Law based Anglo-American tradition comes with an entrenched array of devices for limiting freedom of expression, including a complex and developing defamation case law, as well as a political tradition in which the freedom of the press plays only a spasmodically powerful part. Within this family there are instructive current differences between the United Kingdom and Australia, where there is no powerful presumption in favour of freedom of expression once consequential reputational harms are identified, and the United States with its strong cultural emphasis on the right to criticise and the right to know, whatever the consequences, as partially instantiated in the distinctive application of the First Amendment in recent times. This divergence evidently derives to some extent from the role of the Supreme Court in its application of the First Amendment, but also reflects a deep ideological commitment which is quite general throughout the United States.

There are, nevertheless, aspects of all defamation regimes which can be viewed as contributions to, rather than inhibitions of, freedom of communication. In traditional Common Law systems, defendants may plead that their words are 'fair comment', that is, something that a reasonable person, however prejudiced, could have believed. This extends to protecting comments which are actually unfair, provided that they could have honestly been believed by a fair-minded person on the facts as they were known at the time.[36] The defence of fair comment can be rebutted by malice, and extreme irrationality may be accepted as evidence of malice, as may failure by a newspaper to publish a reply. The legal standard here is 'objective' fairness, which depends on whether a hypothetical honest (albeit prejudiced) person *might* genuinely hold such an opinion, although the plaintiff might also seek to prove subjective malice, namely that the plaintiff did not believe or did not care about the truth of what was published.[37] Fair comment also requires that the defamatory comments be on a matter of public interest, but this only excludes the private lives of persons who are not public figures.

Overall, the defence of 'fair comment' can be viewed as a concession to freedom of speech rather than an actual encouragement of debate, particularly as the defendant has to establish the factual basis for the comment. In this and in many other respects, in the United States there are now major divergences from the Common Law of defamation which largely derive from the Supreme Court's use of the First Amendment, and particularly the jurisprudence subsequent to *New York Times* v. *Sullivan*. The most important differences are that, in the United States:

1 there is a public official and public figure rule which enables the publication of defamatory falsehoods about such figures provided that 'actual malice' is not involved, actual malice involving knowledge that the material is false or recklessness in relation to its truth or falsity;
2 the burden of proof is on the plaintiff to establish the falsity of the allegedly defamatory material; and
3 strict liability has been replaced in relation to defamation in general, so that the mere fact that a defamatory statement is published is insufficent to establish liability.

At least in recent times, therefore, defamation liability has been considerably curtailed in the United States, while in the United Kingdom, despite a recent report which recommends some substantive and procedural changes to tilt the balance of defamation law in favour of defendants, the dominant political mood is hostile to enlarging press freedom, owing in part to the public reaction to media intrusions into the private affairs of royalty and other sensationalised reporting.[38]

While debate in the public arena is now more open in the United States than in those Common Law jurisdictions which have not been liberalised by constitutional interventions, it still cannot be said that US free speech jurisprudence makes common cause with defamation law with respect to free speech values. By seeking to exclude courts from dealing with the factual content of defamations in the public arena, attention has been refocussed on journalistic practice, making defamation suits costly to defend. And, since the First Amendment deals exclusively with alleged restrictions on speech and the press imposed by governments, it is little help to furthering open discussion in the privately owned media. In particular, there is a general hostility to imposing a right of reply or court-ordered correction, devices which can be used in some jurisidictions to reduce damages, but which are considered to be intrusions into press freedom if they are required by law.

If a more positive view is taken of the state's role in promoting freedom of speech, it becomes possible to view any steps which may be imposed to encourage diversity and balance of view as promoting freedom of expression. In the defamation arena this means requiring those whose reputations are under attack to have the material opportunity to respond. Thus, with a defamation law which can order steps to be taken which counter and minimise damage to reputation, we have a genuine coming together of defamation and free speech objectives. Often, however, the mere right of reply will not settle the issue because the relevant evidence is not testable in the sort of debate that can be conducted in newspapers and in the media. To protect a reputation it may be necessary to have a trial of the alleged facts which can only be done satisfactorily in a court. Following out this line of thought it can be argued that defamation law ought to centre on that which courts are best able to do, namely establish the truth or falsity of particular matters of fact. Instead of focussing on the issue of damages, particularly punitive damages, especially where these are set at levels which are clearly designed to deter open debate of reputational matters, defamation law should be a resource to settle factual disputes bearing on reputation. This would be to make the declaratory judgment, not the award of damages, the controlling objective. The thesis is that the prioritising of a specific objective, such as enhancing reputational truth, may enable us to make progress towards more positivistic defamation law.

The suggestion is that policy selection can be made and concretised in a manner which proves more efficacious and certain than existing regimes. This may apply both to the trial process, by directing the issues towards issues of truth, with which courts are adept at dealing, and to the pre-trial process which is designed to head off litigation in ways which promote socially useful and individually protective means of establishing relevant truth. For instance, publishing a correction as setting up a bar to further litigation effectively deals with chance errors. But such retractions cannot be trusted as concessions to truth, as they may be made to avoid costly litigation. They may also have a serious 'chilling' effect, since the retraction may be coerced by the threat of a suit in the event of non-compliance with the demand for a published retraction. We are likely, therefore, to have dishonest admissions of error which do nothing to further the cause of truth.

Theoretically more satisfactory is the proposal that defamation proceedings centre on a declaration of fact. The idea here is that the courts should be used primarily as a means of establishing the truth in cases where individual reputation is seriously at risk. On one proposal this could be required by either party to a potential action. No damages would be awarded, but the authority of the court would become available to ward off or substantiate the defamatory assertion.[39] The merit of this proposal from the point of view of freedom of communication is that it makes truth the central contention and offers a positive way forward in terms of free speech values. Its problems arise from the enormous cost of such proceedings, and the uncertainty as to who should pay. The determination of truth does not in itself establish if the publication was negligent, yet award of costs would have to reflect the reasonableness of the publication, otherwise we are back in the strict liability that serves to inhibit publication of important but unprovable material. Yet to raise such issues for the apportionment of costs would in effect extend the trial issues far beyond the mere truth or falsity of the defamation. If each party were to pay their own costs, however, the chilling effect of the action would remain. The major question remaining therefore concerns the equality of communicative power in a world of material inequality. Mechanisms are required for financing trials, financing retractions and moving towards equality of communicative capacity.[40]

In all this the public/private distinction remains significant with respect to who should pay for the cost of declaratory judgments. Poor individuals suffer serious defamation damage and have need of declaratory judgments to correct the harmful consequences. However, where there are matters of public importance at stake, there are added reasons for triggering mechanisms to settle the facts at issue. Here, as the matter is of public importance, it seems right that the public should bear the cost of the proceedings.[41] With respect to private matters, then, the absence of a public interest in the publication of defamatory material should mean that the publisher is at risk for the cost of the action, and for any actual damages.

Conclusion

The lines of debate sketched above are an example of the sort of policy discussion that is necessary for the articulation of the specific goals on which good positivist laws can be based. Explicit formulation of purposes is a prerequisite of the good legislative drafting and bounded interpretation. If, for instance, the determination of reputational truth is adopted as the central purpose of defamation law, we have an objective which can give sharpness and direction to the rules and procedures that ought to be selected through political debate and legislative activity. It also gives direction and limits to such interpretative problems as arise in the course of the application of legislation. The result should be a clear and systematic set of rules establishing morally and politically relevant distinctions in empirically determinable criteria. Ideally, this would result in a defamation regime in sharp contrast to the convoluted mess of overlapping principles, rules, defences and procedures which have emerged in the development of the Common Law of defamation.

Formulating precise policy objectives in terms of empirically determinable outcomes does not in itself enable us to read off specific rules, but it does provide a basis for selecting precise rules and for their interpretation in cases of ambiguity and vagueness. Thus the criteria for defamation itself can be refined to cover only matters of fact which have a bearing on the opinions and conduct of those whose good opinion affects the legitimate (non-criminal) and explicitly identified interests of the individual (or group) concerned. Thereafter the focus would be on the effective determination of the truth or falsity of the factual content of the defamation. A range of defences could be developed in terms of such factors as the availability of evidence relating to the truth of the factual implications involved and the extent to which the public significance of the reputational truth involved justified placing the matter in the public domain on the basis of incomplete evidence. Focussing on reputational truth also points us towards certain types of remedy, such as declaratory judgments or rights of reply, rather than others, such as punitive damages aimed at 'punishing' journalists.

Of course, there may be other objectives which ought to be secured through the same course of action. In particular, the need to deter negligent or malicious defamation arguably runs counter to the concerns of truth by pointing attention more to the practice of journalists than to the truth of their factual premisses, although good journalistic practice must itself be defined in part through its effectiveness at checking information. Giving priority to reputational truth may also give insufficient attention to demands for just compensation for reputational injury to public officials. LEP must acknowledge that there are difficult choices to be made here between partly conflicting objectives and sometimes incommensurable values. The theory maintains, however, that these choices be made in an open political manner and not be left to emerge from the discretionary space left to judges in deciding particular cases on the basis of inadequate rules.

Central to this line of development is the much-criticised distinction between public and private matters, but there is no reason why a distinction suited to the particular objectives of defamation law cannot be formulated. In this context, the public/private divide is not being used to exclude the state from 'private' matters. In fact, the object is to identify as 'private' those persons who are to be more thoroughly protected by the relevant laws.

The challenge for LEP is to produce ways of arriving at a workable and morally relevant distinction which does not involve the courts in deciding which persons or issues they consider to be of morally legitimate public interest.[42] What is wanted is an empirical rather than a normative test of what constitutes a public issue. The first step is to focus on the definition of a public issue, although it will follow from this that the conduct of certain persons, such as public officials, is within the public domain for the purpose of defamation law.[43] A definition simply in terms of what most people already know about is too restrictive, as it must be possible to introduce new information into democratic debate. It is also too restrictive to cover only matter that relates directly to government policy or personnel.[44] While this is pleasingly empirical, it excludes a wider range of matters which are of social and therefore ultimately of political concern.[45] In a democracy, anything is potentially of legitimate public concern because legitimacy has to be decided on the basis of what is generally accepted as a matter for social and political debate. It is not for the law to make that choice for citizens. On the other hand, it is insufficient to leave the determination of what is a matter of public concern to actual existing majorities, as any plausible theory of democracy recognises the rights of minorities to raise isues which concern them but not others. This points us in the direction of Post's suggestion that we settle on a descriptive content for a matter of public concern in terms of the actual concerns of a significant number of persons.[46] This can be more precisely if somewhat arbitrarily defined for the sake of predictability. This test may be regarded as overinclusive, but it is in such choices that priority is given to such matters as free speech values over the protection of what the majority may regard as private interests.

Similar priority choices fall to be made between choosing the right of reply in the interests of open discussion and protecting the property rights of media owners and their employees with respect to editorial control.[47] Free publication in the media is a valuable commodity, access to which could be abused for personal gain and narrow political advantage. On the other hand, there is no difficulty in principle in holding that existing capacity to control the content of principal media outlets carries with it responsibilities to standards of factual accuracy and hence the duty to make available counter-evidence.[48] Nevertheless, there has to be some means of determining when a right of reply is justified. We are not dealing here, however, with something so indefinable as achieving a balance of coverage on matters of public moment, but solely on material which appears to be defamatory of individuals. This leads us into issues which are central to defamation action, namely the defamatory nature of the material and the identity of the person defamed. Moreover, if such a system is to work at all then the reply must be published in close temporal proximity to the original publication and speedy decision making will be required.

This is a matter, however, on which rough and ready decision making is adequate, given that what is at stake is no more than an extended, more prominent, form of reader's letter. A tribunal system, funded by the media and administered by a body such as a Press Council, could serve to exclude those petitioners for an opportunity to reply who are taking unreasonable advantage of the system. Erring on the liberal side has no serious disadvantage since it affects no significant liberties or other substantial material interests and may help to stimulate truth-serving discussion. The application of clear and precise rules is not paramount in such circumstances.

However, the mere publication of competing views may not be sufficient to provide the public with evidence to determine the credibility of the conflicting assertions. Hence the need for a right of action geared to a declaratory judgment as to the truth of defamatory facts. Not only may the procedures of discovery and trial bring relevant evidence to light, but courts constitute a relative impartial forum for the evaluation of evidence. For the plaintiff this can have the advantage of vindicating reputation, for the defendant it can have the advantage of vindicating the assertion, and for the public there can be the advantage of receiving a considered view on the matter which has a certain neutrality with respect to the contending parties. Courts, it may be argued, are suitable fora for determining questions of fact relating to particular events.[49]

Continuing this analysis would require detailed attention to the question of costs, which bring back in all the difficulties associated with the payment of damages, such as the chilling effect of defamation actions on those who would engage in public debate and the shifting of attention from questions of truth to questions of negligence and good faith.[50] However, the objective of this chapter has been to indicate what progress can be made towards defamation rules which go some way towards meeting the positivist standards. Such progress as we have made in this direction indicates that there are improvements could be made in terms of precision and predictability, and in the reduction of the scope for bias in the legal process. This promises important gains both with respect to limiting the scope of the chilling effect and in relation to the development of a system which is better adapted to achieving at least some politically identified objectives. The contention is that these improvements are best prompted and directed by an approach to law which incorporates the values and priorities of LEP.

Notes

1 It can be argued that privacy and defamation are simply confused, but it is dogmatic simply to assume that defamation law cannot be concerned with privacy. This matter crystallises in the contrast between jurisdictions which have truth as a defence in defamation actions and those which require proof of public interest as well as truth.

2 Of course, libel may be treated separately as a crime and as a tort, and different purposes apply.

3 A variant is the argument that speech causes no real harm or, if it does, that harm is always mediated through voluntary human conduct. See Baker (1989, p.47): 'the constitutional protection of free speech is justified not merely because of the values served by free speech but because freedom of speech serves these values in a particular, humanly acceptable manner, that is, nonviolently and noncoercively'.

4 The problems we encounter in dealing with the interpretation of rules are compounded when the rules which require interpretation deal with linguistic phenomena which themselves require interpretation. This complication can be exaggerated, however, as similar problems arise in any attempt to regulate conduct which can seldom be analysed without reference to its intelligibility, which is also a matter of understanding meanings. See Neill (1991, p.iv): 'Words can be spun into an infinite variety of patterns. The meaning of words and shades of meaning can depend on small changes in arrangement or emphasis. It is not surprising therefore that the law of defamation is a difficult subject.' And, ibid., pp.7–8: 'There are at least two very obvious differences which mark out defamation. We consider that the most important factor is the complexity and subtlety of language, and the infinite variety of allegations and innuendo which can be combined one with another. The raw material of a libel action is generally quite different from that of other claims, and in particular from those based on contract.'

5 Defamation is distinctive amongst torts in that resulting harm does not have to be proven for liability to be established, although this clearly has an impact on the level of damages awarded. A possible positivist reform is to require the proof of actual harm resulting from defamatory statements, but this may be thought to diminish the significance of the subjective hurt caused by personal criticism.

6 Equality of communicative power would diminish this problem but not remove it. Absent regulation, it is unfair to disregard the fact that not everyone makes the same use of communicative power and such use as is made may be justified or unjustified in terms of its truth or significance. See Sunstein (1993b, Chapter 2).

7 While the quantum of damages can be legislatively controlled, the costs of

defamation actions can be even more substantial and less easily controlled. Forer (1987) suggested $20 000 for a contested case in the United States.

8 Paradoxically, there may be no way of getting to the evidence regarding their truth or falsity without placing the issue in the public domain.

9 Notorious examples include Robert Maxwell, but gagging writs are a familiar part of political life in many jurisdictions. See John Wicklein (1992, p.29): 'By a recent count, 142 defamation actions against newspapers, most of them filed by politicians and businessmen, were pending in Sydney, which has been called the libel capital of the world ... In 1989, the John Fairfax Group, which publishes the *Sydney Morning Herald* in Sydney and the *Age* in Melbourne, paid out $2.6 million in settling such suits.' On the topic of SLAPS ('Strategic Lawsuits Against Public Participation') see Canan and Pring (1988).

10 It is a concomitant of high legal costs that there must be the prospect of substantial awards of damages to balance the risk of losing a defamation action.

11 The problem here is similar to that posed by contempt of court. See Chesterman (1989).

12 The specifically positivist form of this problem is the tendency of juries to see the matter in terms of their own moral views of the conduct criticised and the motives of the defendants.

13 For a more optimistic view of the work of Press Councils, see David Flint, 'Media Self-Regulation', in Campbell and Sadurski (1994, pp.281–96).

14 Noteworthy here is the view of the European Court on the intepretation of 'prescribed by law', which they take to mean 'precision and accessibility'. 'It means that any restricting norm must be formulated with sufficient precision so that the citizen is able, if need be with appropriate advice, to foresee the consequences which a given action may entail to a degree that is reasonable in the circumstances' (*Sunday Times* v. *United Kingdom*, Publ.Court, Series A, vol.139).

15 See Meiklejohn (1962, p.259); *Garrison* v. *Louisiana*, 379 US 64, 75 (1964).

16 *New York Times* v. *Sullivan*, 376 US 64, 75 (1964).

17 *Hustler Magazine* v. *Falwell*, 108 S.Ct. at 879.

18 Robertson and Nicol (1992, p.46); Walker (1989, pp.149–63).

19 For a textbook exposition, see Fleming (1992).

20 Thus *Mycroft* v. *Sleight* (1921) 90 LJKB 883, relating to the use of 'scab' with respect to fellow workers in a mining community.

21 Walker (1993, p.54).

22 Dictionary definitions do reflect usage but also have a normative role in relation to correct usage, making them potentially irrelevant to defamation, although there is some protection here for defendants against strict liability for unintended slights.

23 *Gertz* v. *Robert Welch Inc*, 418 US 323 (1974) and *New York Times* v. *Sullivan*, 376 US 254 (1964), 280 and 269–70, which actually quotes J.S. Mill's view that the assertion of falsehoods has value in providing us with the opportunity to better grasp the truth.

24 As in a cartoon lampoon: *Hustler Magazine* v. *Falwell*, 108 S.Ct. 876 (1988). See also *Myerson* v. *Smiths Weekly* (1923) 24 SR (NSW) 20 at 26. Note Robertson and Nicol (1992, p.80): 'there is no hard and fast rule'.

25 Titus (1962, pp.1205–6).

26 *Information Control Corp* v. *Genesis One Computer Corp*, 611 F.2d 781 (9th Cir. 1980) at 784.

27 *Greenbelt* v. *Co-operative Publishing Association and Bresler*, 398 US 6 (1970).

28 Searle (1979, p.67).

29 *Immuno A.G.* v. *Moor-Jankowski*, 145 AD 2d. 114, 143, 537 NYS 2d. 129, 147 (1989).

30 Oddly, this makes opinions useless in the market-place of ideas: see Post (1990, p.655).

31 Ibid., p.660.

32 Note *Obershlick* v. *Austria*, Judgment of 23 May 1991, Series A, no. 204, where it was held that the requirement that a journalist prove the truth of a value judgment is impossible and 'in itself an infringement of freedom of expression' (para. 63).

33 Note *Garrison* v. *Louisiana*, 379 US 64, 75 (1964).

34 *New York Times* v. *Sullivan*, 376 US 254, 270 (1964).

35 See *Gardiner* v. *John Fairfax and Sons* (1942) 42 SR (NSW) 171 at 174): 'The question the jury must consider is this – would any fair man, however prejudiced he may be, however exaggerated or obstinate his views, have said that which this criticism has said?'

36 See Robertson and Nicol (1992, p.84) and Walker (1989, pp.174–8).

37 However note the affirmation of free speech in *Derbyshire Council* v. *Times Newspapers* [1991] 2 NLJ Law Reports 275; also the introduction of a weak form of the public figure defence in *Andrew Theophanous* v. *The Herald and Weekly Times*, 12 October, 1994.

38 See Annenberg Washington Program (1988).

39 Ibid., p.32.

40 See Sunstein (1993a, Chapter 2) and Kairys (1993, p.55).

41 See Schauer (1992).

42 This is acknowledged in *Gertz* v. *Robert Welch Inc.*, 418 US at 346.

43 Schauer (1991, p.173) notes that the argument from democracy 'provides justification for special treatment of discussion of public issues and the conduct and qualifications of public servants'; and p.177: 'To take as a remedy, for example, for the abuses that may occur when criticism of government is concerned is in some sense to extend to the majority the determination of what is right against the majority.' The classifications are not to do primarily with status but with activity: engaging in public discourse, being part of the public scene. It is partly a matter of the ability to gain access to and benefiting from publicity, but is more a matter of the what is properly part of the public domain.

44 Bork (1971) wants to keep the public figure defence for those matters 'concerned with governmental behaviour, policy or personnel'.

45 Hanna Pitkin (1981) extends it to matters concerning collective self-definition and decision making.

46 Post (1990, p. 703).

47 The right of reply is an entitlement which is resisted by the media as an infringement of editorial rights if it goes beyond the existence of a letters section under full editorial control. These objections are untenable when they are based on rights of ownership as would appear to be the case in the United States: see *Miami Herald* v. *Tornillo* 418 US 241 (1974). Publishing replies may or may not be commercially beneficial, but publication is an activity whose nature gives rise to good reasons for particular property rules, which can readily include such a responsibility. Nor is appeal to a right to freedom of expression, constitutional or otherwise, definitive, because what is at stake is in part a matter of what regime best furthers such expression. It is noteworthy that the right of reply is firmly established in continental Europe: see Danzinger (1986).

48 This takes us back to the issue of whether freedom of expression is to be construed as a negative right which privileges the holder with respect to government 'interference' or as involving effective rights of access with correlative duties to facilitate such access.

49 The desire to get such a public affirmation may be the motivation which explains the prevalence of public figure plaintiffs in the United States who believe

that they have 'won' even if they do not prove actual malice and therefore get any damages. Indeed it can be said that, systemically, the reason why damages are important is that it gives private parties a reason to undertake costly litigation in the course of which the public is benefited by an authoritative determination of fact.

50 On issues of public concern, there is the argument, mentioned above, that the cost should be borne by the state, perhaps through a tax on communications. In a system where each party pays their own costs there may not be sufficient incentive for plaintiffs to bring a suit which cannot lead to a monetary remedy. This is avoided if costs are transferred to the losing party, but this could produce a significant chilling effect on publications unless the burden of disproof in relation to fact is on the plaintiff, or the defendant has to establish only that it was a reasonable factual belief in the light of evidence available.

10 Conclusion: A Unifying Prescription

Introduction

The legal theory of Ethical Positivism (LEP) centres on the significance of specific rules as the appropriate medium for the exercise of political power. The theory is positivistic in requiring that authoritative rules be outcomes of objectively identifiable legitimated political process and in its insistence that these rules be in general utilised without recourse to the personal, group or class value judgments of the citizen/enforcer/adjudicator. The theory is ethical, in the first place because this model of law is an aspirational ideal which requires moral justification, including justification of the roles and institutional mechanisms involved, but also because it is an ideal which cannot be operationalised without adherence to a professional ethic by a politically and socially aware judiciary and legal profession, and a comparable citizen ethic in relation to public understanding of and compliance with the law. There is no implication that laws ought to be ethically neutral in content; indeed, ideally they encapsulate the outcome of overt and considered political choice. Laws are to be understood as expressions of, often contentious, conduct maxims whose enforcement requires moral justification. The intelligibility of rules is dependent on the capacity to understand, but not necessarily endorse, the context of the conduct they regulate, the sort of purposes they serve and the moral principles they embody.

The justification of the model is not directly definitional or conceptual, but moral and political. The rationales for preferring government through rules have to do with fundamental political values, particularly the fair and effective pursuit of objectives which have sufficient significance to justify mandatory social coordination and control. Adding a democratic dimension, having rule making the proper focus of political rather than legal choice, gives more effective, because more specific, implementation to the institutionalisation of equality in decision making.

LEP will seem to the postmodern readers to be naive and unsophisticated for failing to take adequate account of the problematics of communication and the inevitability of ideological bias in any regulatory system. To traditional lawyers LEP is more likely to appear rather obvious, but perhaps mildly reassuring in the context of insistent denigration of the claimed impartiality of legal process. The former are steeped in reaction against false and self-serving claims to objectivity. The latter, in their reflective moments, are beset by doubts as to the professional nature of their occupation. There may, however, be some common ground to be found in a theory which, while acknowledging the grave difficulties involved, sets out to present a usable intellectual and moral framework for a rule-centred approach to law making, law implementation and, in case of dispute, law adjudication. By concentrating on the notion of rules and regulation, LEP presents a perspective on legal systems which makes possible both critique and aspiration. It is contended that the ideal of principled political decision making which manifests itself in rules that can often be followed unproblematically and frequently adjudicated with some impartiality sets up a model against which we can identify at least some kinds of bias and oppression, and which can be acknowledged as desirable by citizens with radically different moral and political views.

This unifying objective is unattainable unless we are able to unshackle Legal Positivism from limiting caricatures and ideological pigeon-holes, and genuinely explore the prospect of an agreed framework for law reform and legal practice. This book does not go beyond the point of outlining an approach which is relatively clear, philosophically tenable and of some use to those who seek to persist with the ideals associated with government through rules. It would be repetitious to rehearse at this point the basic insight that the powerful critiques of Legal Positivism as a sociological theory have dubious relevance when matters of prescriptive political philosophy are at issue. If government through rules is a vulnerable human creation which grasps at a smattering of purposeful and just cooperative achievement in a world which is routinely unresponsive to and destructive of such projects, then it cannot be put to one side on the grounds that even the best legal systems often fail adequately to instantiate its aspirations. Instead of reiterating that theme, this concluding chapter ventures briefly into the contemporary ideological landscape to consider the prospects for the legal theory of Ethical Positivism as a unifying democratic philosophy, and in particular seeks to forge some unlikely alliances with approaches to legal philosophy whose starting point is normally a ritual rejection of the positivist tradition.

Socialist Positivism

Prior to the spectacular collapse of communist regimes in eastern Europe and the transformation of democratic socialist parties of the West into liberal lookalikes, the socialist historian E.P. Thompson had already shocked many traditional socialists with his declaration that the rule of law is an 'unqualified human good'.[1] Thompson's dictum is mainly to do with the mitigating effects of the Common Law process with respect to some of the nastier aspects of the historical breakdown of the traditional system of land tenure in the early stages of capitalist development in England. Others have since mounted rather more comprehensive accounts of the affinities of law and socialism. These accounts centre in the main on the crucial role of government in providing a regulatory framework for any industrial and post-industrial society that seeks a measure of social and economic equality and tolerably harmonious social relationships.[2]

The main steps in the argument are a critique of the idea that there is some identifiable minimalist role for states which stops at providing a neutral framework for individual competition[3] and the demonstration of the compatibility of potentially pervasive but by no means totalitarian regulation of economic and social life with the goals of economic efficiency and democratic consent.[4] Within this overall picture there are more specific debates to be explored in relation to the ideological ties of the legal concepts central to regulatory systems. Central to these debates are the concepts of law, rights and obligation which have absorbed our analysis of Ethical Positivism. What has to be directly addressed at some stage is the claim that this system of thought is inextricably tied to a version of liberal individualism that has no logical room for the egalitarian, communal and non-coercive aspects of the socialist tradition.

I have traversed this ground in *The Left and Rights*, in relation to the alleged amoralism, legalism, coerciveness and individualism of rights and, a fortiori, the interest-protecting rules which constitute rights.[5] Many of these themes have also emerged in the course of this book, particularly with respect to the institutionalisation of democratic inequality through the close connection of choice of government and choice of rules. One theme which has not been emphasised so far is the role of rights in relation to non-competitive situations. While we have stressed the way in which rules are pivotal for most standard cooperative social situations which are routine rather than individually negotiated, there remains the lingering assumption that rights mark the boundaries of legitimate selfishness in a world populated by cognitively self-sufficient egoistic hedonists.[6]

This prejudice against rule-governed rights remains, despite the evidence that is readily adduced about the cooperative advantages of rules as a basis for coordinated actions in complex social situations. There is a reluctance to accept that these rules concern rights because rights are defined, in terms of the critique, as the source of competing claims. But once we break out of this unrewarding circularity, and take rights to include entitlements under coordination rules, then all the participatory activities of egalitarian societies fall within the rights framework.

Further, if we regard rights as rule-protected interests, the right to speech can become the right to the material opportunity actually to participate in a complex organisation of social communication.[7] The right not to be defamed can be related to the existence of effective social mechanisms for ensuring a proper resolution of factual disputes about criticised conduct.[8] The sense of interest involved here relates to what the individuals involved are interested *in* or concerned about, but they are by no means essentially selfish in the sense that they are hostile to the concerns of other people, or self-centred in the sense that they do not take into account the wellbeing of other members of society. There is nothing in the idea of rule-protected interests that is peculiarly the province of classical liberal individualism.

Further, the significance of public goods is dominant in socialism.[9] The organisation of benefits to which, ideally, all contribute and from which none can be excluded is an aspect of social life which is as rule-dependent as any other. The fact that the pursuit of public goods involves duties as well as rights is confirmation that here we are dealing with real matters of societal coordination rather than the sort of political rhetoric which uses the language of rights to block welfare-oriented government programmes. Positive and humane rights are more demanding of the active cooperation of other people than are the narrowly negative versions of traditional human rights.

If we retreat from these intimations of altruism to the stronger realities of class conflict, then rules, although powerless in themselves, provide an essential element in the principled way of transcending these tensions in an enduring way. The fact that we often fail in such endeavours would be decisive if there were acceptable alternatives. But situation-by-situation political contest is even less likely to result in victory for the losers in the inequalities of the societal status quo than is the attempt to correct these inequalities through systematic, that is rule-directed, redistribution, in the context of an otherwise overwhelming natural tendency to social and economic inequality. Moreover, rule-based rights provide a basis for confidence that the protections and services they guarantee are something to be relied upon to the extent that the citizens have grounds for their assurance that they are not vulnerable to the forms of domination excluded by the rules.[10] The fact that rules in themselves make little difference if the economic and political constitution is unfavourable and unreceptive, and that legislative reforms can be foiled by unconscious as well as deliberative misunderstandings of the political purposes involved by those charged with their implementation, is simply a familiar part of a social and political scene which places the success of government through law firmly in the context of adequate education, genuine communication and the taming of economic power.

Critical Legal Positivism

While some readers may go along with the idea of Socialist Positivism it may seem perverse to float the rash oxymoron 'Critical Legal Positivism' in relation to the idea of a positivist version of Critical Legal Studies (CLS). Given that CLS is basically a critique of the liberal tradition in which Positivism is embedded, it seems incongruous to look for any reconciliation of view here. However, if we dissect the many interwoven strands of this movement it is possible to regard many of the powerful critical analyses of existing legal systems as connected with some underlying assumptions about rules and legitimacy which connect with LEP.

CLS draws on many disparate traditions, and it is certainly impossible to reconcile some of the more extreme versions of the indeterminacy thesis with the idea that governments, judges and citizens can be limited and directed by rules.[11] But a central theme of CLS is not so much the indeterminacy of rules as the determinacy of judicial decisions which are viewed as the outcomes of systematic class bias, determined and dominated by ideology rather than authentic agreement on shared criteria. Where there is sharing of criteria, it is amongst the oppressing elite, and through false consciousness, in society generally. At its most forceful and encompassing, the thesis is that, as on the Realist analysis, rules never decide cases and that, despite any psychological impulses to the contrary, it is always open to judges to get the result that their political judgment dictates. Such limitations as there are arise from a need to sustain legitimacy by gaining wider judicial and political acceptance for their decisions, rather than from any exclusions indicated in the rules. Law is a dirty trick played, more or less consciously, by the judicial hierarchy which disguises the indefensible inequalities of the society in which they operate.[12] It is possible to read this as an emancipatory enterprise, seeking to liberate us from the dominance of fetishism by exposing the real basis of the legal process. For Duncan Kennedy, at least, this has the effect of delegitimising the system and thus reducing the assumptions as to the naturalness or necessity of social inequalites. Judges are in one way or another engaged in a bad faith exercise of pretending that what they do is required by law, whereas in fact it is all an elaborate and expensive manipulative facade.

This radical theme is, in itself, compatible with prescriptive Positivism. Indeed, the 'outing' of bias is often achieved in critical analysis by showing that judges ignore the evident contextual meaning of rules when the outcome is not to their liking. What is not compatible with Ethical Positivism is the further claim that all the assumptions of such critiques are illusory in that there is no such thing as contextually evident meaning and, therefore, no way in which bias can be demonstrated by pointing to failures to exhibit fidelity to such meanings. On the most radical CLS premisses, there can be no basis for saying that judges, in seeking to present legal argument which gets the result that they want, are being unethical. Kennedy may argue that all judging is a matter of bad faith, in that it involves the pretence that legal argument produces a determinate result, but this cannot be taken as a moral condemnation for there is no way that there could be such a thing as good faith judging. CLS and LEP may agree as to the deconstruction of many 'we-have-no-choice' decisions, but they part company over the thesis that judges cannot be anything but ideological. The alternative for CLS is not better judging but, on the model of government through law, no judging. For Kennedy this is a better outcome because it may help to remove a cause of oppression by opening the way for politicising each legal decision.[13]

A rapprochement may be possible here, in that this pragmatic approach rests on an assumption of the philosophical impossibility of objectively successful communication. Appealing to Wittgenstein, it is argued that rules do not foreclose any possibilities for choice and are firmly rooted in specific ways of life. However, we have seen that it is a mistake to read Wittgenstein in this radically sceptical way, in that his objective was to explain the phenomenon of successful communication, not to negate its possibility.[14] Indeed, Kennedy himself accepts that communication can succeed at the level of intersubjective agreement. If we move forward from this to accepting that such agreement is in principle sufficient for a working system of law, this makes it possible to arrive at a situation where legislators are understood as they wish to be understood and the rules they create are applied as they intended them to be applied. The claim that, in different contexts and different ways of life and on different assumptions, intersubjective agreement would not occur, does not show that effective communication does happen or undermine the thesis that it is part of a healthy political system that it should. Nor is there much force in endless exposure of the political agendas at work in American Constitutional Law, given that Positivism is at its most critical with respect to systems which give courts the power to apply highly abstract and imprecise principles to override more specifically articulated legislative enactments.

However, it may well be that the prospects for agreement on the idea of Critical Legal Positivism run out at the point where CLS theorists claim that, even if judges can follow a rule in good faith and demonstrate a measure of interpretative fidelity, they do not get, and are not going to get, the sort of rules which can be approached in this way. Here the background thesis is that societies are riven with conflicting ideological tendencies, such as the tension between egoism and altruism, which means that no unequivocal outcome can ever be expected to emanate from the political process.[15] In other words, the positivist legislative ethic is unattainable. Rules will always be internally inconsistent, with flexible and manipulable let-out clauses, or be incompatible with each other, enabling judges to pick and choose which rule they wish to follow, at what level of generality and on which interpretation. The analysis here does not depend on showing that it is actually cognitively impossible to strike a balance in terms of specific conduct between such disparate motivations as altruism and egoism, but that the social forces at work will not permit this to be done. This is a grandiose claim, reminiscent of Marx's affirmations about the internal contradictions of the capitalist system, a claim that has plenty of evidence to support it but not enough to make it so convincing that it gives us no choice but to go along with its fatalistic implications.

And so, without suggesting that Kennedy would for one moment agree, we can argue that there are elements in his theories which can be used to build a positivist model with considerable critical edge. Agreed mechanisms are there with respect to intersubjective rule understanding and communication. The agreed motivation may be there, in so far as rules can be used to combat prejudice and oppression by redistribution and affirmative action. A beneficial effect of a Critical Legal Positivism might be that the critique of law is directed not only towards the elimination of systematic bias in legal process, but also towards critiques of the inadequacies of legislative process and democratic decision making. Perhaps, for instance, the development in the United States of a more decisive polity and a judicial culture which reduced the status and authority of judges to a more European stature might produce a system which has more scope for the virtues of Ethical Positivism. For Kennedy there is no prospect of this happening, but at least we can speculate on what changes would have to occur to prepare for such an eventuality. The question is not whether a particular political/legal system is characterised by a manageable division of functions as between legislation and adjudication, or whether, in current conditions, oppression is more readily tackled in a piecemeal way through exploiting de facto Realism, whereby rules are mere guideposts which feature to prompt rather than determine legal outcomes, but whether there is a part of the CLS manifesto which could be implemented by the pursuit of legislative reform and the development of a culture in which rules are seen as potentially legitimate norms rather than fetishisms to be exposed and avoided.

Feminist Positivism

In its repudiation of the values of competition and the postmodern assumptions of many of its current advocates, current feminism is readily counterposed to Positivism as a masculine and gender-oppressive theory. Particularly evocative is Gilligan's account of boys quarrelling over the rules of the game while girls seek to preserve the mutually supporting interactions of the group.[16] Yet there are few political movements in recent times that have contributed more ideas for positivist-style legal change than feminism.[17]

I do not suggest that the focus of feminism is now or should be primarily on legal change. Clearly feminist concerns are bound up with a broader agenda of social and economic reform to which rule change is largely peripheral. Gender consciousness raising, articulation and communication of the unacknowledged realities of gender bias, and effective political organisation are more pressing feminist concerns than legal reform. But when, in these very activities, the apparent objectivity of male line drawing is revealed to be nothing more than a cloak for male power, the next step is not necessarily the repudation of all line drawing. There may be other lines which are more sensitive to women's lives and ways of applying rules which are less subvertible by male prejudice. The fact, for instance, that some ways of distinguishing private and public have been used as a technique for excluding women from the protection of the law does not mean that other definitions, in other contexts, could not empower women by, for instance, restricting the control which men exercise over their reproductive concerns.[18]

To conjure up a vision of Feminist Positivism is not to assert the superiority of liberal feminism with its emphasis on equal rights, by which is meant gender-blind rules which apply to all, irrespective of gender, class or racial differences.[19] There is nothing within Positivism that excludes making gender distinctions in the formulation of rules and rights, thus making it possible to implement devices, such as employment quotas, for combating gender discrimination and dealing with matters which have an impact primarily upon women. Gender is, on the whole, a distinction which can be defined and operationalised, in a predominantly objective manner. Further, feminist viewpoints can be brought to the fore in the political discourse of legislation to bring out what it is about a social situation that is unacceptable and what remedies are required, thus paving the way for good, that is precise and determinate, political decision and less readily subvertible legal implementation.

This aspect of Positivism is missed by a recent feminist critique of Legal Positivism in which Margot Stubbs castigates the pretence of trans-historicity and universality of Positivism, arguing instead for a view of law which takes it to be a praxis through which people define or change their world which I take to be, in fact, a fundamentally positivist position. The identification of the distinctions and differences that matter to us and creating the meanings through which we can express our own view of a properly ordered society can be seen as part of that radical positivist tradition which seeks to change the world as a matter of understanding as well as action. Once we get behind attribution to 'Positivism' of the view that 'meaning is a property of – and is embedded in – texts' which can be applied in a 'mechanical' way, and fasten on that aspect of the positivist tradition which is an effortful articulation of a view of the world in which the rules of language are as much human creations as the rules of law, then, however conservative law may be in so far as it serves as a transmitter of existing (no doubt male-dominated) culture, it also has the potential, as Bentham realised, to play a part in the radical transformation of existing social relationships as well as sustaining such structures as we wish to preserve.[20]

Those aspects of Positivism which generate feminist disquiet at the abstractions which conceal the social realities of women's situations fit well with feminist aspirations to provide context-specific remedies for gender oppression. Both movements share a concern for identifying the decisive factors which bear on the injustices to be remedied. Thus there is much of this positivist impulse in the attempt by Catherine MacKinnon to bring precision and definition into the positivistically problematic area of obscenity.[21] Her concern to identify what it is about pornography that is unacceptable and to concentrate upon this phenomenon in terms which make it clear what sort of material is at issue is, despite its drafting weaknesses, something of a model for the sort of selection of priority purposes and formulation of precise rules which accurately convey legislative intention which we have identified as a hallmark of LEP.

The terms 'obscene' and 'pornographic' are often said to be hopelessly indeterminate and largely indefinable even by those who advocate their legal restriction in arguments which use this terminology throughout.[22] This is cited as a convincing positivist reason for having no regulation in this area. In pluralistic societies it is increasingly difficult to brush aside the practical difficulty of arriving at objectively applicable definitions in this area on the grounds that everyone can recognise obscenities when they come across them, and of the alleged measure of agreement on, for instance, the distinction between 'hard-core' and 'soft-core' pornography.[23] This simple-minded reliance on personal certainty has often resulted in an unhappy ambiguity between definitions which deal with terms such as 'obscenity', 'indecency' and 'pornography' as labels for anything which causes certain forms of reaction, such as disgust, revulsion and abhorrence, and definitions which seek to identify the nature of those actions, words, depictions or sounds which tend to arouse such reactions, such as 'sexually explicit material', 'gross violence' or 'nudity'. The former, subjectivist, approach means that we can all be against obscenity as objectionable by definition without agreeing as to what it is that is objectionable. The latter, more objective or ostensive, approach means that we can more readily agree on what materials are, according to the definitions, obscene but not on whether these materials are offensive and therefore targets for censorship.

The subjectivist approach serves best for those who are concerned to control certain materials simply because they are 'disgusting'. Those who have this objective think they can work well enough with the idea of obscenity simply as a label for what they and others of like mind find revolting. The objectivist approach is preferred by those who are more concerned with the socially harmful effects of obscenity, such as 'perverse' sexual practices, which go beyond mere disgust and revulsion. In order to argue that obscenity causes social harm it is necessary to identify the causes of this harm in a way which enables us to examine the claimed causal connections between, say, sexually explicit material and, say, increased teenage pregnancies. However, once this approach is taken, the tendency is to identify whatever causes socially harmful conduct as 'obscene', so that depictions of war or dangerous driving or conspicuous consumption are candidates for 'obscenities', thereby removing the term from its normally understood ambit.

It is common to try to escape from this morass by stipulating that what we are dealing with is confined to sexual materials as the peculiar locus of the combination of the disgusting and the harmful. For this reason the term 'obscenity' is often put to one side, as irredeemably indefinable, in favour of 'pornography', which has the advantage of being more readily confined to the sphere of sexual conduct.[24] Thus pornography may be defined as sexually explicit material designed to arouse sexual desire, sometimes referred to as appealing to 'prurient interests'.[25] Success in this design may itself be regarded as an undesirable consequence, especially if the desire in question relates to 'abnormal' sexual activity. In modern society concern focusses more on the possibility of the desire for and the execution of violent sexual conduct. The marginal status of violence as perhaps obscene and pornographic can be taken care of by noting that violence has a role in certain forms of sexual behaviour and may therefore be considered as pornographic in these instances.

This conceptually restrictive approach may have some justification if there are distinctive problems with sexual materials because of their powerful role in arousing sexual feelings and conduct. Yet it is a very weak moral basis for the control of pornography to hold that sexual desire and/or behaviour is in itself wrong or undesirable. Indeed materials which simply stimulate lust are normally labelled 'erotic' and are not thought to warrant censorship. Further, it is clear that these phenomena can be induced by materials which are not in themselves sexually 'explicit'. The logic of such stratagems is therefore to suppress whatever are the cultural cues for sexual arousal.

Moreover, the concentration on sexually explicit materials can often represent an unexamined value judgment that, for instance, control of sexual materials is more important that control of depictions of violence. If it is the control of harm that is the concern, there may be a stronger case for the control of violent materials than of sexual ones. Yet, once we include violence within the ambit of obscenity, it is hard to see why other forms of unacceptable conduct whose depiction may cause imitative behaviour should not be drawn within the area. Representations of theft, fraud and illegal parking may all serve as examples for real-life conduct. It seems, however, that these do not arouse the sort of response that is readily thought of as characterising obscenities. Such considerations drive us back to definitions which concentrate on revulsion and disgust, even if such materials may not lead to any harm beyond the distress of those who are revolted by it.

The advantage of MacKinnon's approach is that it cuts through this tangled justificatory and conceptual mess, identifies a specific type of evil and proposes a legal definition to feature in its legal control:

> What Andrea Dworkin and I mean by pornography is rather well captured in our legal definition: Pornography is the graphic sexually explicit subordination of women, whether in pictures or in words, that also includes one or more of the following: (i) women are presented as dehumanized sexual objects, things, or commodities; or (ii) women are presented as sexual objects who enjoy pain or mutilation; or (iii) women are presented as sexual objects who experience sexual pleasure in being raped; or (iv) women are presented in postures of sexual submission, servility or display; or (v) women's bodily parts – including but not limited to vaginas, breasts and buttocks – are exhibited, such that women are reduced to those parts; or (vi) women are presented as whores by nature; or (vii) women are presented as being

> penetrated by objects or animals; or (viii) women are presented in scenarios of degradation, injury, torture, shown as filthy or inferior, bleeding, bruised, or hurt in a context that makes these conditions sexual.[26]

This is a self-confessed stipulative definition, a perfectly acceptable technique in a positivist context where the emphasis is on rendering manageable precise fuzzy evaluative terminology.[27] It is certainly not a definition that captures what many other people find objectionable in what they regard as pronography, but in representing a particular selection of priorities it makes feasible the articulation of acceptably precise rules which provide usable tests for identifying the material that it is proposed to ban. This is not to say that it is not without its problems with respect to the subjective imprecision of many of its terms. In particular, it is by no means easy to envisage agreement as to whether or not particular depictions, taken out of context, exhibit subordination or inequality. Theoretically also, it may be weak in failing to identify why this sort of subordination should be singled out for censorship while depictions of other oppressions, such as women performing all the lowly occupations, are exempt. However, it is a strength of MacKinnon's bold theory that she locates the core of male domination in the sexual nature of men,[28] so that what others (mainly men) see as peripheral material, scarcely worthy of serious attention, is, in her view, fundamental to gender relationships in society. In identifying this, and making clear the priority purpose of her legislative proposal, MacKinnon exemplifies Feminist Positivism. Whether or not MacKinnon's commendations carry conviction, they serve as a model for positivist law reform. It therefore fits uneasily with the claim that it is only 'male culture' which 'thrives on argument and prides itself on distinctions'.[29]

Interestingly, the legal technique which was used to strike down the legislation that was enacted in the famous Indianapolis ordinance was the First Amendment-based prohibition on the censorship of viewpoint, a classic example of the impact of a supposedly neutral Bill of Rights on the actual inequalities of social relationships.[30] This has given rise to an impressive feminist response which seeks to explicate a more progressive view of freedom of expression by identifying social practices which silence women and not just legislative measures which seek to limit the traditional negative conception of free speech.[31] The debate has thus been moved on, from the dismissal of pornography as not worthy of First Amendment protection because it is not really speech at all, to the thesis that pornography is very effective, and very harmful, speech and that this is one reason why it must be controlled. Behind the formalistic debates about speech and non-speech lie basic political questions, answers to which are not to be found by reading off solutions from conceptualisations as to what does or does not constitute speech, but by framing terminology which captures the distinctions that feminists wish to make. Again, this illustrates a genuinely positivist rather than formalist approach in which language is used to convey the purposes of legislation in such a way that it can produce the social results that are intended rather than as a normative phenomenon from which we can derive legal rules.

Alternative Dispute Resolution

Many of the criticisms of Legal Positivism only make sense if we make the erroneous assumption that Positivists necessarily regard law as the principal mechanism for attaining social cooperation and control. In fact, even the most sanctions-minded Positivists place great store on non-legal sanctions. In particular, the sanctions of adverse social opinion operating in conjunction with a code of positive morality are frequently ascribed more impact on behaviour than the almost supervenient system of physical sanctions associated with law. On the classical model, even more powerful are the primary sanctions of pleasure and pain which drive the economic conduct of individuals.[32] Modern Positivists have more complex theories of human behaviour which allow for substantial measures of interactive social controls and a measure of moral autonomy which makes law little more than a background framework which rarely intrudes into everyday conduct. Further, it is evident that, for liberal Positivists at any rate, there are strong Positivist reasons for keeping that 'intrusion' to a minimum.[33]

This suggests that it is not a criticism of Positivism to insist that there may be better ways of dealing with social problems than legislation and litigation. Negotiated agreements, spontaneous cooperation, self-restraint, all of which may be encouraged by education and appropriate systems of economic and political life, may prove simpler, more effective and better adapted to individual circumstances than the more cumbersome and often threatening processes of law. And so, while the introduction of alternative methods of dispute resolution cannot be regarded as itself a positivist trend, it is far from incompatible with Positivism. In the first place, the positivist view of law is far wider than dispute resolution. Not only are the rule-focussed methods of social cooperation designed more to avoid disputes than to resolve them, but the central purpose of law is to affect the conduct of individuals and corporations and only secondarily to deal with disputes between them. Theories of law which dwell almost entirely on disputes about law or resolving disputes by means of law are blind to the wider social functions of law and rather limited in their view of the activities of lawyers and courts. In the second place, it is not denied that litigation and law enforcement is a very expensive and often very unsatisfactory matter, partly because human conduct is affected to a limited extent by legal regulation and also because the disputes generated in the enforced application of laws are often hard to resolve owing to the lack of appropriate factual evidence and poorly drafted laws. Mediation, arbitration and conciliation without the rigorous applications of substantive or adjectival law can be commended on grounds of cost, speed and the merits of the outcomes, which foster agreement, continuing good social and economic relations and consideration of the merits of particular cases.[34]

There is no doubt that litigation is a very expensive matter and no way to go about normal social interactions. However, if litigation is regarded merely as the tip of an iceberg which makes up the daily, non-lawyer-mediated operations of law in society, then litigation is not the normal modus operandi of law and is not to be criticised in isolation but seen as something which we require to have as part of a wider advantageous package. The crucial question for the Positivist is whether Alternative Dispute Resolution (ADR) is actually proposed as an alternative to this background possibility of civil litigation or legal bargaining in the imminent shadow of such litigation.[35]

At one level, ADR is simply an agreed cheaper way of dealing with the fact-finding aspect of law which makes sense when the stakes are not high and the means of contestants are limited. It is not worth litigating over disputes involving small sums of money where the factual evidence is complex. Mutual interest suggests that an independent arbiter making an informed judgment to which both parties agree to be bound may be quicker and cheaper and perhaps just as accurate as the legal alternatives. In other situations it seems less important to get the facts right than to patch up a quarrel or reach a compromise that enables working relationships to continue. Thus Calcutt talks of conciliation and adjudication without delay[36] in place of defamation actions. The Neill Report also suggests arbitration as a cheap and informal machinery to obtain damages up to £1000, at no risk to the complainant, although it argues that it cannot be expected to deal with 'lengthy and complicated issues of fact'.[37]

In general, LEP has no problem with methods of dispute resolution which seek to avoid formalities. Having rules and rights does not exclude agreeing to dispense with them where only the private interests of the parties are at stake. Having rights does not require that individuals insist on enforcing them. Even in matters of criminal law, objectives, such as rehabilitation, may suggest the utility of adopting a socially negotiated conclusion to minor, particularly juvenile, crime.[38] However, these non-legal activities do not thereby become systemic alternatives to law in the sense that they can replace rather than supplement law. Mediating in the shadow of ways of actually enforcing rules is quite different from mediation in the absence of rules. Now some mediation can be rule-centred, the difference from court process being in informality and the consenting involvement of the parties, in which case it is an alternative to law but not an alternative to Positivism, for no Positivist wants to deny the role and efficacy of social rules, enforced by public opinion, mutual agreement or educational processes.

However, LEP is not amenable to the idea that, in situations of disparity of power where a great deal is at stake for any of the participants, it is right to have disputes determined without rules which protect the interests of the weaker parties. Without the background possibility of legal enforcement, bargains will reflect the interests of the stronger party. Moreover, informal procedures are poor at gathering evidence, as there is no practical method of discovery, and weak in their capacity to exclude evidence which is irrelevant to the settlement but psychologically imposing and influential. It is for such reasons that institutionalising methods of ADR become increasingly legalistic.[39] Nor can LEP accept that it is efficient as a matter of social organisation to have no authoritative way of determining and implementing the rules which apply where there is a lack of agreement, where there is a socially or economically coercive relationship and where there is a societal need for authoritative guides to be followed with some reliance on their enforceability. If ADR operates without rules, without precedent and without effective methods of fact finding, the social value of cooperative rules will be undermined, as ADR becomes a legitimate way of free-riding by enabling you to bargain your way out of the unhappy outcomes of economic and social interactions that, for these purposes, now lie outside the law.[40]

As far as expense goes, it can be argued that the absence of rules will in the long run be very expensive, and the processes of mediation become increasingly costly as a result. Already there is tension between those who wish to have rules within ADR and those who wish to avoid rules and exclude lawyers. These tensions will increase if significant areas of commercial practice, for instance, are taken outside a legal framework and subjected to a private system of informal determination. Nor is it easy to see how the public interest is to be protected where such methods dominate, to say nothing of what happens to the interests of third parties excluded from the settlement.

Conclusion

The general conclusion of this book is that Positivism, understood as an ethical or prescriptive ideal, is worth persevering with in contemporary conditions as a unifying prescription. In some respects the argument is designed to be eclectic and all-encompassing, in that it is hoped that people of many different political persuasions may agree to resolve their differences within a framework of democratic Positivism. In other respects LEP is partisan and exclusive, particularly in relation to the significance of enacting precise rules rather than general standards and retaining control of the articulation and concretisation of human rights within the democratic process. There is no suggestion that governments are not capable of great evil, or indeed that they do not systemically promote such evil, or that there are not deep human interests that are worthy of their paramountcy. But it is argued that the most hopeful pathway through the paradox of politics is to enhance and focus dialogue within the democratic process on progressive rule-centred government, rather than seeking to set up judges as watchdogs who argue over again the legislative issues in an unaccountable and circumscribed fashion. This is a process which is in the end illegitimate and likely to be unprogressive with respect to the realisation of humane values in the conditions of contemporary societies.

Notes

1 Thompson (1975, p.265). See Horowitz (1977).
2 Thus Wright (1986) and Sypnowich (1990).
3 As in Hayek (1960) and Nozick (1974). See Jeffrey (1981).
4 See Miller (1989).
5 Campbell (1983).
6 For such critiques, see Kingdom (1991).
7 As with the 'New Deal' for free speech: Sunstein (1993b).
8 See Franklin (1986).
9 Hardin (1982). See pp.58–61.
10 Pettit (1993).
11 Klare (1982, p.34): 'legal reasoning is a texture of openness, indeterminacy and contradiction'.
12 This pocket summary of Duncan Kennedy's complicated and changing theory is constructed from Kennedy (1976, 1979, 1980) and an unpublished paper.
13 Kennedy (1976, pp.560–62).
14 See pp.126–9.
15 Kennedy (1979, p.213).
16 Gilligan (1982).
17 For an overview, see Naffine (1990).
18 See Wacks (1993, p.99–180).
19 As Kingdom (1991 Chapter 7) seems to suggest. See also Orford (1994).

20 Stubbs (1986). Her view is that Positivism offers a fictitious description of law as autonomous and politically neutral. She insists that this applies to the form as well as the substance of law, but her critique actually centres on the *facade* of formality, and she is happy to formulate her objections by saying that capitalist Positivism treates unlike cases alike (p.69), indicating that there could be a correct substance expressed in a sufficiently discriminating rule format.

21 Thus MacKinnon (1984) and Dworkin, A. (1981).

22 Robertson (1979), Williams (1979), Dworkin, R. (1981) and Feinberg (1987).

23 *Jacobellis* v. *Ohio*, 378 US 184, 197 [1964]; see Hawkins and Zimring (1988).

24 Williams (1979, pp.104–5).

25 *Miller* v. *California* (1973).

26 MacKinnon (1987, p.262).

27 See pp.137–8.

28 MacKinnon (1987, p.113): 'sexuality is the linchpin of gender inequality'.

29 Dworkin, A.(1981, p.127).

30 See Brest and Vandenberg (1987).

31 Such as Rae Langton, 'Speech Acts and Unspeakable Acts', in Campbell and Sadurski (1994, pp.95–130). See MacKinnon (1987, pp.154–5): 'If pornography is an act of male supremacy, its harm is the harm of male supremacy made difficult to see because of its pervasiveness, potency, and success in making the world a pornographic place. Specifically, the harm cannot be discerned from the objective standpoint because it is so much of 'what is'. Women live in the world pornography creates ... So the issue is not whether pornography is harmful, but how the harm of pornography is to become visible.'

32 Bentham (1970a).

33 See MacCormick (1985).

34 For an overview of Alternative Dispute Resolution, see Freeman (1995) or Sander (1985).

35 See Aubert (1963) and Gallanter (1986).

36 Calcutt (1990, 15.24).

37 Neill (1991, XVIII).

38 See Braithwaite and Pettit (1990).

39 See Bryans (1992) and Brunet (1987).

40 See Fiss (1984).

Bibliography

Aarnio, A. (1981), 'The Foundations of Legal Reasoning', *Rechtstheorie*, **12**, 131.

Abel, Richard L. and Philip S.C. Lewis (1988–9), *Lawyers in Society*, Berkeley: University of California Press.

Ackerman, Bruce A. (1977), *Social Justice in the Liberal State*, New Haven: Yale University Press.

Ackerman, Bruce A. (1984), 'The Storrs Lectures: Discovering the Constitution', *Yale Law Journal*, **93**, 1013–72.

Acton, H.B. (ed.) (1969), *The Philosophy of Punishment*, London: Macmillan.

Aleinikoff, T. Alexander (1988), 'Updating Statutory Construction', *Michigan Law Review*, **87**, 20.

Alexander, Larry (1987), 'Striking Back at the Empire: A Critical Survey of the Problems in Dworkin's Theory of Law', *Law and Philosophy*, **6**, 419.

Alexander, Larry and Emily Sherwin (1994), 'The Deceptive Nature of Rules', *University of Pennsylvania Law Review*, **142**, 1191.

Alexy, Robert (1989a), *A Theory of Legal Argumentation*, Oxford: Clarendon.

Alexy, Robert (1989b), 'On Necessary Relations between Law and Morality', *Ratio Juris*, **2**, 167–83.

Allan, T.R.S. (1993), *Law, Liberty and Justice: Legal Foundations of British Constitutionalism*, Oxford: Clarendon.

Annenberg Washington Program (1988), *Proposals for the Reform of Libel Law*, Washington, D.C.

Anscombe, G.E.M. (1958), 'On Brute Facts', *Analysis*, **18**, 69–72.

Aquinas, T. (1966), *Summa Theologica*, London: Blackfriars.

Aristotle (1912), *Politics*, ed. by A.D.Lindsay, London: Dent.

Atiyah, P.(1986), 'Form and Substance in Legal Reasoning', in D.N. MacCormick and P. Birks (eds), *The Legal Mind*, Oxford: Clarendon.

Aubert, Vilhelm (1963), 'Competition and Dissensus: Two Types of Conflict anmd Conflict Resolution', *Journal of Conflict Resolution*, **7**, 26–42.

Aubert, Vilhelm (1966), 'Some Social Functions of Legislation', *Acta Sociologica*, **10**, 99–110.

Austin, J. (1954), *The Province of Jurisprudence Determined*, ed. by H.L.A. Hart, London: Weidenfeld and Nicolson.

Axelrod, R. (1984), *The Evolution of Cooperation*, New York: Basic Books.

Ayer, A.J. (1936), *Language, Truth and Logic*, Harmondsworth: Penguin.

Baker, C. Edwin (1989), *Human Liberty and Freedom of Speech*, New York: Oxford University Press.

Balkin, J.M. (1987), 'Deconstructive Practice and Legal Theory', *Yale Law Journal*, **96**, 748.

Barak, A. (1989), *Judicial Discretion*, New Haven: Yale University Press.

Barendt, Eric (1985), *Freedom of Speech*, Oxford: Clarendon.

Barnes, Annette (1988), *On Interpretation*, Oxford: Blackwell.

Bell, John (1983), 'Policy Arguments in Judicial Decision', *Oxford Journal of Legal* Studies, **3**, 405–16.

Bell, John (1986), 'The Acceptability of Legal Arguments', in D.N. MacCormick and P. Birks (eds), *The Legal Mind*, Oxford: Clarendon.

Bentham, Jeremy (1970a), *An Introduction to the Principles of Morals and Legislation*, ed. by R. Burns and H.L.A. Hart, Oxford: Clarendon.

Bentham, Jeremy (1970b), *Of Laws in General*, ed. by H.L.A. Hart, Oxford: Clarendon.

Berlin, I. (1969), *Four Essays on Liberty*, Oxford: Clarendon.

Bernstein, R. (1978), 'Legal Utilitarianism', *Ethics*, **89**, 127–46.

Bernstein, R. (1983), *Beyond Objectivism and Relativism*, Oxford: Blackwell.

Beyleveld, Deryck and Roger Brownsword (1986), *Law as a Moral Judgment*, London: Sweet and Maxwell.

Beyleveld, Deryck and Roger Brownsword (1989), 'Normative Positivism: The Mirage of the Middle Way', *Oxford Journal of Legal Studies*, **9**, 463–512.

Bix, Brian (1993), *Law, Language, and Legal Determinacy*, Oxford: Clarendon.

Blasi, Vincent (1977), 'The Checking Value in First Amendment Theory', *American Bar Foundation Research Journal*, 521

Bollinger, Lee (1986), *The Tolerant Society: Freedom of Speech and Extremist Speech in America*, New York: Oxford University Press.

Bork, Robert H. (1971), 'Neutral Principles and Some First Amendment Problems', *Indiana Law Journal*, **47**, 1–35.

Boyle, James (1992), 'Thomas Hobbes and the Invented Tradition of Positivism: Reflections on Language, Power and Essentialism', *University of Pennsylvania Law* Review, **135**, 35–76.

Boyle, James (ed.) (1992), *Critical Legal Studies*, Aldershot: Dartmouth.

Braithwaite, John and Phillip Pettit (1990), *Not Just Deserts*, Oxford: Clarendon.

Brest, P. and A. Vandenberg (1987), 'Politics, Feminism and the Constitution: The Anti-Pornography Movement in Minneapolis', *Stanford Law Review*, **39**, 607.

Brink, O. (1989), *Moral Realism and the Foundations of Ethics*, Cambridge: Cambridge University Press.

Brunet, Edward (1987), 'Questioning the Quality of Alternative Dispute Resolution', *Tulane Law Review*, **62**, 1–56.

Bryans, N. (1992), 'Killing Us Softly: Divorce Mediation and the Politics of Power', *Buffalo Law Review*, **40**, 441–523.

Burke, E. (1990), *Reflections on the Revolution in France*, Harmondsworth: Penguin.

Burnheim, J. (1985), *Is Democracy Possible?*, Cambridge: Polity.

Calcutt Committee (1990), *On Privacy and Related Matters*, London: HMSO, Cmnd 1102.

Campbell, Tom (1970), 'The Normative Fallacy', *Philosophical Quarterly*, **20**, 368–77.

Campbell, Tom (1971), 'John Stuart Mill and Freedom of Speech', *Il Pensiero Politico*, **4**, 443–50.

Campbell, Tom (1974a), 'Humanity Before Justice', *British Journal of Political Science*, **4**, 1–16.

Campbell, Tom (1974b), 'Equality of Opportunity', *Proceedings of the Aristotelian Society*, **75**, 51–68.

Campbell, Tom (1983), *The Left and Rights*, London: Routledge.

Campbell, Tom (1988a), 'Ethical Positivism', in S. Panou G. Bozonis, D. Scorgas and P. Trappe (eds), *Theory and Systems of Legal Philosophy*, Stuttgart: Steiner.

Campbell, Tom (1988b), *Justice*, London: Prentice-Hall.

Campbell, Tom (1990), 'Obligation: Societal, Political and Legal', in P. Harris, (ed.), *Political Obligation*, London: Routledge.

Campbell, Tom (1994a), 'Legal Change and Legal Theory: The Context for a Revised Legal Positivism', in W. Krawietz, N. MacCormick and G.H. von Wright (eds) *Prescriptive Formality and Normative Rationality in Modern Legal Systems*, Berlin: Dunker and Humbolt.

Campbell, Tom (1994b), 'Democracy, Human Rights, and Positive Law', *Sydney Law Review*, **16**, 195–212.

Campbell, Tom and C. Hegginbotham (1991), *Mental Illness: Prejudice, Discrimination and the Law*, Aldershot: Dartmouth.

Campbell, Tom and W. Sadurski (eds) (1994), *Freedom of Communication*, Aldershot: Dartmouth.

Campbell, Tom, G. Goldberg, G. Maher and Y. Mullen (1986), *Human Rights: From Rhetoric to Reality*, Oxford: Basil Blackwell.

Canan, Penelope and George W. Pring (1988), 'Strategic Lawsuits Against Public Participation', *Social Problems*, **35**, 506.

Cardozo, B. (1921), *The Nature of the Legal Process*, New Haven: Yale University Press.

Cass, R. (1987), 'The Perils of Positive Thinking: Constitutional Interpretation and Negative First Amendment Theory', *UCLA Law Review*, **34**, 1905.

Chambers, S. (1993), 'Talking about Rights: Discourse Ethics and the Protection of Rights', *Journal of Political Philosophy*, **1**, 229–41.

Chapman, J. and R. Wertheimer (1990), *Majorities and Minorities*, New York: New York University Press.

Chesterman, Michael (1989), 'The Law of Media Contempt: What Should It Protect?', *Communications Law Bulletin*, **9**, 5.

Coase, R. (1977), 'Advertising Free Speech', *Journal of Legal Studies*, **6**, 1.

Coleman, Jules (1981), 'Legal Formalism and Instrumentalism: a Pathological Study', *Cornell Law Review*, **68**, 949–72.

Coleman, Jules (1982a), 'Negative and Positive Positivism', *Journal of Legal Studies*, **11**, 139–64.

Coleman, Jules (1982b), 'Moral Aspects of Legal Theory', *Midwestern Studies in Philosophy*, **VII**, 223–54.

Coleman, Jules (1989), 'On the Relationship Between Law and Morality', *Ratio Juris*, **2**, 66–78.

Collins, Hugh (1986), 'Democracy and Adjudication', in D.N. MacCormick and Peter Birks (eds), *The Legal Mind*, Oxford: Clarendon.

Craven, G. (1992), 'The Crisis of Constitutional Interpretation in Australia', in H.P. Lee and George Winterton (eds), *Australian Constitutional Perspectives*, Sydney: Law Books.

Cross, Rupert (1987), *Statutory Interpretation*, 2nd edn, London: Butterworths.

Cunningham, R.L. (ed.) (1979), *Liberty and the Rule of Law*, Texas: Texas University Press.

Dahl, R.A. (1957), 'The Concept of Power', *Behavioral Science*, **2**, 201–15.

Dahl, R.A. (1965), *A Preface to Democratic Theory*, New Haven: Yale University Press.

Daniels, N. (1975), *Reading Rawls*, Oxford: Blackwell.

Danzinger, C. (1986), 'The Right of Reply in the U.S. and Europe', *International Law and Politics*, **19**, 171.

Davidson, Donald (1984), *Inquiries into Truth and Interpretation*, Oxford: Clarendon.

Detmold, Michael (1984), *The Unity of Law and Morality: A Refutation of Legal Positivism*, London: Routledge.

Dicey, A.V. (1959), *Introduction to the Study of the Law of the Constitution*, 10th edn, ed. by E.C.S. Wade, London: Macmillan.

Dilthey, W. (1970), *Selected Writings*, ed. by H.P. Rickman, Cambridge: Cambridge University Press.

Douzinas, Costas and Ronie Warrington (1991), *Postmodern Jurisprudence: the Law of the Text in the Text of the Law*, London: Routledge.

Downie, Robert S. (1971), *Roles and Values: An Introduction to Social Ethics*, London: Methuen.
Downs, A. (1957), *An Economic Theory of Democracy*, New York: Harper.
Drahos, Peter and Stephen Parker (1992), 'Rule Following, Rule Scepticism and Indeterminacy in Law: a Conventional Account', *Ratio Juris*, **5**, 109–19.
Dummett, M.A.E. (1978), *Truth and Other Enigmas*, London: Duckworth.
Dummett, M.A.E. (1986), 'A Nice Derangement of Epitaphs: Some Comments on Davidson and Hacking', in E. LePore (ed.), *Truth and Interpretation*, Oxford: Blackwell.
Durkheim, E. (1933), *The Division of Labour in Society*, trans. by G. Simpson, Illinois: Macmillan.
Duval, B. (1972), 'Free Communication of Ideas and the Quest for Truth: Towards a Teleological Approach to First Amendment Adjudication', *George Washington Law Review*, **41**, 161.
Dworkin, Andrea (1981), *Pornography: Men Possessing Women*, New York: Putnam.
Dworkin, R. (1977), *Taking Rights Seriously*, London: Duckworth.
Dworkin, R. (1981), 'What is Equality?', *Philosophy and Public Affairs*, **10**, 198.
Dworkin, R. (1986), *Law's Empire*, London: Fontana.
Dworkin, R. (1990), *A Bill of Rights for Britain*, London: Chatto.
Dyzenhaus, D. (1991), *Hard Cases in Wicked Legal Systems: South African Law in the Perspective of Legal Philosophy*, Oxford: Clarendon.
Ebenstein, W. (1971), 'The Pure Theory of Law', *California Law Review*, **59**, 65–88.
Ely, J.H. (1980), *Democracy and Distrust: A Theory of Judicial Review*, Cambridge: Harvard University Press.
Emerson, Thomas I. (1963), 'Toward a General Theory of the First Amendment', *Yale Law Journal*, **72**, 877–956.
Emmett, Dorothy (1966), *Rules, Roles and Relations*, London: Macmillan.
Eskridge, William N. and Philip P. Frickey (1990), 'Statutory Interpretation as Practical Reasoning', *Stanford Law Review*, **42**, 321.
Ewing, A.C. (1953), *Ethics*, New York: Free Press.
Feinberg, Joel (1985), *Harm to Others*, New York: New York University Press.
Feinberg, Joel (1987), *Offence to Others*, New York: Oxford University Press.
Finnis, John M. (1980), *Natural Law and Natural Rights*, Oxford: Clarendon.
Finnis, John M. (1989), 'Law as Co-ordination', *Ratio Juris*, **2**, 97–104.
Fish, Stanley (1982), 'Working on the Chain Gang: Interpretation in Law and Literature', *Texas Law Review*, **60**, 551.
Fish, Stanley (1983), 'Wrong Again', *Texas Law Review*, **62**, 299–316.
Fish, Stanley (1984), 'Fish v. Fiss', *Stanford Law Review*, **36**, 1325–47.

Fish, Stanley (1987), 'Still Wrong, After all these Years', *Law and Philosophy*, **6**, 401.

Fiss, Owen M. (1984), 'Against Settlement', *Yale Law Journal*, **93**, 1073–90.

Fiss, Owen M. (1985), 'Conventionalism', *Southern California Law Review*, **58**, 177–97.

Fiss, Owen M. (1987), 'Why the State?', *Harvard Law Review*, **100**, 781.

Fleming, John (1992), *The Law of Torts*, 8th edn, Sydney: Law Books.

Forer, Lois G. (1987), *A Chilling Effect*, New York: W.W. Norton.

Franklin, M. (1986), 'A Declaratory Judgment Alternative to Current Libel Law', *California Law Review*, **74**, 809.

Freedman, Monroe H.(1966), 'Professional Responsibility of the Criminal Defense Lawyer: The Three Hardest Questions', *Minnesota Law Review*, **64**, 1989.

Freedman, Monroe H. (1978), 'Personal Responsibility in Professional Systems', *Catholic University Law Review*, **27**, 191–205.

Freeman, Michael (ed.) (1995), *Alternative Dispute Resolution*, Aldershot: Dartmouth.

Frey, R.G. (1980), *Interests and Rights, the Case Against Animals*, New York: Oxford University Press.

Fried, Charles (1976), 'The Lawyer as Friend: The Moral Foundations of the Lawyer–Client Relation', *Yale Law Journal*, **85**, 1060–89

Fuller, Lon (1934), 'American Legal Realism', *University of Pennsylvania Law Review*, **82**, 429–76.

Fuller, Lon (1958), 'The Separation of Morality and Law: A Reply to Professor Hart', *Harvard Law Review*, **71**, 595–639.

Fuller, Lon (1969), *The Morality of Law*, New Haven: Yale University Press.

Gabel, P. (1979), 'Reification in Legal Reasoning', *Research in Law and Society*, **3**, 25.

Gabel, P. (1980), 'Reification in Legal Reasoning', *Research in Law and Sociology*, **3**, 25–51.

Gabel, P. and P. Harris (1982–3), 'Building Power and Creating Images: CLS Theory and Practice of Law', *Review of Social Change*, **11**, 25.

Gaete, Roland (1993), *Human Rights and the Limits of Critical Reason*, Aldershot: Dartmouth.

Gallanter, Marc (1986), 'Compared To What? Assessing the Quality of Disputes Processing', *Denver University Law Review*, **60**, xi–xiv.

Galligan, B. (1987), *The Politics of the High Court*, New York: University of Queensland Press.

Gans, Chiam (1981), 'The Normativity of Law and its Coordinative Function', *Israel Law Review*, **16**, 333–55.

Gavison, Ruth (ed.) (1987), *Issues in Contemporary Legal Philosophy: The Influence of H.L.A. Hart*, Oxford: Clarendon.

Gewirth, A. (1978), *Reason and Morality*, Chicago: University of Chicago Press.

Giddens, A. (1984), *The Constitution of Society*, Berkeley: University of California Press.

Gilligan, Carol (1982), *In a Different Voice*, Cambridge: Harvard University Press.

Gillmor, Donald M. (1992), *Power, Publicity and the Abuse of Libel Law*, New York: Oxford University Press.

Goldsworthy, Jeffrey (1991), 'The Self-Destruction of Legal Positivism', *Oxford Journal of Legal Studies*, **10**, 449–86.

Goldsworthy, Jeffrey (1993), 'Is Jurisprudence Liberal Ideology?', *Oxford Journal of Legal Studies*, **13**, 548–70.

Goodwin, Barbara (1992), *Justice by Lottery*, Hemel Hempstead: Simon and Schuster.

Gould, Carol (1988), *Rethinking Democracy: Freedom and Social Cooperation in Politics, Economy and Society*, Cambridge: Cambridge University Press.

Graycar, R. and J. Morgan (1990), *The Hidden Gender of Law*, Sydney: Federation Press.

Green, Leslie (1983), 'Law, Co-ordination and the Common Good', *Oxford Journal of Legal Studies*, **3**, 299–324.

Greenawalt, Kent (1989), *Speech, Crime and the Uses of Language*, New York: Oxford University Press.

Greenawalt, Kent (1991), *Law and Objectivity*, Oxford: Clarendon.

Grice, H.P. (1957), 'Meaning', *Philosophical Review*, **66**, 377–88.

Griffith, J. (1977), *The Politics of the Judiciary*, Glasgow: Collins.

Gutman, Amy (1985), 'The Communitarian Critics of Liberalism', *Philosophy and Public Affairs*, **14**, 308–22.

Habermas, Jurgen (1984), *The Theory of Communicative Action.*

Habermas, Jurgen (1987), *The Philosophical Discourse of Modernity*, Cambridge: Polity.

Habermas, Jurgen (1989), 'Toward a Communication-Concept of Rational Collective Will-Formation', *Ratio Juris*, **2**, 144–54.

Hardin, R. (1982), *Collective Action*, Baltimore: Johns Hopkins University Press.

Hare, R.M. (1963), *Freedom and Reason*, Oxford: Clarendon Press.

Hare, R.M. (1963), *Morality and Freedom*, Oxford: Clarendon.

Harris, J. (1980), *Legal Philosophies*, London: Butterworths.

Hart, H.L.A. (1957–8), 'The Separation of Law and Morals', *Harvard Law Review*, **71**, 593–629.

Hart, H.L.A. (1961), *The Concept of Law*, Oxford: Oxford University Press (2nd edn 1994).

Hart, H.L.A. (1973), 'Bentham on Legal Rights', in A.W.B. Simpson (ed.), *Oxford Essays in Jurisprudence*, Oxford: Oxford University Press, 171–201.

Hart, H.L.A. (1982), *Essays on Bentham*, Oxford: Clarendon.

Hawkins, G. and F.E. Zimring (1988), *Pornography in a Free Society*, New York: Cambridge University Press.

Hayek, F.A. (1960), *The Constitution of Liberty*, Chicago: University of Chicago Press.

Hayek, F.A. (1976), *Law, Liberty and Legislation*, vol. 2, London: Routledge and Kegan Paul.

Hobbes, T. (1990), *Leviathan*, ed. by R. Tuck, Cambridge: Cambridge University Press.

Hohfeld, W. (1919), *Fundamental Legal Conceptions*, New Haven: Yale University Press.

Hollis, M. and S. Lukes (1982), *Rationality and Relativism*, Oxford: Blackwell.

Honore, A.A. (1973), 'Groups, Law and Obedience', in A.W.B. Simpson (ed.), *Oxford Essays in Jurisprudence*, 2nd series, Oxford: Oxford University Press, chap. 1.

Horowitz, M. (1977), 'The Rule of Law: An Unqualified Human Good?', (book review) *Yale Law Journal*, **86**, 561.

Hume, David (1978), *A Treatise on Human Nature*, ed. by L.A. Selby-Bigge, Oxford: Clarendon.

Hunt, Alan (1992), *Reading Dworkin Critically*, New York: Berg.

Hutchinson, A.C. and P. Monohan (1986), *The Rule of Law: Ideal of Ideology?*, Toronto: Toronto University Press.

Jeffrey, P. (1981), *Reading Nozick*, Totowa: Rowan Littlefield.

Jori, Mario (1990), 'Paradigms of Legal Science', *Rivista internationale di filosofia del diritto*, **LXVII**, 230–54.

Kairys, D. (1984), 'Law and Politics', *George Washington Law Review*, **52**, 243.

Kairys, D. (1993), *With Liberty and Justice for Some*, New York: New Press.

Kant, I. (1948), *The Moral Law*, ed. by H.J. Paton, London: Hutchinson.

Kelman, M. (1987), *A Guide to Critical Legal Studies*, Cambridge: Harvard University Press.

Kelsen, H (1957), *What is Justice?*, Berkeley: University of California Press.

Kelsen, H. (1967), *The Pure Theory of Law*, trans. by Max Knight, Berkeley: University of California Press.

Kelsen, Hans (1992), *An Introduction to the Problems of Legal Theory*, Oxford: Clarendon.

Kennedy, Duncan (1973), 'Legal Formality', *Journal of Legal Studies*, 351–98.

Kennedy, Duncan (1976), 'Form and Substance in Private Law Adjudication', *Harvard Law Review*, **89**, 1685.

Kennedy, Duncan (1979), 'The Structure of Blackstone's Commentaries', *Buffalo Law Review*, **28**, 209.

Kennedy, Duncan (1980), 'Freedom and Restraint in Adjudication: A Critical Phenomenology', *Journal of Legal Education*, **36**, 513–62.

Kerruish, Valerie (1991), *Jurisprudence as Ideology*, London: Routledge.

Kingdom, E. (1991), *What's Wrong with Rights?*, Edinburgh: Edinburgh University Press.

Kinley, D. (1993), *The European Convention on Human Rights: Compliance without Incorporation*, Aldershot: Dartmouth.

Klare, K. (1979), 'Law Making Praxis', *Telos*, **40**, 123–52.

Klare, K (1982), 'The Law School Curriculum in the 1980s: What's Left?', *Journal of Legal Education*, **32**, 34.

Kramer, Matthew H. (1991), *Legal Theory, Political Theory and Deconstruction: Against Rhadamanthus*, Indiana: Indiana University Press.

Kripke, Saul (1982), *Wittgenstein on Rules and Private Language*, Cambridge: Harvard University Press.

Kronman, Anthony T. (1980), 'Contract Law and Distributive Justice', *Yale Law Journal*, **89**, 472.

Kronman, Anthony T. (1987), 'Living in the Law', *University of Chicago Law Review*, **54**, 835–76.

Lamont, W.D. (1981), *Law and the Moral Order*, Aberdeen: Aberdeen University Press.

Lee, Keekoh (1989), *The Positivist Science of Law*, Aldershot: Gower.

Lester, A. (1968), *Democracy and Individual Rights*, London: Fabian Society.

Lewis, David K. (1969), *Convention: A Philosophical Study*, Cambridge: Harvard University Press.

Lindley, R. (1987), *Autonomy*, London: Macmillan.

Llewellyn, K.N. (1934), 'Some Realism about Realism', *Harvard Law Review*, **44**, 1222.

Llewellyn, K.N. (1950), 'R and the Theory of Appellate Decisions and the Rules of Law about how Statutes are to be Construed', *Vanderbilt Law Review*, **3**, 395.

Llewellyn, K.N. (1960), *The Common Law Tradition*, Chicago: University of Chicago Press.

Locke, John (1689), *An Essay Concerning Human Understanding*, ed. by Peter Niddich, Oxford: Clarendon, 1975.

Locke, John (1690), *Two Treatises of Government*, ed. by Peter Laslett, New York: Mentor, 1960.

Luban, David (ed.) (1994), *The Ethics of Lawyers*, Aldershot: Dartmouth.

Lyons, David (1977), 'Principles, Positivism, and Legal Theory', *Yale Law Journal*, **87**, 415

Lyons, David (1984), *Ethics and the Rule of Law*, Cambridge: Cambridge University Press.

Lyotard, J-F. (1984), *The Postmodern Condition*, trans. by G. Bennington and B. Massuri, Manchester: Manchester University Press.

MacCallum, Gerald C. (1970), 'Legislative Intent', in R. Summers (ed.), *Essays in Jurisprudence*, Oxford: Basil Blackwell, pp.237–73.

MacCallum, Gerald C. (1986), *Political Philosophy*, Englewood Clifs: Prentice Hall.

MacCormick, D. Neil (1978), *Legal Reasoning and Legal Theory*, Oxford: Clarendon.

MacCormick, D. Neil (1981), *H.L.A. Hart*, London: Edward Arnold. .

MacCormick, D. Neil (1982), *Legal Rights and Social Democracy*, Oxford: Clarendon.

MacCormick, D. Neil (1985), 'A Moralistic Case for Amoralistic Law?', *Valparaiso University Law Review*, **20**, 1–42.

MacCormick, D. Neil (1989), 'The Ethics of Legalism', *Ratio Juris*, **2**, 184–93.

MacCormick, D. Neil (1990), 'Reconstructing after Deconstruction: A Response to CLS', *Oxford Journal of Legal Studies*, **10**, 539–58.

MacCormick, D. Neil and R.S. Summers (eds) (1992), *Interpreting Statutes*, Aldershot: Dartmouth.

MacCormick, D.N. and O. Weinberger (1984), *An Institutional Theory of Law: New Approaches to Legal Positivism*, Boston: Reidel.

Mackie, J.L. (1977), *Ethics: Inventing Right and Wrong*, Harmondsworth: Penguin.

MacKinnon, Catharine (1980), *Toward a Feminist Theory of the State*, Cambridge: Harvard University Press.

MacKinnon, Catharine (1984), 'Not a Moral Issue', *Yale Law and Policy Review*, **2**, 321.

MacKinnon, Catharine (1987), *Feminism Unmodified: Discourses on Life and Law*, Cambridge: Harvard University Press.

Marmor, Andrei (1992), *Interpretation and Legal Theory*, Oxford: Clarendon.

Mayo, B. (1960), *Democracy and Political Theory*, New York: Oxford University Press.

Meiklejohn, Alexander (1960), *Political Freedom: The Constitutional Powers of the People*, New York: Harper.

Meiklejohn, Alexander (1962), 'The First Amendment is an Absolute', *Supreme Court Review*, 245–66.

Menlowe, Michael and A. McCall-Smith (eds) (1993), *The Duty to Rescue*, Aldershot: Dartmouth.

Mensch, Elizabeth (1980), 'The History of Mainstream Legal Thought', in D.Kairys (ed.), *The Politics of Law*, New York: Pantheon.

Michelman, Frank I. (1986), 'The Supreme Court 1985 Term: Foreword: Traces of Self-Government', *Harvard Law Review*, **100**, 4–77.

Mill, James (1821), 'Liberty of the Press', *Encylopaedia Britannica*, 5th edn, 258–72.

Mill, J.S. (1910), *Utilitarianism, Liberty, Representative Government*, London: Dent.

Miller, D. (1984), *Anarchism*, London: Dent.
Miller, D. (1989), *Market, State and Community*, Oxford: Clarendon.
Moore, G.M. (1908), *Principia Ethica*, Cambridge: Cambridge University Press.
Moore, Michael S. (1981), 'The Semantics of Judging', *Southern California Law Review*, **54**, 151–294.
Naffine, N. (1990), *Law and the Sexes*, Sydney: Allen and Unwin.
Neill, Lord Justice, Chairman (1991), *Supreme Court Procedures Committee, Report on Practice and Procedure in Defamation*, London.
Nelson, W. (1975), 'On the Alleged Importance of Moral Rights', *Ratio*, **18**, 145–55.
New South Wales Law Reform Commission (1993), *Defamation*, Discussion Paper 31, Sydney.
Norris, C. (1988), 'Law, Destruction and the Resistance of Theory', *Journal of Law and Society*, **15**, 165–87.
Nozick, R. (1974), *Anarchy, State and Utopia*, Oxford: Blackwell.
Olson, M (1965), *The Logic of Collective Action*, Cambridge: Harvard University Press.
Orford, Anne (1994), 'Liberty, Equality, Pornography: The Bodies of Women and Human Rights Discourse', *The Australian Feminist Law Journal*, **3**, 72–102.
Parfit, D. (1984), *Reasons and Persons*, Oxford: Clarendon.
Parsons, T. (1937), *The Structure of Social Action*, New York: McGraw-Hill.
Parsons, T. (1951), *The Social System*, New York: McGraw-Hill.
Pateman, Carol (1970), *Participation and Democratic Theory*, Cambridge: Cambridge University Press.
Pearce, Dennis and Harry Geddes (1988), *Statutory Interpretation in Australia*, 3rd edn, Sydney: Butterworths.
Peczenick, A. (1983), *The Basis of Legal Justification*, Lund: University Press.
Perelman, Chiam (1980), *Justice, Law and Argument*, Dordrecht: Kluwer.
Pepper, S.L. (1986), 'The Lawyer's Amoral Ethical Role: A Defense, Some Problems and Some Possibilities', *American Bar Foundation Research Journal*, 613–35.
Perry, T. (1976), *Moral Reasoning and Truth*, Oxford: Clarendon Press.
Pettit, Philip (1993), *The Common Mind: From Folk Psychology to Social and Political Theory*, Oxford: Clarendon.
Pitkin, Hanna (1981), 'Justice: On Relating Public and Private', *Political Theory*, **9**, 343.
Posner, R. (1977), *Economic Analysis of Law*, Boston: Little Brown.
Posner, R. (1985), *The Federal Courts: Crisis and Reform*, Cambridge, Mass.: Harvard University Press.
Posner, R. (1986) 'Free Speech in an Economic Perspective', *Suffolk University Law Review*, **20**, 1–18.

Post, Robert C. (1990), 'The Social Foundations of Defamation Law Reputation and the Constitution', *California Law Review*, **74**, 691.

Postema, Gerald J. (1982), 'Coordination and Convention at the Foundations of Law', *Journal of Legal Studies*, **XI**, 165–203.

Postema, Gerald J. (1986), *Bentham and the Common Law*, Oxford: Clarendon.

Pound, R. (1908), 'Mechanical Jurisprudence', *Columbia Law Review*, **8**, 605.

Putnam, H. (1983), *Realism and Reason*, Cambridge: Cambridge University Press.

Quine, W.V. (1960), *Word and Object*, Cambridge: Massachusetts Institute of Technology.

Radin, M. (1989), 'Reconsidering the Rule of Law', *Boston University Law Review*, **69**, 781.

Rawls, J. (1972), *A Theory of Justice*, Oxford: Clarendon.

Rawls, J. (1993), *Political Liberalism*, New York: Columbia University Press.

Rawls, J. (1994), *Political Liberalism*, New York: Columbia University Press.

Raz, Joseph (1975), *Practical Reason and Norms*, London: Hutchinson.

Raz, Joseph (1979), *The Authority of Law: Essays on Law and Morality*, Oxford: Oxford University Press.

Raz, Joseph (1985), 'Authority, Law and Morality', *Monist*, **68**, 296.

Raz, Joseph (1986), *The Morality of Freedom*, Oxford: Oxford University Press.

Raz, Joseph (1991), 'Free Expression and Personal Identification', *Oxford Journal of Legal Studies*, **11**, 303–24.

Reynolds, Noel B. (1989a), 'Grounding the Rule of Law', *Ratio Juris*, **2**, 1–16.

Reynolds, Noel B. (1989b), 'Law as Convention', *Ratio Juris*, **2**, 105–20.

Reynolds, William L. (1992), 'A Practical Guide to Statutory Interpretation Today', *West Virginia Law Review*, **94**, 927–45.

Rhode, Deborah L. (1985), 'The Ethical Perspectives on Legal Practice', *Stanford Law Review*, **37**, 589–652.

Richards, D.A.J. (1986), *Toleration and the Constitution*, Oxford: Oxford University Press.

Richards, D.A.J. (1989), 'Robert Alexy, A Theory of Argumentation: The Theory of Rational Discourse as Theory of Legal Justification', *Ratio Juris*, **2**, 304–17.

Rifkin, J. (1980), 'Towards a Feminist Jurisprudence', *Harvard Women's Law Journal*, **3**, 83–91.

Robertson, Geoffrey (1979), *Obscenity*, Weidenfeld and Nicolson.

Robertson, Geoffrey and Andrew Nicol (1992), *Media Law*, 3rd edn, London: Penguin.

Rorty, R. (1989), *Essays on Heidegger and Others*, Cambridge: Harvard University Press.

Rostow, Eugene V.(1952), 'The Democratic Character of Judicial Review', *Harvard Law Review*, **66**, 193–224.

Rousseau, J.J. (1963), *The Social Contract*, London: Dent.

Sadurski, W. (1985), *Giving Desert its Due*, Dordrecht: Reidel.

Sadurski, Wojciech (1990a), 'Joseph Raz on Liberal Neutrality and the Harm Principle', *Oxford Journal of Legal Studies*, **10**, 122–33.

Sadurski, Wojciech (1990b), *Moral Pluralism and Legal Neutrality*, Dordrecht: Kluwer.

Sadurski, Wojciech (ed.) (1991), *Ethical Dimensions of Legal Theory*, Dordrecht: Kluwer.

Sandel, Michael (1982), *Liberalism and the Limits of Justice*, Cambridge: Cambridge University Press.

Sander, Frank (1985), 'Alternative Methods of Dispute Resolution: An Overview', *University of Florida Law Review*, **37**, 1–18.

Sartorius, Rolf (1968), 'Justification of the Judicial Decision', *Ethics*, **78**, 173.

Scanlon, Thomas (1972), 'A Theory of Freedom of Expression', *Philosophy and Public Affairs*, **1**, 284.

Scanlon, Thomas (1979), 'Freedom of Expression and Categories of Expression', *University of Pittsburgh Law Review*, **40**, 519.

Schauer, Frederick (1982), *Free Speech: A Philosophical Enquiry*, Cambridge: Cambridge Unversity Press.

Schauer, Frederick (1983), 'Must Speech be Special?', *Northwestern University Law Review*, **78**, 1284.

Schauer, Frederick (1985), 'Slippery Slopes', *Harvard Law Review*, **99**, 361.

Schauer, Frederick (1988), 'Formalism', *Yale Law Journal*, **97**, 509–46.

Schauer, Frederick (1991), *Playing By The Rules: A Philosophical Examination of Rule-Based Decision-Making*, Oxford: Clarendon.

Schauer, Frederick (1992), 'Uncoupling Free Speech', *Columbia Law Review*, **92**, 1321–57.

Schlag, Pierre (1985), 'Rules and Standards', *University of California Law Review*, **33**, 379.

Schlag, Pierre (1987), 'Fish v Zapp: The Case of the Relatively Autonomous Self', *Gerogetown Law Journal*, **76**, 37.

Schumpeter, Joseph (1950), *Capitalism, Socialism and Democracy*, 3rd edn, London: Allen and Unwin.

Schutz, A. (1970), *On Phenomenology and Social Relations*, ed. by H.R. Wagner, Chicago: University of Chicago Press.

Searle, J. (1969), *Speech Acts: An Essay in the Philosophy of Language*, Cambridge: Cambridge University Press.

Shaffer, Thomas L. (1987), 'The Legal Ethics of Radical Individualism', *Texas Law Review*, **65**, 963–91.

Shanck, Peter C. (1990), 'The Only Game in Town: An Introduction to Interpretative Theory, Statutory Construction and Legal Histories', *Kansas Law Review*, **38**, 815.

Shapiro, Ian (ed.) (1994), *The Rule of Law: Nomos XXXVI*, New York: New York University Press.

Shiffrin, S.H. (1990), *The First Amendment: Democracy and Romance*, Cambridge: Harvard University Press.

Shiner, Roger A. (1992), *Norm and Nature: The Movements of Legal Thought*, Oxford: Clarendon.

Shklar, Judith (1986), *Legalism*, rev. edn, Cambridge: Harvard University Press.

Simmonds, Nigel (1993), 'Bringing the Outside In', *Oxford Journal of Legal Studies*, **13**, 147–65.

Simon, William H. (1978), 'The Ideology of Advocacy: Procedural Justice and Professional Ethics', *Wisconsin Law Review*, **29**, 30–144

Simpson, A.W.B. (1973), 'The Common Law and Legal Theory', in R.S. Summers, *Oxford Essays in Jurisprudence*, 2nd series, Oxford: Oxford University Press.

Singer, Peter (1984), 'The Player and the Cards: Nihilism and Legal Theory', *Yale Law Journal*, **94**, 9–25.

Smart, Carol (1989), *Feminism and the Power of Law*, London: Routledge.

Smith, Adam (1976), *The Theory of Moral Sentiments*, ed. by D.D. Raphael and A.L. Macfie, Oxford: Clarendon.

Smolla, R.A. (1993), *Free Speech in an Open Society*, New York: Knopf.

Soper, Philip (1977), 'Legal Theory and the Obligation of a Judge: The Hart/Dworkin Dispute', *Michigan Law Review*, **75**, 473.

Soper, Philip (1984), *A Theory of Law*, Cambridge: Harvard University Press.

Soper, Philip (1986), 'Choosing a Legal Theory on Moral Grounds', *Social Philosophy and Policy*, **4**, 31–48.

Soper, Philip (1988), 'Legal Theory and the Claim of Objectivity', *Philosophy and Public Affairs*, **18**, 209–37.

Sorensen, Roy (1989), 'The Ambiguity of Vagueness and Precision', *Pacific Philosophy Quarterly*, **70**, 174–83.

Strossen, Nadine (1986), 'A Defence of the Aspirations – But Not the Achievements – of the U.S. Rules Limiting Defamation Actions by Public Officials and Public Figures', *Melbourne University Law Review*, **15**, 419.

Stubbs, Margot (1986), 'Feminism and Legal Positivism', *Australian Journal of Law and Society*, **3**, 63–91.

Summers, Robert S. (1982), *Instrumentalism and American Legal Theory*, Ithaca: Cornell University Press.

Summers, Robert S. (1984), *Lon L. Fuller*, Stanford: Stanford University Press.

Summers, Robert S. (1992), *Essays on the Nature of Law and Legal Reasoning*, Berlin: Dunker and Humbolt.

Summers, Robert S. with P.S. Atiyah (1987), *Form and Substance in Anglo-American Law*, Oxford: Oxford University Press.

Sunstein, Cass (1985), 'Interest Groups in American Public Law', *Stanford Law Review*, **38**, 29–87.

Sunstein, Cass (1989), 'Interpreting Statutes in the Regulatory State', *Harvard Law Review*, **103**, 405.

Sunstein, Cass (1993a), *The Partial Constitution*, Cambridge: Harvard University Press.

Sunstein, Cass (1993b), *Democracy and the Problem of Free Speech*, New York: Macmillan

Sypnowich, C. (1990), *The Socialist Concept of Law*, Oxford: Clarendon.

Thompson, E.P. (1975), *Whigs and Hunters: The Origins of the Black Act*, New York: Pantheon.

Titus R. (1962), 'Statement of Fact – Statement of Value – A Spurious Dispute in Fair Comment', *Vanderbilt Law Review*, **15**, 1203.

Tribe, L. (1989), *American Constitutional Law*, 2nd edn, New York: Foundation Press.

Tucker, D.F.B. (1985), *Law, Liberalism and Free Speech*, Totowa NJ: Rowman and Allanheld.

Tur, Richard (1985), 'Paternalism and the Criminal Law', *Journal of Applied Philosophy*, **2**, 173.

Tur, Richard (1986), 'Common Law and Legal Theory', in William Twining (ed.), *Legal Theory and Common Law*, Oxford: Blackwell.

Tur, Richard and William Twining (eds) (1986), *Essays on Kelsen*, Oxford: Clarendon.

Tushnet, Mark (1988), *Red, White and Blue*, Cambridge: Harvard University Press.

Tushnet, Mark (ed.) (1993), *Constitutional Law*, Aldershot: Dartmouth.

Tyler, T.R. (1990), *Why People Obey the Law*, New Haven: Yale University Press.

Ullmann-Margalit, Edna (1977), *The Emergence of Norms*, Oxford: Oxford University Press.

Unger, R. (1986), *The Critical Legal Studies Movement*, Cambridge: Harvard University Press.

U.S.A. President's Commission on Obscenity and Pornography, Report (1970), Washington, D.C.: US Government Printing Office.

US Department of Justice (1986), *Attorney General's Commission on Pornography Final Report*, vols 1 and 2, Washington, D.C.: US Government Printing Office.

Wacks, R. (ed.) (1993), *Privacy*, Aldershot: Dartmouth.

Waismann, F. (1945), 'Verifiability', *Proceedings of the Aristotelian Society*, **19**, supplementary volumes, 119–50.

Waldron, Jeremy (1989), 'The Rule of Law in Contemporary Liberal Theory', *Ratio Juris*, **2**, 79–96.

Waldron, Jeremy (1990), *The Law*, London: Routledge.

Waldron, Jeremy (1991), 'Rights and Minorities: Rousseau Revisited', in J. Chapman and R. Wertheimer (eds), *Majorities and Minorities*, New York: New York University Press, 44–75.

Waldron, Jeremy (1993), *Liberal Rights: Collected Papers 1981–91*, Cambridge: Cambridge University Press.

Walker, G. de Q. (1987), *Initiative and Referendum: The People's Law*, Sydney: Centre for Independent Studies.

Walker, Neil (1993), 'Discovering the Intention of Parliament', *Scots Law Times*, **14**, 121–8.

Walker, Sally (1989), *The Law of Journalism in Australia*, Sydney: Law Book.

Waluchow, W.J. (1994), *Inclusive Legal Positivism*, Oxford: Clarendon Press.

Warnock, G. (1971), *The Object of Morality*, London: Methuen.

Wasserstrom, Richard (1975), 'Lawyers as Professionals: Some Moral Issues', *Human Rights*, **5**, 1–24.

Weber, Max (1947), *The Theory of Social and Economic Organization*, edited by T. Parsons, Glencoe: Free Press.

Weber, Max (1968), *Economy and Society*, two vols, trans. and ed. by G. Roth and C. Wittich, New York: Bedminster Press.

Westmorland, Robert (1991), 'Dworkin and Legal Pragmatism', *Oxford Journal of Legal Studies*, **11**, 174–92.

Wicklein, J. (1992), 'Fun and Profit with Liberl', *Communications Law Bulletin*, **12**, (1), 29

Williams, B. (1981), *Obscenity and Film Censorship*, Cambridge: Cambridge University Press.

Williams, Bernard, Chairman (1979), *Report of the Committee on Obscenity and Film Censorship*, London: HMSO Cmnd 7772.

Williams, Bernard (1985), *Ethics and the Limits of Philosophy*, Glasgow: Collins.

Williams, Glanville (1945), 'The Controversy concerning the Word "Law"', in P. Laslett (ed.), *Philosophy, Politics and Society*, 1st series, Oxford: Blackwells.

Williams, Susan H.(1991), 'Content Discrimination and the First Amendment', *University of Pennsylvania Law Review*, **139**, 614–730.

Wilson, W.A. (1992), 'Trials and Try-ons: Modes of Interpretation', *Statute Law Review*, **13**, 1–10.

Wittgenstein, L. (1968), *Philosophical Investigations*, 3rd edn, trans. G.E.M. Anscombe, New York: Macmillan.

Wolff, R.P. (1976), *In Defence of Anarchism*, New York: Harper and Row.

Wood, Malcolm (1988), 'Rule, Rules and Law', in M. Leith and P. Ingram (eds), *The Jurisprudence of Orthodoxy*, London: Routledge, 27–59.

Wright, A. (1986), *Socialism: Theories and Practices*, Oxford: Oxford University Press.

Wroblewski, Jerzy (1992), *The Judicial Application of Law*, Dordrecht: Kluwer.

Yablon, C. (1985), 'The Indeterminacy of Law: Critical Legal Studies and the Problem of Legal Explanation', *Cardozo Law Review*, **6**, 917.

Young, I.M. (1990), 'The Ideal of Community and the Politics of Difference', in L.J. Nicholson (ed.), *Feminism/Postmodernism*, London: Routledge.

Yudof, Mark G. (1983), *When Government Speaks: Politics, Law and Government in America*, Berkeley: University of California Press.

Zines, L. (1992), *The High Court and the Constitution*, 3rd edn, Sydney: Butterworths.

Index